Extraordinary Hearts

Extraordinary Hearts

Reclaiming Gay Sensibility's Central Role in the Progress of Civilization

The 100 Collected "Nick Benton's Gay Science" Essays

Nicholas F. Benton

LETHE PRESS
MAPLE SHADE NJ

Published September, 2013 by Lethe Press, 118 Heritage Ave, Maple Shade NJ 08052
lethepressbooks.com lethepress@aol.com

Book Design by Toby Johnson
Cover Design by Nick Gatz (based on an ancient Greek rendering of Ganymede)
Mr. Benton's back cover photo by Brenda Schrier

ISBN-13 978-1-59021-392-6
ISBN-10 1-59021-392-0

_____

Library of Congress Cataloging-in-Publication Data

Benton, Nick.
  [Essays. Selections]
  Extraordinary hearts : reclaiming gay sensibility's central role in the progress of civilization : the 100 collected "Nick Benton's gay science" essays / Nicholas F. Benton.
     pages cm
   ISBN-13: 978-1-59021-392-6
   ISBN-10: 1-59021-392-0
   1. Gays. 2. Gay rights. I. Title. II. Title: Nick Benton's gay science.
   HQ76.25.B46 2013
   306.76′6--dc23
                                    2013020457

About This Book

This book is a compilation of 100 chapters published under the title, "Nick Benton's Gay Science" on consecutive weeks from October 14, 2010 through September 4, 2012 on the website of the *Falls Church News-Press* and in print in the *Metro Weekly*, one of two prominent LGBT weeklies that pervades the Washington, D.C. Metropolitan area LGBT community.

In that time frame, "Don't Ask, Don't Tell" was repealed, Larry Kramer's powerful play written in the midst of the AIDS crisis, *The Normal Heart,* was revived on Broadway, the President of the United States came out explicitly in favor of gay marriage and just two months afterward, citizens of four U.S. states, for the first time, voted in favor of gay marriage. While these entries don't presume to take credit for any of this, by circulating widely in the nation's capital then, they did perhaps contribute to a new dialogue on shaping LGBT identity and self-esteem going forward into a new world of equality.

—The Author

Contents

Dedicated to the Great
Truth Tellers
Of Our Cause

Oscar Wilde
Christopher Isherwood
Tennessee Williams
Randy Shilts
and
Larry Kramer

We *Can* Handle the Truth!

Foreword

by Joey DiGuglielmo,
Feature Editor, *The Washington Blade*

I had a wonderful professor for Biology 102 in college. Actually right now, off the top of my head, I'm struggling to pull her name up from the cobwebs of my memory, but she was a lovely person, a good teacher, a good scientist and also a Christian.

She was a member of one of the mainline Protestant churches, though I don't recall, nor does it matter, which. What struck me so much about this woman was her willingness to indulge any question that might come up during her lectures—it was a small class so this was possible without it getting out of control and endlessly delaying her lectures. And both during class and in post-lecture discussions in her office, she was willing to talk *ad infinitum* about any related topic even if it went beyond the realm of science.

This was revolutionary to me in the context. The clergy at the Bible-thumping evangelical (non-denominational) church of my youth—which my parents and adult sisters and their families still attend in small-town West Virginia—were also willing to have those discussions but only in retrospect did I realize they were only telling us part of the story. This was a fairly black-and-white world as far as that line of thinking was concerned. They would concede there were "gray areas" where two good Christians might come to different conclusions, but the things they were talking about were not powder keg topics like evolution or homosexuality—they were talking about Christians dancing, going to movies or listening to pop and rock music.

And they had (and indeed have!) an answer for everything—
"Nature clearly teaches us that homosexuality is not God's plan
for human sexuality!," "Yes, Hollywood or Nashville may manage
to produce a decent movie or hit song occasionally, but why wade
through all the muck and filth they constantly peddle to find it?,"
or one of my simplistic favorites, "Evolution is just a theory—
they've never found the missing link, so they can't prove a thing."

I bought into all this for a long time—I was green, a rather
average student, not as intellectually curious as I would later become
and had a limited world view. In so many arenas, previously, it was
only the church of my youth that was willing to have any sort of
all-encompassing conversation. My high school biology teachers
would have said certain questions were beyond the realm of what
was appropriate for a public school science classroom. And the
folks who were willing to indulge more far-ranging questions—at
least the ones I'd encountered—had been in this evangelical, the
Bible-is-the-answer-to-everything-and-gives-man-everything-he
needs-type of mindset that, while good intentioned, was almost
smug in its self assuredness.

The aforementioned college biology professor proved a
watershed figure for me, though. Because she was a Christian
and also believed evolution was scientifically valid, I was highly
curious to hear how she reconciled all this in her own mind. She
was perfectly willing to discuss all that at length, read and refute
the anti-evolution literature my church and its type had armed me
with and not limit our discussions to "just science."

Having just re-read dozens of Mr. Benton's columns, the sense
I'm left with is that he's providing us with that same beautiful
forum in these great writings, which to me are endlessly fascinating.
I read them all each week in *Metro Weekly* as they appeared. He and
I had not discussed this series before he started publishing them.
When they began appearing in *Metro Weekly*, I was delighted with
them and it became by far my favorite feature in that publication.

The great beauty of the series—as you will discover—is that
he is doing, on a much broader level, exactly what my college

professor was doing: taking on all sorts of LGBT topics without any borders and without the slightest concern that he might be getting too wonky, too esoteric, too academic, too historical, too autobiographical or whatever. Initially published each week on the website of Mr. Benton's own newspaper, the *Falls Church News-Press*, they were reprinted by the Benton Foundation as paid ads in *Metro Weekly*. As such, Mr. Benton could write as he wished and was not beholden to an editor. Granted I'm not saying editors are bad—I'm one myself and I do believe that keeping an audience in mind and not veering off too far on any rabbit trail is generally a good idea. Art and commerce have always been uncomfortable bedfellows, but editors, record company and network execs are not always the bad guys.

Still isn't it fun to think about what movie Hitchcock would have made had he been left entirely to his own devices (actually we know—it's called *Mary Rose,* based on the Barrie play and you can read Jay Presson Allen's script for it online)? Or what orchestral configuration Leonard Bernstein (gay, by the way) might have kept at his recording disposal were money no object? You get the idea. In a way, that's exactly what we have here from Mr. Benton—you'll find in these pages, he's deliciously and refreshingly all over the place, from the great works of Tennessee Williams and Christopher Isherwood, to his friendships with famous gay figures like Don Bachardy (speaking of Isherwood—not sure of whom I refer? Keep reading—Mr. Benton will fill you in) and the great figure skater Johnny Weir, to what led to AIDS and the toll it exacted on gay culture, to what else was going on when Stonewall happened and why it was anything from an isolated fluke in a cultural vacuum, to what it really means to be gay, to his own life choices to, at the very core of the writings, why gays and lesbians exist in the first place.

I'm not going to get into specifics—you'll get plenty of that in this volume. And do keep in mind, as Mr. Benton also points out, if it feels a tad repetitive at times, realize it was initially unveiled in serial format. Mr. Benton tells me he purposefully kept these writings as they initially appeared to maintain their historic nature. The editor in me wants to streamline things a few times here and there, but he has a valid point. And trust me—there are enough new angles and insights that emerge throughout the series to justify the presence of several recurring themes.

There are a lot of silver linings to the gay experience. For me, the simple fact of being gay was the catalyst for escaping the hard-and-fast religious teachings of my upbringing. Even today, I don't fault my parents for this teaching nor do I criticize my sisters for bringing my nieces and nephews up in the same tradition. Children can only process so much at their stages of development—it's a good starting point and hopefully they'll keep reading and exploring beyond the church as they mature.

For me, had I been straight, I don't know the degree to which I would have done that. I see the straight counterparts with whom I grew up in church and I see most of them very much following the paths of their parents. If not all go to the same church, they go to sister-type churches (officially or unofficially) that teach much the same thing. I come from that world so I understand it—I can see how on a superficial level, many of the scriptural interpretations they espouse seem to make sense, especially if you're straight.

Whether one has had sex with a person of the same sex or not, this orientation is a staggering thing to behold. One sees it everywhere—both overtly and covertly—and it truly does bring an alternate perspective to the world that Mr. Benton explores brilliantly in this series. Were all LGBT people indistinguishable—as some are—from straights unless you knew with whom they had sex, the world would be a much different place.

I see it all the time in ways as simple as how the table looks when I set it versus the way it looks when my straight mother sets it. She has a good eye, she dresses well, she's not a hack—yet she lacks a certain panache that a gay man would bring to it. It's not merely aesthetic either—it's an attention to detail, a heightened awareness that so often goes missing among our straight counterparts. I see it in all mediums, in all arenas, though its dearth is often heightened in anti-gay spaces. It's almost always still there in some miniscule fashion, just not as extensively. As controversial as it was in its day, there really was something to the makeover show *Queer Eye for the Straight Guy.* Many gays condemned it for pigeonholing and stereotyping us. I loved it and found it dead on.

And yet queer sensibility is not *just* that. That's merely how it's sometimes manifested on the most superficial level. As you'll read in these pages, it goes far beyond that.

Asking why is such a basic human impulse—my sister has triplets who are three. When they were about two and a half, they started asking, "Why?" constantly. It became a running joke in our family. Whatever my sister happened to be doing at any given time, I'd mimic their toddler coo and ask her "Why?" With the kids, it's rather hilarious the frequency with which it comes up— they see me flossing my teeth, peeling a banana, keeping ear plugs beside my bed, whatever. Why? Why? Why? It's not a frustrated question—it's merely a thirst for basic information.

It's interesting how that impulse stays as we mature and get a good understanding of the basics of life. Practically anything you've ever wondered about the gay experience and the whys of it all, will be addressed by Mr. Benton in the coming pages. You may not always agree with him, but he's a staggeringly well-read and well-informed intellectual who will delight you with his theories and convictions.

I hope at some point he considers in some arena the transgender experience as well for surely evolution and the cosmos has something equally intriguing up its sleeve in that evolutionary riddle as well.

For now, I'm off to pop as many societal balloons of male chauvinist-dominated tyranny with as much constitutional, egalitarian and democratic ideals as my beautiful gay soul can muster.

Joey DiGuglielmo
Washington, DC
December, 2012

Testimonials

From Don Bachardy,
Portrait Artist, Long-Time Partner of Christopher Isherwood

Nick Benton's outspoken accounts of our tribe's issues are not only intelligent and articulate but candid and compassionate. Such exciting and informative writing is a benefit to all humanity, and a challenge to us, and to everyone.

From Steven F. Dansky,
Gay Pioneer, publisher of Christopher Street Press

Over the decades, Nick Benton has been a pioneer, daring to express points of view few would risk, the consequences too grave. Fundamental at the beginning of the LGBT movement, as now, is the affirmation of our core values, defined Nby Benton as the desire for love, truth, commitment, and compassion. Benton and I share a bond as early activists and proponents of "effeminism." As early as 1970, during the first year post-Stonewall Rebellion, small groups of like-minded men began to question the direction of the newly formed LGBT movement. Never before, had there been a coalition of lesbians, gay men, and transgender people, and in New York, Gay Liberation Front (GLF) meetings were a hotbed of contention, bringing together people, racially diverse, from different class backgrounds, often with irreconcilable antithetical political beliefs. His newspaper, *The Effeminist,* inspired me as it did other anti-sexist men to course a direction into unchartered territory. The publishing of his thematically-linked collected essays, *The 'Gay Science' Papers*, should be considered an important event for our movement.

From Gay Pioneer Lilli Vincenz and Nancy Davis

Considerable expertise on behalf of our Gay community, and humanity, in general.

From Johnny Weir,
Openly Gay Olympic Figure Skater,
Author and Newspaper Columnist

Nick Benton's voice is a shining light into our culture. His voice is that of reason and invaluable experience, witness and strength. *'Gay Science'* is a project of love and admiration for the community that shouldn't be missed. Wisdom is a gift that shines so brightly in this work.

From Randy Shulman,
Publisher, Metro Weekly

Honored to be the launching pad.

From Hon. Adam Ebbin,
First Openly-Gay Member of the Virginia State Senate

Gay Science is provocative, enlightening and intriguing. Nick Benton's personal and cultural histories, theories and 'gay sensibility' put LGBT history into a unique, contemporary context. While some will nod in agreement, others will be troubled by his theory on the precipitation of the AIDS crisis. You are sure to reflect as you read his unique take on our world. Benton is an American original and *Gay Science* reflects not just the history of Nick and his times, but that of 'gay sensibility' and culture. The book is provocative, enlightening and intriguing--like Benton himself.

From Barbara Brown Zikmund,
Dean of Students, Pacific School of Religion, 1981-1990
(where Nick Benton graduated with honors)

This book is grounded in personal experiences that will inform, challenge and enrich future conversations about homosexuality. Nick Benton's story and passion for the gifts of homosexual persons throughout human history is inspiring. His analysis of how homosexuals moved beyond lives of privacy and secrecy into what he calls hedonistic promiscuity in recent decades is controversial. Yet his hope is that the natural gift of a "gay sensibility," that expresses love beyond the erotic, might be celebrated and cultivated in new ways. He suggests that "being different" can allow the flourishing of a "constructive non-conformity."

Nicholas F. Benton
Portrait by Don Bachardy (August 7, 2010)

Extraordinary Hearts

Reclaiming Gay Sensibility's Central Role
in the Progress of Civilization

Nick Benton, 1972

Author's Introduction

1

I intended the title, "Nick Benton's Gay Science," of my 100-part series published weekly in a Washington, D.C. gay magazine from October 2010 to September 2012 to have a multi-layered meaning. First, it was to set *my* "gay science," so to speak, against the 19th century philosopher Friedrich Nietzsche's. That is, it was the signal of a wholesale philosophical engagement with Nietzsche and the Western philosophical/psychological/scientific current of which he was a seminal part. He had his "gay science" (a book by that name published in 1869), and I have mine, as I wrote in the first installment of my series.

Nietzsche use of the term "gay" was not in the homosexual sense, of course, nor was his "science" (it was a reference actually to the "joy of poetry" as almost a form of anti-science). But that evokes the ironic part of my, as opposed to his, "gay science." My series was about the homosexual sense of the term, but also not limited to it. So with the term "science": it is about the natural universe, and same-sex attraction's central role in it, but also about alternative perception and, as it were "artful" ways of knowing. It was Plato who said that "poetry is nearer to vital truth than history."

As a 100-part weekly series, the reader will find readily in this gathered version a seeming lot of recapitulation of points, designed to connect the content from week to week, but there is a story being unfolded here that comes through loud and clear.

2

Central to my case in this work is the social phenomenon I describe
as the "anarcho-hedonist counterculture." This is the best, most
succinct way I came up with for identifying what I encountered
as a San Francisco Bay Area-based pioneer Gay Liberation Front
activist first hand in the late 1960s and which through the post-
Stonewall era came to sweep over the Gay Liberation movement
with a relentless, bullying imperative for "sex, drugs and rock and
roll."

This was not a "counterculture" in the constructive sense that
many of us associated with the civil rights and anti-war movements
of the earlier 1960s. It was the "anarcho-hedonist" invasion of that
constructive counterculture by the madness of Ken Kesey's LSD-
laden "Merry Pranksters" and their "Magic Bus" tour and their
mindless offshoots that helped to undermine and destroy the civil
rights movement. By "anarcho" I mean the opposite of genuine
concern for positive social change, that is, an anarchistic impulse
to destroy, not transform, any form of authority. By "hedonist" I
mean the rejection of notions of trust, love and fidelity with angry
demands for "edge experiences" in the pursuit of pleasure for its
own sake.

Nietzsche-inspired   postmodernism   is   the   philosophical
overlay under which all of this was subsumed.

3

There are important signs that cynical, anarcho-hedonist, right-
wing fueled postmodernism's grip on American culture is giving
way. Whatever marginally constructive contribution it made was
far more than outweighed by its denial, at its core, of the very
existence of the human soul. With its angry rejection of anything
authoritative, including science or justice, it despised the concept of
universals, scoffed at love, respecting only power and the pursuit
of pleasure for its own sake, and became the radical "divide and

conquer" weapon of global elites to rip asunder impulses of humanity to find common grounds for unity and solidarity against the plunder, brutality and injustice of their overlords. In its first wave, it involved the mainstreaming into American culture of a soulless, anarcho-hedonist counterculture in the 1960s deployed against the rising civil rights and anti-war movements of that era and it morphed into the Reagan revolution and its worst excesses of the worship of greed and selfishness.

But now, there is evidence of a new yearning for meaning and a cautious optimism is arising to overthrow the postmodern era.

This work is a contribution to a hoped-for new dialogue shaping a fresh, post-postmodern consciousness. The problem for the modern LGBT movement is that all of its theory, its self-identification and its history arose and were defined from within the parameters of postmodernism at its height, from the Stonewall Riots era of 1969 onward. For a new consciousness to take root, the deep flaws of the pretexts of that thought must be challenged and reconsidered, as I have sought to do in this series.

As one gay liberation pioneer activist who resisted the postmodern capture of the gay movement from the earliest post-Stonewall days, I presented my thoughts, updated with the benefit of much reflection and study, in this 100-part weekly series that appeared in print between October 2010 and September 2012 and is compiled in a single volume here.

4

Popular Western sociological/psychological epistemology commensurate with the Industrial Revolution and following has been grounded in the notion of a duality defining human behavior and desire in terms of law abiding versus law breaking. This dualistic construct permeated all areas of social sciences with the dishonest aim of taming the human spirit against powerful impulses for social equality and universal justice.

Thus arose the "science" of sexology and the theories of Freud that, among other things, circumscribed same sex erotic attraction within these bounds. In the last forty years since the eruption of the modern post-Stonewall Riots gay movement, this expressed itself in the mainstreaming of a radical anarcho-hedonist counterculture fueled by the cynical theories of post-modernism.

The core insight in my *Gay Science* essays shatters this construct by asserting that same sex erotic attraction is the embodiment of a socio-physical impulse of self-development, a manifestation of the very nature of the universe and the evolution of humanity toward equality, justice and ultimately love in its truest form. As such, contrary to the dualists and anarcho-hedonists who define behavior in terms of either duty-bound law abiding (Apollonian, in terms of Greek mythological archetypes) or pleasure-seeking law breaking (Dionysian), this view sees same sex erotic attraction as at its core Promethean, as that which gives life and progress to humanity as transformative and revolutionary. Thus, it is not a variant or deviation of the heterosexual impulse for biological reproduction. It is an expression of our species' natural impulse for preservation and advancement through social, not biological, reproduction.

The Promethean aligns with the modern social currents of civil rights, especially the emancipation of women from the shackles of the male chauvinist social paradigm, advocating what I defined as 'effeminism' in the early days of the post-Stonewall gay liberation movement. These essays explore a wide panorama of the gay experience from this point of view.

5

It is unusual, perhaps, to anticipate the publication of a book whose impact has, at least to a degree, already been felt. In this case, this volume is a collection of 100 weekly newspaper columns I wrote that were published between October 2010 and September 2012 in two Washington, D.C. media sources—my own *Falls Church*

News-Press general interest paper, *via* its website, and the *Metro Weekly* news magazine that serves the D.C. area gay community. Thus they bypassed the sanctions of any academic, editorial or acknowledged institutional movement leadership to speak directly and unfiltered to the grassroots, so to speak, of the gay world. The "butterfly effect" of those columns has already been set loose, although they may await future generations to be fully appreciated.

These columns introduced some unique content and ideas, challenged numerous prevailing assumptions and engaged in "truth telling" that make them controversial for some in the ranks of the current established gay community hierarchy. But the design was to help my readers to discover that the very notion of same-sex erotic attraction is vastly more important and valuable than gay culture since Stonewall has acknowledged.

The case was made in many ways in the columns themselves, and it is basically this: same-sex erotic attraction is a vital and inherent component of creation, itself, derived from a visible "lefthanded" negative-entropic impulse on the macro-cosmic level, and manifested in human societies in the progress toward equality, justice and democracy. It derives not as a variant of, or deviation from, the impulse toward species reproduction, but from the equally valid and scientifically-documented impulse toward species survival through the exercise of heightened empathy and altruism. Same-sex erotic attraction works, socially, to stand against an otherwise unbridled militaristic male dominion that subjugates women, children and the elderly in a relentless quest for territorial and resource control, helping to preserve and advance those societies that would otherwise devolve and self-destruct.

Thus, same-sex erotic attraction has been around since before the beginning as a temporizing, compassionate and equalizing force in civilization, even if it is not evident in the way it is recognized in the post-Stonewall era. Evidence shows that comparatively rarely has it ever been manifested as explicit sexual acts. Instead, it is mostly found in history through the elevation of art, poetry, music, science and the exercise of fair and just governance. Empathy is not, of course, the sole property of our tribe, but central to our same-sex erotic attraction as a heightened sense of it, to the point of forming bonds, loyalties and loves more profound than bonding for purposes of strengthening male dominion and marriage.

A sharp same-sex erotic attraction also naturally produces an alternate sensual perspective to the norm and naturally evokes an inclination toward a constructive non-conformity that seeks general social betterment through constructive change.

6

As for evidences of explicitly sexual expressions of same-sex erotic attraction that modern historians have uncovered since Stonewall, given that close to eight percent of all the populations is born with an inherent impulse toward same-sex erotic attraction, the number of such persons through all history renders the few documented cases of actual sexual acts less than miniscule. Even today, the number of "open" gays participating in urban gay culture, it can be presumed, is but a tiny fraction of what permeates our entire culture.

My columns documented, uniquely, the relationship between the emerging gay movement of the 1960s and two other social currents, the civil rights movement (among other things, citing the members of the then-tiny Mattachine Society who attended Martin Luther King Jr.'s "I Have a Dream" speech in 1963) and anti-Vietnam War movement (noting the unrecognized fact that the same weekend as the Stonewall Riots in June 1969, *Life* magazine published its provocative, controversial yearbook-style photographs of young American men killed in one week in Vietnam). Such obvious and instructive interconnections in an era of progressive social ferment are ignored in our recent histories because of postmodernism's insistent compartmentalization, the fallacious notion that we must write our own history as if nothing else mattered.

The truth is that post-Stonewall gay culture emerged as a double-edged sword, something I saw from the inside as a high-profile pioneer in that culture in the San Francisco Bay Area from 1969 to 1973. Details of my involvement were presented in this series. Primarily through my tireless writing for counterculture newspapers such as the *Berkeley Barb, Gay Sunshine, Berkeley Tribe, San Francisco Kalendar* and my own *The Effeminst,* I quickly became one of, if not the most, high profile advocate for the gay liberation cause in the San Francisco Bay Area in the period between Stonewall and prior to the rise of Harvey Milk, whom I knew and interacted with. Much of the record of my role was purged after I withdrew from the movement in 1973. For example, the second edition of the Ramparts Press' *Gay Liberation Book:* having more entries (three) than anyone else in the first edition, all my work was deleted from the second.

On the one hand, the Stonewall Riots came to represent the social inflection point that opened the barn door for everyone in our tribe for the first time in history to "come out," to claim the fullness of an internal integrity, no longer marginalized, forced to lie or hide our natural erotic attractions. On the other hand, this historically important turning point occurred in a climate governed by the radical hedonism of the "sex, drugs and rock and roll" counterculture that was being mainstreamed in Western culture at the same time.

That meant that "coming out," rather than unleashing far more powerful kinds of cultural and institutional betterments as we'd forwarded all along in history, was instead hijacked by the radical anarcho-hedonistic impetus of that period to be subordinated to a dominant obsession with self-centered, pleasure-seeking sexual acts. No love, no romance, no relational commitments, but sheer carnality for its own sake.

7

Anyone in that era who suggested any restraint on a veritable mandate of limitless sexual acts was denounced as "sex negative" and "counter-revolutionary." Urban gay culture rapidly morphed into a place where one felt pressured to abandon any creative career pursuits to devote virtually every waking hour plunging headlong into unbridled sexual pursuits, with growing dependency on whatever forms of intoxicants helped along the way. I lived in this world.

The sexual license that went unchecked favored the aggressive predator over all others, and it was those predators, far too often also rapists and human traffickers, who angrily enforced the "no-rules, no restraints" laws of the urban gay culture. Countless sensitive and naïve young gay men, like myself, and women were no match for this, victimized in countless ways, including by falling under its suasion almost like mind-controlled victims of a cult. Venereal diseases were rampant and unchecked. Predators and their prey, together, tumbled into compulsive behaviors driven by *bonafide* addictions, and those addictive habits compelled them to adopt the readily-available philosophies justifying their excesses, the postmodernism of Michel Foucault and others who insisted on "no limits" and that sexual acts were grounded not in love, but hate, a defiance against authority, even the "repressive" authorities of science and public health.

This led to the spread of the HIV virus and outbreak of AIDS in 1981, as I described in this series, and even with its horrible spread, the stubborn refusal of the predatory gay community leaders to place any public health restraints on the lifestyles they'd cultivated in public bathhouses and sex clubs. That insured that millions of as-yet-uninfected gays would subsequently become infected and die before drugs enabling victims to live with the HIV virus became effective in the mid-1990s.

8

I had "come out" in 1969, jumping headlong into the emerging post-Stonewall gay liberation movement after graduating from a progressive graduate theological seminary around the same time. It was in the context of the 1960s civil rights and anti-war struggles. But by 1973, I resigned my role as an early gay liberation leader with a commentary in a San Francisco gay newspaper entitled, "Homosexuality Vs. Socialism." In it I described the predatory nature that had taken over the urban gay culture, and I counterposed to it a compassionate, humanitarian notion of ideal socialism. I wrote that I preferred the latter, while in no way suggesting that I was attempting to change my sexual orientation. In fact, it was part of my struggle to redeem my same-sex erotic attraction, my "gay soul," from the predatory context I found myself overwhelmed by.

Having been declared *persona non grata* by my family upon coming out in 1969, and remaining a harsh critic of the unjust, war-mongering wider culture that hated and discriminated against gays, my choices were few upon departing my gay leadership role in the mid-1970s (I got by writing for counterculture and gay newspapers), and I aligned on the margins of a fringe, ostensibly pro-socialist current that held me at arm's length because of my homosexuality and which devolved into a slavish cult. Ironically, that experience helped me to eventually grasp how urban gay scenes had fallen under a similar sort of influences, although ostensibly "leaderless," evidenced by hyper-conformist clone-like fads in clothing, appearance, tastes and social and sexual behaviors.

Simultaneously desiring a higher calling for my life and communion with my fellow tribesmen, on the other, I lived with great internal stresses in that era. The 1981 outbreak of the AIDS epidemic and the unspeakable, subsequent horror I saw unfolding kept me in a state of virtual exile, emotionally and physically, until, after I feared that I had come down with AIDS in 1985, a sure death sentence, the first test for exposure to the HIV virus became available. Clearing that test, only then did I begin afresh to claim my life. Completely disassociating from the cult, I incorporated my own news service in 1987 and I began, along lines I'd hoped to in 1969, doing, as I like to put it, "what any good gay boy (or girl) would do." I founded a weekly community newspaper in 1990 to make a positive difference in people's lives the way we are all supposed to.

9

My *Falls Church News-Press* has, to the present day, provided genuine and meaningful coverage of its local community, and an effective advertising medium for local businesses, addressing editorials and national affairs columns to matters of social justice, compassion and equality, introducing a weekly gay issues column, founding a "Diversity Affirmation Education Fund" in my name in the local school system, sponsoring the 1990s AIDS Rides and much more.

Meanwhile, by 2003 sorting through experiences I'd come through since 1969, I began taking on my "post-traumatic stress" by beginning an autobiographical blog called "Notes from the Future by Gay Jesus" ("Gay Jesus" being a nickname I was saddled with in my early gay liberation days).

In 2009, I contributed an essay to an anthology published by the City Lights Books on the 40th anniversary of Stonewall. The book was entitled, "Smash the Church, Smash the State: the Early Days of Gay Liberation," and my essay was called, "Berkeley and the Fight for an Effeminist, Socially Transformative Identity."

But it was in the summer of 2010 that I had a critical "Aha!" moment, reading a May 1977 exchange published in the *Village Voice* between Tennessee Williams and William Burroughs. It is described in detail in my columns. Looking back on my travails from the early post-Stonewall era with fresh eyes, I felt an urgency and to offer others the benefit of my experiences and insights. Thus, in October 2010, my weekly "Nick Benton's Gay Science" series began.

Too much of what passes for urban gay culture today has not really changed since the post-Stonewall, pre-AIDS era. Shallow hedonism reigns supreme on the pages of gay newspapers, magazines and other media outlets. Foucault continues to be worshiped by too many who have never been introduced to a competent criticism of his work. Young gay people still do not find in urban gay culture a social connection reinforcing and compelling the achievement of their full potentials, or in terms of what it really means to be gay, to be empowered to grow through resistance to those who would exploit them and make their best marks on the world. Still, the push for gay marriage signals a hopeful revival of our core desires for the love, truth, commitment and compassion that our movement ignored in its earlier years.

These 100 columns represent an attempt by me to "give back," to being a "truth teller" out of a supreme gratitude for life, for the love and opportunities it affords through struggle, and for being gay.

10

Since the completion of my *Gay Science* series in September 2012, the third volume of the diaries of Christopher Isherwood was published, *Liberation, Diaries, Volume 3, 1970-1983,* covering the 1970s into the early 1980s when he stopped writing (he died of prostate cancer in early 1986). As much as my series drew from the Isherwood diaries of the 1940s, 50s and 60s, and conversations with his surviving long-time partner Don Bachardy based on them, the 1970s diaries have a great deal more to offer, and there is so much that I would have loved to include from them.

Included are Isherwood's disdain (he was "repelled," in his words) for the "Gay Elite" leadership of establishment gay rights organizations (that only months later began to so horribly botch the response to the AIDS crisis). As he wrote in October 1980, "They all seem to be psychiatrists, either professional or amateur, and were archly knowing about the problems of gay married life. You were made immensely conscious, however, that at least one out of each pair had *money*—lots. And that this, and not psychology, was what ultimately settled all the marriage problems."

A decade earlier, in December 1970, Isherwood wrote warmly of a close gay liberation collaborator of mine, Michael Silverstein. "I liked him, He is very intelligent, in a belligerent Jewish way," Isherwood wrote, and noted (as perhaps prescient given who soon became the "Gay Elite") that Silverstein "says that psychoanalysis is ultimately political because it judges the patients according to the standards of the establishment." Silverstein's "Open Letter to Tennessee Williams" became a classic of early gay liberation literature of that era, and sadly, he eventually took his own life.

Isherwood also expressed his disdain (a "slob," "insulting," a "waste...of my hours") for Winston Leyland, who'd hijacked the *Gay Sunshine* newspaper from the collective, including myself, that founded it.

The decade of diaries attest to Isherwood's perpetual commitments to his relationship with Bachardy (regaling his "genius for expressing love") and his Vedanta faith (quoting William Penn, "They that love beyond the world cannot be separated by it"), his conviction that, besides his faith, "my only salvation lies in...purposeful activity," and his first encounters with friends who'd come down with AIDS. Suffice it to say that there is nothing I found in his 1970s diaries that contradicts, or in fact does anything other than further confirm, insights or conclusions that I derived from Isherwood's other works.

11

In the effort on this work over a two year period, I wish to thank Jody Fellows, my loyal, reliable and talented managing editor, who kept the *Falls Church News-Press* on an even keel while my focus on this series and book sometimes distracted me more than a little. Then there have been special cherished friends, among other things masters of the art of the question, whose substantial intellects and gentle criticisms spurred me, that include more than those I name here: Simon Van Steyn, Jonathan Harper, Janine S. Benton, Chris and Carol White. Thanks to Barbara Brown Zikmund for her encouragement and Nick Gatz for his patience with me while skillfully formatting and submitting my weekly entries, often enduring urgent calls to make last minute modifications, substitutions or corrections.

Thank you also to Rep. James P. Moran of Virginia for entering into the U.S. Congressional Record of November 2, 2011 the entirety of Chapter 54 of these offerings honoring the legacy of my late friend and gay movement founder Franklin Kameny.

Of note, finally, is the news that beginning in October 2012, Johnny Weir began writing a weekly column exclusively for my *Falls Church News-Press*, which so far has continued well over 40 consecutive weeks into late summer 2013.

Nicholas F. Benton
Falls Church, Virginia
December 27, 2012

"It has been my experience that gay and lesbian people who have fought through their self-hatred and their self-recriminations have a capacity for empathy that is glorious and a capacity to find laughter in things that is like praising God. There is a kind of flagrant joy about us that goes very deep and is not available to most people."

Paul Monette, *On Becoming* (1990).

~

"I believe in aristocracy, though—if that is the right word, and if a democrat may use it. Not an aristocracy of power, based upon rank and influence, but an aristocracy of the sensitive, the considerate and the plucky. Its members are to be found in all nations and classes, and all through the ages, and there is a secret understanding between them when they meet. They represent the true human tradition, the one permanent victory of our queer race over cruelty and chaos. Thousands of them perish in obscurity, a few are great names. They are sensitive to others as well as for themselves, they are considerate without being fussy, their pluck is not swankiness but the power to endure, and they can take a joke..."

E.M Forster, "What I Believe" (1939)
(I take this to be about gays like himself
when writing openly was forbidden.)

Chapter 1

Saint Foucault?
Are You Kidding? Part 1

This new column is a supplement to the global affairs column I've been writing and publishing weekly in the *Falls Church News-Press* since 1997. This new commentary series focuses on LGBT issues, reflecting on the future, the present and the past, especially the forty years since I was a "gay pioneer," who as a seminary graduate co-founded the Berkeley, Calif., chapter of the Gay Liberation Front in 1970 and founded *The Effeminist* newspaper in 1972. I founded in 1991, and continue to own and edit the weekly *Falls Church News-Press*, a general interest Washington, D.C. regional newspaper, which celebrated its 1,000th consecutive weeks of publication, and counting, this July.

"Gay Science" is the title of an 1882 book by Frederich Nietzsche, and I am not a fan. So he has his "Gay Science," and I have mine. The term comes from a common usage pertaining to the "science" of writing poetry. Nietzsche was an influential figure in a current running from Max Stirner through Martin Heidegger that was a cornerstone thread of anti-socialist, pro-individualist, "will to power" thought and policy in the emergence of the modern industrial state that fueled the rise of European fascism. Following World War II, it morphed into modernist and the infamous post-modernist currents in philosophy and social policy, bonding with the works of Ayn Rand, the Structuralists and others to espouse an extreme form of anarchism and nihilism, merging with notions of libertarianism and radical hedonism, and brought to us in the emerging 1960s counter-culture through the influence of the Beats and the likes of gay French philosopher Michel Foucault (see James Miller's "The Passion of Michel Foucault").

Not coincidentally these currents, and their powerful social influences, cohered with those in the corridors of the most powerful financial institutions in the world who demand the elimination of government oversight and regulation in their pursuit of greed and Social Darwinist objectives. The Reagan revolution brought these elements into national power. Federal Reserve chief Alan Greenspan was a devotee of Rand. People were put in charge of regulatory agencies who were angrily and ideologically opposed to regulation. The Heritage Foundation and Cato Institute took control of the intellectual and policy debates in Washington.

This is the same force of history that hijacked and almost killed the LGBT movement in the earliest days of the post-Stonewall era, and may do it again. Tirelessly expounding a relentless demand for excess, for pushing beyond the limit against social convention, its proponents drove sex from romance to mechanical excess in the major urban centers, converting a happy, burgeoning LGBT community into a string of financially-lucrative businesses catering to what Foucault, best known for his "History of Sex Part I," and his kind pushed as the revolutionary nature of unbridled sexual excess. So-called sexual "core groups" became the consequence in major cities, and their multiple STD infections spread to the wider gay population through "bridges." Larry Kramer described all this in his warning-shot book, *Faggots*, published in 1978 and more recent documentary, *Gay Sex in the '70s*.

Efforts to contain this descent into a social context in which exotic infectious diseases exploded were angrily decried as reactionary and homophobic by leaders of gay organizations who were often owners or friends of owners of these sex-related businesses, even as it became clear that an unbridled continuation of the practices was wantonly subjecting young gay men to horrible disease and certain death by the scores of thousands. This was all well documented by respected gay journalists from that era, including Randy Shilts (*And the Band Played On*) and Gabriel

Rotello (*Sexual Ecology*), and others. None of this is academic for me. I lived through it and experienced it up close and personally.

HIV infections and frank AIDS are again on the rise—not only devastating the African subcontinent and Third World, generally, but once again increasing exponentially in large U.S. cities. Young gay men say they needn't be concerned because it is now curable.

I heard this line participating in a *Washington Blade* inter-generational symposium that I participated in as part of the events marking the 40th anniversary of Stonewall in the summer of 2009. Hardly alone in this, I warned them of the threat of therapy-resistant mutations of the virus. The seeds of another, even more horrible explosion of mass suffering and death within the U.S. LGBT world are being sewn as we speak.

The way forward is to step away from the unquestioned core notions of our popular culture, as defined both from within and without by forty years of radical hedonistic dominance, including that being LGBT is all about sex, alone, and not sentiment, romance, sensibility and purpose.

Chapter 2

Saint Foucault?
Are You Kidding? Part 2

The gay world didn't know what hit it in the period immediately following Stonewall in the summer of 1969, and generally doesn't even to this day.

But being lesbian or gay in one of the major U.S. cities went from the dominant paradigm of a socially-marginalized private life on weekends with a creative public career to one where the pursuit of random sex became a 24-7 obsession, with career pursuits often kicked overboard in the process. The modern gay culture still bears a strong imprint of that transformation.

Carrying forward my characterizations of the forces behind that transformation comes now the scenario for how it was carried out, and what the ulterior motives behind it were. As one who was a pioneer of the modern post-Stonewall gay movement, but as one who tried unsuccessfully to buck the prevailing trend, I saw this up close and personal. For me, personally, I observed the process unfolding from the point I entered graduate theological seminary in the San Francisco Bay Area in 1966.

Through a concerted social engineering process, powerful forces deployed, including covert ones, to transform U.S. society from one which was energized by Martin Luther King's historic "I Have a Dream Speech" on the national mall in 1963, to one driven by Gordon Gekko's memorable speech on the virtues of greed in the 1987 film, *Wall Street*.

The transformation of society from the social consciousness of the early to mid-1960s, fighting for civil rights, the War on Poverty and against an emerging war in Vietnam, to the self-centered, personal greed obsessed 1980s did not happen by accident, and what was done to the post-Stonewall gay movement was pivotal to the process.

There are two relevant, publicly-documented factors when, if overlaid upon one another, tell the story in a startling and straightforward manner.

The first is what, in a 1980 book by that name, involved what was called the *The Aquarian Conspiracy*. The book was written by Marilyn Ferguson as a comprehensive catalog of how a new social movement, which began to take off in the 1960s under the rubric of the "human potential movement," had successfully insinuated itself into the fabric of American public life.

This self-described "Aquarian conspiracy" elevated the philosophies and social mores of the individual over social consciousness, and was regaled against, for example, more traditional struggles of trade unions and anti-poverty and war and pro-civil rights liberal Democrats with what it called a so-called new "radical middle" in politics. It drew on the teachings of Aldous Huxley, the Beat generation poets and other "postmoderns" like Michel Foucault and Ayn Rand, as I mentioned in my last column, in specially-formed places like the Esalen Institute south of San Francisco as well as on campuses across the U.S.

The second factor is another matter of public record and of an even more insidious nature, outlined in thousands of pages of declassified internal Central Intelligence Agency documents which came to light in the late 1970s at the result of Congressional hearings by Sen. Frank Church's committee, revealing a massive CIA covert operation known by the code name, MK ULTRA.

That involved the CIA's massive assault on the domestic U.S. population, operating on no less than forty U.S. college and university campuses, using unsuspecting U.S. citizens for mass experimentation in the proliferation of LSD and other mind-altering drugs. These drugs were tested and proliferated as sort of mass "liquid lobotomies" (lobotomies, or surgical incisions into the frontal lobe, being widely practiced well into the 1950s as a form of taming unruly persons). The goal was to turn social consciousness into personal inward-directedness, and it was found to work.

These two publicly-documented forces of the "human potential movement" and the covert MK-Ultra operation melded into the same force during the infamous 1967 Summer of Love in San Francisco, when "sex, drugs and rock-and-roll" became new mantra of American youth. It was followed by the urban riots of 1968 in wake of the assassination of Martin Luther King and pushed forward to wound and eventually leave the idealism of the civil rights, War on Poverty and early anti-Vietnam War struggles in the dust.

What role did the imposition of all this on the gay movement play? Specifically, being unable to foist this massive social "paradigm shift" on the mainstream U.S. population directly, the masters behind these efforts chose to insinuate them through socially marginalized groups, mainly African-Americans, gays and displaced youth.

By targeting these already socially-alienated groups as portals, so to speak, these forces leveraged their influence to have a greater bearing on overall society.

All three of these marginalized segments tended to be progressive-minded and in favor of social movements to aid the downtrodden. In the case of gays in the major U.S. cities, strides to gain wider social acceptance were already well underway and gay culture tended to bond with the plights of African-Americans, displaced youth and the poor.

But what came out of the Summer of Love and hit the gay movement like a giant tsunami shifted the dominant emotional content of these sub-cultures from themes of justice, peace and love to anger and the wanton, angry pursuit of boundless pleasure for its own sake.

Chapter 3

Saint Foucault? Are You Kidding? Part 3

Assessing the emergence over the last forty years of contemporary gay culture, including the recent rise of a more robust right-wing, anarcho-libertarian current, it is instructive to examine how two powerful cross-currents energized the earliest days of the post-Stonewall movement. Their differentiation is by and large cloaked, but still exists to this day.

As a seminary-graduated co-founder of the Berkeley, Calif., Gay Liberation Front in 1970, I was deeply involved in promoting one of those currents, as reflected in the title of my chapter in the collection, "Smash the Church, Smash the State: The Early Years of Gay Liberation," published by City Lights Books on the 40th anniversary of Stonewall in the summer of 2009. My chapter was entitled, "Berkeley and the Fight for an Effeminist, Socially-Transformative Gay Identity."

For myself and my allies, what the post-Stonewall explosion of the gay movement stood for was an empowerment of what we felt was a core identity of LGBT people, who have a special role in creation, their powerful capacity to transform the larger society in the direction of greater economic and social justice, compassion and peace. With a long string of role models in Western Civilization as guides, from Socrates to Leonardo da Vinci to Tennessee Williams and many others, we felt the emergence of the Gay Liberation movement offered an historic opportunity to ally with the anti-war, civil rights and feminist movements to wrest the dominant social paradigm away from the militaristic white male "chauvinists" on all levels of society, from individual households to the most powerful governments of the world.

Because of the special importance in this cause of identifying with the liberation of women, and our natural affinity with their plight and struggles, we branded ourselves "Effeminists," and I and my close friend produced two editions of a newspaper that we sold on the streets of Berkeley and San Francisco in 1972 and 1973 called *The Effeminist.*

In the editorial I wrote in the first-ever edition of the *Gay Sunshine* newspaper in 1970, I proclaimed the purpose of that *Gay Sunshine* was to represent "those who understand themselves as oppressed—politically oppressed by an oppressor that not only is down on homosexuality, but equally down on all things that are not white, straight, middle class, pro-establishment...It should harken to a greater cause—the cause of human liberation of which homosexual liberation is just one aspect—and on that level make its stand."

This reflected an alignment with the current that extended from the idealism of the civil rights and anti-war movements of the 1960s, their urgency underscored by the assassinations of Martin Luther King and Bobby Kennedy in the spring of 1968. However, there was the other current to contend with, which I wrote about in Part 2. That was the psychedelic, radical hedonism of, as author Marilyn Ferguson called it, in the title of her 1980 book, *The Aquarian Conspiracy,* an overwhelming force of radical hedonism, of the proliferation of "drugs, sex and rock and roll," which was launched in an entirely different direction, with an entirely different objective.

This social engineering force, driven by covert intelligence interests, including the CIA's MK Ultra domestic drug proliferation project, was aimed as derailing, defanging and defusing the great 1960s social force for civil rights and peace in Vietnam. U.S. intelligence forces feared these movements would threaten the U.S. in the context of the Cold War, and unleashed a great wave of self-centered hedonism to counter it. The post-Stonewall gay movement was targeted and overwhelmed by this. The pitch was not for love and romance, but for impersonal, promiscuous sex as pleasure and angry power. Resisting the relentless calls for "more, more, more" was called counter-revolutionary, and soon in the major cities sex clubs and baths exploded, as did sex in public places like the trucks at the Greenwich Village piers, and epidemics of every variety of STDs along with them. The only politics anyone wanted were those that would help protect their ability to keep on doing this.

Postmodernist Pied Pipers like the gay Michel Foucault were in the *avant garde* of urging this on. Foucault died of AIDS in 1984 after making it his practice to visit S&M gay bathhouses in San Francisco virtually every day in the fall of 1983, even as clear evidence exists that he knew he was infected.

Any notion of a unique gay sensibility was trampled under, with "gay" being a sexual orientation, nothing more. To many, the very identity of the gay movement underwent just the transformation those pushing all this wanted.

Up against this, we "effeminists" and our allies were like hapless students at the barricades in *Les Miserables*. We were completely outgunned and routed. Some went underground, others tried rear-guard efforts at maintaining a link between the gay movement and other progressive causes. For me, being smack in the middle of one of the fiercest of the hedonistic tempests in San Francisco, I had no choice but to bail out decisively. I went into virtual exile, publishing my resignation from the gay movement in a local gay newspaper, saying I would fight for my ideals in a wider pro-socialist context.

Chapter 4

Who Are We, Really? Part 1

The purpose of this exercise is to contribute to a frank conversation about where LGBT people have come from, how we got to where we are now, and where we're headed.

The explosion of self-affirmation among homosexuals leading up to and immediately following the Stonewall moment in the summer of 1969 was the most powerful and positive development for our kind in recorded history.

With it, the unique role for same-sex oriented people in the natural order gained an incredible boost, a lightning-like shot of energy propelling our innate creative, empathetic, care-giving and socially-transformative propensities. Unleashing a cascading process of "coming out" that rippled out to wider and wider waves of our population, it was without precedent.

We happily and positively embraced our difference in its many manifestations with no more shame or self-loathing in public ways never seen before.

Alas, it did not last. Within only a couple of years, the seeds of what would soon decimate this remarkable human movement were sewn. Those like myself who were there, riding the crest of this colorful gay liberation explosion, saw these changes with our own eyes.

In her one-person autobiographical play about her life through the gay liberation era, entitled *A Life in Three Acts*, transvestite performer Betty Bourne describes how a happy commune of young gay men in London in the early 1970s suddenly and quickly began succumbing to heavy drugs and angry discord.

Later in her retrospective, she goes into the AIDS epidemic, as it impacted her living in Manhattan. She knew more than 100 friends who died. But what she did not connect was the relationship between what started disassembling her commune in the early 1970s, and the unleashing of the AIDS Dark Age in 1981.

The connection was direct, and strong evidence exists that it was driven by an intentional intervention of covert U.S. intelligence operations plowing a petri dish-cultivated "sex, drugs and rock-and-roll" synthetic anarcho-radical hedonist culture like a nuclear-tipped Trojan Horse into the gay movement, and into the wider elements of what had been the powerful anti-war, pro-civil rights current of the previous decade.

They did not invent the AIDS virus, most likely, but they deliberately created the social contexts for its emergence and spread.

In his epochal work about the AIDS epidemic, *And the Band Played On*, the late journalist Randy Shilts describes what I also witnessed repeatedly in the early 1970s by telling the story of one Ken Horne:

"Ken Horne had always wanted to be a dancer, performing a dazzling array of pirouettes, entrechats, and arabesques before a rapt audience that would nod approvingly at his grace and beauty. A glowingly optimistic sort, he loved everything about the theatre, with its romance and costumes and fairly-tale happy endings. Maybe he could even be a star, a guy people cheered and wrote about.

"That's why he left his blue collar family in Oregon and moved to San Francisco in 1965, when he was 21, to study at the San Francisco Ballet School...The sheer contrast between his childhood plainness and his adult beauty made Ken's introduction to San Francisco gay life rewarding. All these men liked him so much, and he so desperately wanted to be liked. Sometimes, he confided to friends, he felt like a Cinderella who had finally arrived at the ball.

"Maybe that's why it was easier to let go of the dancer's dream in the late 1960s....Ken dropped out of ballet school...In 1969, he took a clerical job...He liked the regular paycheck as well as a work week that was a dream compared to the regimen of 6 a.m. to 9 p.m. he'd followed with the ballet. He had more time to go out at night now. 'This isn't so bad after all,' he told a friend. 'I'm having fun.'

"Ken soon fell in love with a German sign painter and lost touch with his early San Francisco friends, who recalled a sweet young kid who loved romance. They were surprised five years later to happen into Ken at the Folsom Prison, a leather bar. His hair was cut severely and he sported a close-cropped, narrow beard that followed the line of his jaw... His old friends were floored, not only because he was so thoroughly the prototype of the black leather machismo...but also because he looked so wasted. His hair had gone gray and his eyes looked glazed. Ken complained of how tough it was in this 'city of bottoms' to find a man who would screw him.

"His friends decided that Ken had fallen into the trap that had snared so many beautiful gay men. In his twenties, he had searched for a husband instead of a career. When he did not find a husband, he took the next best thing—sex—and soon sex became something of a career. It wasn't love but it felt good... As the focus of sex shifted from passion to technique...sexual practices would become more esoteric. That was the only way to keep it from getting boring."

A few years later in 1981, Ken Horne officially became the first person known in the U.S. to die from AIDS.

Chapter 5

Who Are We, Really? Part 2

The historically unparalleled explosion of self and social affirmation that was suddenly bestowed on all of society's homosexuals in the post-Stonewall Era meant that we faced absolutely uncharted waters.

Never before in the recorded history of mankind were homosexuals, en masse, confronted with such freedom to be open, to be their true selves publicly. The problem, however, was that there was no one to tell us, no historical precedents, no guidelines, for defining who we are and what our purpose on this planet is.

That in part explains why, coming out of the gate rudderless, the movement fell so readily under the influence of the radical hedonists, postmodernist "push pleasure beyond the limit" monsters like Allen Ginsberg, William Burroughs and Michel Foucault. There were, and to this day, are no real guideposts, no founding fathers in the manner of the U.S.'s establishment who've stood for anything but "pride" and equal rights. That is fine and good, but does nothing for defining who we are, really, in the wider context of our culture.

Prior to the Stonewall era, the realities of the closet compelled homosexuals to focus their lives and energies on their creative potentials, and we provided a vital and intrinsic component to society, overall. But once the need for privacy and secrecy about matters of sexual orientation were stripped away, homosexuals found we could focus their lives differently, namely on being homosexual, in and of itself, and the practice of it openly and publicly.

So, in this modern era, compelled by a relentless drum beat of the radical hedonists and entrepreneurs in the business of profiting from the businesses of sex, drugs and rock-and-roll (morphing into disco and club music), countless homosexuals abandoned their creative pursuits in favor of the practice of homosexuality, *per se*. "Pride" was rapidly wed with promiscuity on a level unimaginable before. There were no potent voices offering an alternative definition, of if there were, they were trampled under foot.

The case of Ken Horne, who became the first official victim of death from AIDS in 1981, illustrates this. He came to the big city as a young gay man seeking two things that are classically intrinsic to the gay sensibility: to pursue and creative artistic career (in his case, ballet) and to find true romance.

He found neither. But he did find that there was a lot of impersonal sex and drugs in the institutions that became synonymous with so-called "gay culture," such that he abandoned the idealistic dreams that brought him to San Francisco in the first place. That "culture" fed into a rampant spread of STDs and an environment for the emergence of the HIV virus. With the first reported cases of AIDS in the summer of 1981, and the average incubation period of the HIV virus 5.5 years, journalist Randy Shilts concluded in *And the Band Played On* that HIV infections began occurring around the time of the U.S. Bicentennial in 1976.

But for that to happen, what journalist Gabriel Rotello described from a public health perspective in his book, *Sexual Ecology*, as "active core groups" in New York and San Francisco, in particular, had formed. There, sexual contact by thousands with multiple partners daily in the baths, sex clubs, peep shows, movie theaters, bars with dark back rooms, parks and the West Villages' notorious trucks were key for their "eco-significance" in the "synergy of plagues."

This had become "gay culture." When the AIDS epidemic was in its full fury in the 1980s, gay activists launched pitched battles against any self-imposed or government public health constraints on such behavior in the name of defending "the essence of our liberation."

Shilts documents how grotesque this became in the height of the epidemic, leading to the massive spread of the virus when it could have been curtailed. It was symptomatic of the problem that the business owners of many of sex establishments held positions on the boards of the powerful pro-gay lobby organizations, who followed in lock step their insistence that to provide any modest restraint in the accessibility to limitless impersonal sex was "counterrevolutionary."

"Gay culture," then, had become synonymous with the stubborn right to ensure the spread of the AIDS virus to tens of thousands of unsuspecting other homosexuals.

Fast forward to this day, no one has seriously called the issue of this notion of "gay culture" into question from the standpoint of a positive alternative.

There remains no defining notion of what it means to be gay. The next stage of our freedom requires it. We have to step up and figure out who we are, really, freeing ourselves from internal constraints (our own psyches and profit motive-based institutions from bars to marketers to political parties who gain from a lowest-common-denominator definition of our so-called "community").

Homosexuals, in our many varied ways, are a vital part of the natural order. We're here on behalf of all humanity for a reason. While our new found freedom the last forty years has unleashed an incredible potential, it has ironically also endangered us and our role as never before.

Chapter 6

Who Are We, Really? Part 3

Assessing contemporary so-called "gay culture" from the standpoint of "who we are, really," it is stunning to consider that two people among those most responsible for the shaping of post-World War II American culture, including the era's gains in civil rights, were both proud, if discrete, homosexuals: Eleanor Roosevelt and Tennessee Williams.

1. Eleanor Roosevelt, wife of President Franklin D. Roosevelt, was a delegate to the newly-formed United Nations following the death of her husband and the end of World War II. She headed the committee that drafted the incredibly progressive *Universal Declaration of Human Rights,* adopted by the entire U.N. in 1948. In its preamble, it affirms "the inherent dignity and the equal and inalienable rights of all members of the human family" as "the foundation of freedom, justice and peace in the world." It was created, it says, "To the end that every individual and every organ of society, keeping this Declaration constantly in mind, shall strive by teaching and education to promote respect for these rights and freedoms and by progressive measures, national and international, to secure their universal and effective recognition." The entire world bought into these concepts.

A world weary from war and shocked by the depravity of a Nazi Germany society gone mad, subjecting millions of Jews and others (including homosexuals) to death in concentration camps, readily embraced the formation of the post-war United Nations to put humanity on a better course. Eleanor Roosevelt was a tireless pioneer in this effort, and the Universal Declaration in its entirety (including International Covenants on Economic, Social and Cultural Rights and Civil and Political Rights adopted later) set the cultural tone that resonated globally in the post-war years, and were instrumental in helping to spark the impassioned push for civil rights in the U.S., including for racial minorities, women and homosexuals.

Eleanor Roosevelt was one of us, as was well known in her time by those close to her, and even many in the media and public life, who respected her and lesbian partner's privacy until her death in New York City in 1962. She was comfortable with her homosexuality even as it was hidden from the general public while her husband was alive and for 17 years following his death.

2. Tennessee Williams was the poetic and scriptwriting voice of this same sentiment in the post-World War II era. As a homosexual man, I consider him my hero. His gritty plays, unforgiving in their honesty, challenged the conscience of the nation, depicting as they did, the plight of women and minorities, especially in the south, and of homosexuals, too. His plays won major awards and were made into movies. His first big breakthrough, coming right at the end of World War II and in the context of the founding of the United Nations, was *The Glass Menagerie*, and it was followed by *A Streetcar Named Desire*, and such follow-ons as *Suddenly Last Summer*.

Menagerie and *Suddenly* both spoke to the heinous practice of surgical frontal lobotomies of the brain widely performed on unruly children in that era, as had been done to Williams' own sister. Those plays helped to end that terrible practice.

As his works hit the Broadway stage, were turned into movie hits and were then performed by drama departments on college campuses all over the U.S., they evoked a sensibility that spurred the student civil rights activism of the early 1960s, including the courageous efforts of thousands of college students from the North busing in to register newly-enfranchised African-American voters in the South.

Williams was, like Eleanor Roosevelt, also proudly homosexual, although that did not become public until, in the wake of the gay liberation surge that followed Stonewall in 1969, he "came out" in a big way, beginning to write his memoirs in 1972 that told of the depths of his gay spirit and lifestyle.

I believe he did that partly in response to a written appeal by an early Berkeley Gay Liberation Front friend and collaborator of mine, Mike Silverstein, who wrote a passionate letter published in the *Gay Sunshine* newspaper in 1971, entitled, "An Open Letter to Tennessee Williams" (reprinted in *Come Out Fighting: A Century of Essential Writing on Gay and Lesbian Liberation*, edited by Chris Bull).

Eleanor Roosevelt and Tennessee Williams, these towering pillars of American post-World War II culture and values, transformed the wider, even global, culture and I believe their homosexuality had a lot to do with that, as I will discuss more later.

By contrast to this, today's "gay culture" is a parody of what it really means to homosexual, more like a social marketing charade. It is a consequence of the massive intervention into the emerging gay liberation movement by the reactionary peddlers of radical hedonistic "sex, drugs and rock and roll," designed to derail the impact of the homosexual sensibility on wider society in the post-Stonewall era.

Chapter 7

Tennessee Williams
Vs. William Burroughs, Part 1

Who are we really? Homosexuals are a vital element of natural creation, operating throughout history as the makers and menders of the social fabric of civilizations. Without fully articulating the wider perspective of homosexuality's derivation from the very dissymmetry of the evolving universe itself, suffice it to say for now that not only are we are meant to be, but we fail to fulfill our vital social role only when we try to suppress our true natures, or become desperate to mimic the straight world.

Homosexuals who've loved themselves and others have mediated a world otherwise too sharply divided by testosterone-dominated males and estrogen-infused women, where the natural order trends to a brutal domination of the former over the latter, leading to social systems of militaristic tyrannies fueled by the internal dynamics of systematic abuse of women, children, the weak and the elderly in individual households.

Nature provides for homosexuals by and large with elevated levels of empathy who are not interested in using women for procreation and domination, who tend to offer comfort and care for the proverbial "widows and orphans." They introduce tools of science, medicine and art to ease their plight and to "tame the savage beasts" of male dominated societies.

While no one can insist that this is the case for each and every homosexual person, it does account for the existence of homosexuality as a phenomenon in every human society, even when it is not identified openly.

Thus, a compassionate and civil-rights oriented American society after World War II was shaped to a large degree by the enormous, seminal influence of two prominent homosexuals, Eleanor Roosevelt, co-author and expounder of the 1947 International Declaration of the Rights of Man, and Tennessee Williams, the playwright who spurred the conscience of the entire nation.

But evidences of the socially-efficacious role of homosexuals go way back: to the tyrant-slaying and nation building of David, lover of Jonathan in the Old Testament, to Socrates, the inventor of modern scientific reasoning, to the artistic and scientific giants of the Renaissance, Donatello, da Vinci, Michelangelo and Caravaggio, to the artistic genius of Shakespeare (whose Sonnets are explicit), Whitman and Wilde and the statesmanship of Lincoln, and many others.

In the 20th century, many leaders of women's suffrage, writers, poets and artists like Christopher Isherwood, W.H. Auden and Don Bachardy and statesmen like the United Nations' Dag Hammarskjöld not only advanced humanitarian and just social institutions, but also inspired the first waves of brave women and men standing up for the public recognition and appreciation of homosexuals in the context of striving for social justice for all, heroes like Frank Kameny, Lilli Vincenz and Nancy Davis, Barbara Gittings, Del Martin and Phyllis Lyon, Harry Hay and others.

But the civil rights fervor of the 1960s waned as a massive social engineering offensive was launched by the enemies of progressive values in the U.S. It was spurred by the 1968 assassinations of Martin Luther King and Robert Kennedy and the massive introduction of LSD and other drugs, through the CIA's well-documented MK-Ultra project run on forty U.S. college campuses, of psychedelic rock and disco to substitute for the music of love and social justice, and of radical hedonism and boundless excesses of the angry Beats and their anarchistic and radical libertarian hordes.

America underwent a social transformation under this offensive in the 1970s, which was introduced to wider society through portals on its social margins, including the post-Stonewall gay movement.

That engineered excess led to the urban environments in which AIDS would appear and spread and it has not relented in much of the gay culture even to this day.

Nothing signaled the departure of this offensive from the earlier gay sensibility than a conversation between Tennessee Williams and the gay radical Beat poet, William Burroughs, published in the pages of the *Village Voice* in May 1977, just as the excesses of impersonal gay sex were well on their way to fueling the outbreak of AIDS.

From that exchange:

Burroughs: "Do what thou wilt" is the whole of the Law.

Williams: Regarding drugs, you mean.

Burroughs: Regarding anything..."Nothing is true, everything is permitted." In other words, everything is permitted because nothing is true. If you see everything as illusion, then everything is permitted...

Williams: Provided you want to do the right thing, yes.

Burroughs: Ah, but if you really want to do it, then it's the right thing. That's the point.

Williams: Isn't that an amoralist point of view?

Burroughs: Completely...completely.

Williams: I don't believe you are an amoralist.

Burroughs: Oh yes.

Williams: You do believe it?

Burroughs: Well, I do what I can...

Williams: I don't think it's true.

Burroughs: We were both brought up in the Bible Belt; but it's obvious that what you want to do is, of course, eventually what you will do, anyway. Sooner or later.

Doing the "right thing" versus "everything is permitted" —that sharp contrast defined the separation between the true homosexual sentiment from the horror it became for too many during that awful era.

Chapter 8

Tennessee Williams
Vs. William Burroughs, Part 2

It is instructive that as late as 1977, gay playwright Tennessee Williams recoiled at the discovery his fellow gay writer William Burroughs was as amoral and radically hedonistic as he professed to be in a memorable exchange between Williams and Burroughs published in the *Village Voice* that spring.

Burroughs, a heroin addict and central figure of the so-called Beat Generation writers that included Allen Ginsberg and Jack Kerouac, epitomized the postmodern philosophy grounded in anger and a rejection of all convention, including all laws and prevailing concepts of right and wrong.

There is no "right thing" to do, as Williams suggested in the exchange, Burroughs insisted, only individual desire. Following the urges of such desire is the only way to be real. Williams was startled and couldn't believe his ears.

From the standpoint of an effort to figure out what really happened to homosexuals in America following the magnificent explosion of open self-affirmation that attended the early days of the Stonewall Era, the 1977 Williams-Burroughs exchange functions as a sort of Rosetta Stone. It is the key to unlocking and sorting out how the gay liberation movement went from the highest of the high positive social force to the pit of an AIDS Dark Age, to the lowest of the low, within the course of barely a decade. The implications for today, and the movement going forward, are also profound.

That someone as perceptive and street-savvy as Williams was truly surprised by Burroughs' revelation in that exchange, as late in the gay liberation process as 1977, was indicative of the confused state of the movement, and few people even to this day are aware of this distinction, much less of its significance.

With the outburst of post-Stonewall gay liberation in 1969 came an unprecedented opportunity for homosexuals to massively increase and intensify the unique contributions to a just and compassionate wider society that it is innate to our disposition to provide. Homosexuals' creativity, suddenly bolstered by a new level of self-affirmation and esteem, was poised for unleashing on the world its greatest gifts.

Williams represented that creativity. An active, happy and practicing homosexual since the days he plucked chickens in California and worked as a doorman in New York prior to his 1944 breakthrough as a playwright, Williams led a lively and adventurous gay life, but no matter how much he caroused, he did not compromise on his commitment to his creative work.

He never abandoned, even in his roughest patches, his routine of hard work writing for lengthy unbroken periods every single morning. He often said his creative work was his life, and was amazingly prolific. He did not define himself by his homosexuality, but by his work.

But the counter-cultural ethos that swept over the post-Stonewall gay movement was entirely otherwise. It quickly became grounded entirely in the pursuit of unrestrained gay sex, urged people to "turn on, tune in and drop out" of their creative pursuits, and progressed rapidly to an astounding level of promiscuity and excess.

Efforts by myself and others in my "Effeminist" gay liberation current of the early 1970s, including my literary slug fests with Burroughs' pal Allen Ginsberg on the pages of the *Berkeley Barb,* were overwhelmed.

By 1977, at the time of the Williams-Burroughs dialogue, there was only one voice in the wilderness cautioning that there were emerging, dire consequences to the urban gay scenes' descent into a wanton, unbridled, obsessive drug-induced unending orgy of impersonal and extreme sex.

By 1977, the AIDS virus was already spreading among gay men in these environments, with an average 5.5-year incubation period to surface with so-called "gay cancer" symptoms in the summer of 1981.

Larry Kramer, who in 1969 wrote the Oscar-nominated screenplay for the film version of D.H. Lawrence's *Women in Love*, was writing his biting novel, prophecy and critique of what the gay movement had devolved into, entitled *Faggots*.

The book was reviled by the forgettable leaders of the gay movement, including its political leaders none of whom said a word of caution about what the prevailing "gay lifestyle" had become.

Faggots was written as an unyielding challenge to urban gay men to take a hard, critical, self-reflective look at what they had descended into, written in the form of a brutally-explicit novel about the behavior of such men in the Manhattan of that day. Tragically, its accounts were generally not excessive, compared to the actual reality, and it was incredibly prescient.

Among other things, it has its characters saying things like: "Faggots don't want to know about success. It reminds them of what they're evading." Its sub-stories of young teenagers coming from rural areas to find themselves, to seek creative success and romance, being dragged into the middle of intense sequences of unrelenting drugged sexual activity with no regard for consequences or human emotions is painful to read, even had the resultant AIDS epidemic that killed most of them not resulted.

But even Kramer couldn't see that coming home to roost only three years later.

Chapter 9

Signposts for a Revival of The "Gay Sensibility"

It is refreshing to see prominent young, articulate voices new to the gay scene making public statements about homosexuality that are not filtered through conventional expectations or the hedonist-gripped post-Stonewall gay culture.

In the fall of 2010, when singer Ricky Martin celebrated his recent "coming out" by saying, "God does not make mistakes," in an interview with Ellen DeGeneres, or when U.S. Olympic figure skater Johnny Weir tells a homosexual rights group in California that, "It's an ugly world out there, but we are the people who bring beauty to it," they are saying simple but, in fact, revolutionary things that point to a more positive future for us all. They both suggest that there is a purposefulness to homosexuality that goes beyond sex, and that has been completely missing from any significant discourse in the gay liberation movement since its earliest days, when it first was caught in the grip of the radical hedonist surge that was unleashed by sinister forces to demolish the social consciousness of an entire generation.

Now, both Martin and Weir come to the movement as fully-enfranchised adults, having levels of professional achievement under their belts that add credibility and authority to what they say, especially as they come to speak out in fresh, new ways about their own identities. They are like children in that sense, not jaundiced by forty years of a hedonistic gay culture, and eager to embrace expressions that are rich with purpose and meaning.

They offer hope that new generations of homosexuals, free to be open, expressive and creative in our society, will grow up appreciating themselves not for opportunities to pursue sex and drug use at will, but for their uniquely gay sensibilities and what those will bring to serious professional pursuits.

In the case of Weir, he has for years seen himself as a role model for the young, expressing openly that purpose in his willingness to be "out front" with his sassy but articulate comments and flashy, unconventional costumes, while always in the context of his grueling pursuit of excellence in his sport. It was the crowning achievement of his career to qualify for his second Olympic Games last February, even with three U.S. championships under his belt.

He did not come to where he has by virtue of posturing. His reality TV show was not about idle wealth or voyeurism into the lives of pathetic, mediocre people. It was based in his struggle to excel on the ice, and his accomplishments there have earned him a devoted worldwide following.

The Ricky Martin story is similar. The hard work of building a successful career was, as for Weir, at the core of his identity, just as it was for the likes of Tennessee Williams and others from an earlier era.

Homosexuals, as Weir said in California, bring beauty to an ugly world, and that strikes at the core of our identity and role in the natural order of things.

In my own life, and in the context of having conversations with and reading the words of literally thousands of other homosexuals over the last decades, I am convinced that there is a "gay sensibility" that finds expression in many different ways but can usually be found in the earliest years of development, usually long before there is any awareness of a sexual orientation.

I grew up with an acute sense that I was somehow different. I must commend my parents (meaning my mother) for allowing my difference to play itself out. It took the form of different interests. I pursued interests completely unlike those of any of my family members, or my classmates and teachers at school.

Maybe my fascination with the history and portraits of the presidents of the U.S. had to do with their being powerful and important men. Maybe my interest in producing newspapers, beginning at age seven, was to help my besieged mother's efforts to maintain loving bonds in our household, constantly threatened by my father's brutality. It was at the core of my identity to empathize and support her in these struggles. Maybe my love for classical music was tied to my infatuation, TV having been introduced to our home, with the old *Flash Gordon* movie serials, whose theme music was Liszt's *Les Preludes*. It had something to do with Flash himself, played by the handsome, wavy blond Buster Crabbe.

When I read Tennessee Williams' memoirs, I see clear footprints of similar sensibilities, and have found them in the autobiographical stories of legions of other homosexuals I have known or read.

My difference as experienced in my youth formed the basis of my adult passion for beauty and social justice, beginning with my seminary training. While "coming out" in the Stonewall era was the best thing that ever happened to me, my creative contribution to society was temporarily derailed by the radical hedonistic takeover of the gay movement. Still, unlike so many other young, beautiful creative homosexual souls, I somehow survived, luckily enough to publish my own newspaper in the nation's capital for the last 20 years.

Chapter 10

"Gay Sensibility" and Socrates
On "The Science of Love"

The issue is how a notion of "gay sensibility" can replace or at least be elevated against sexual hedonism as the default paradigm that has prevailed in the gay movement from Stonewall to the present.

It is important to consider, when positing that some rough percentage of human populations are naturally born as homosexual, the following: for the vast, vast majority of homosexuals throughout history on this planet, and in all over it even at this time, acting out sexually is and has simply not been an option.

These countless souls have had to live out their lives resigned to no sexual component, at least in terms of same-sex, facing penalties of unbearable social ostracism, brutal punishment, torture and death. Only in the tiniest slivers of human history have there been brief exceptions to this, and of course there has never been a period in history comparable to the last forty years since Stonewall.

But for all history, in what ways have homosexuals managed to manifest their unique identities to their societies?

I propose that, taking sex out of the equation, the term, "sexual orientation" can be substituted for with a valid alternative. The term "orientation" pertains to a disposition, or a vantage point, and can be replaced with "perspective." The term "sexual," with sex not an option, can be replaced with "sensual," maintaining the qualities associated with attraction that leads to sexual desire.

So, we can suggest that homosexuals throughout history have expressed their unique natures not through "sexual orientation," except rarely, but far more prominently through "sensual perspective," instead.

Behold, this is completely valid and coherent with qualities of "gay sensibility" as I identified it in earlier segments. The unique "sensual perspective" of homosexuals has informed our poetry, art, music, governance, scientific method, and sympathies for the downtrodden and oppressed throughout history.

Our rock-star "founder," the homosexual Socrates, by way of Plato perhaps the most influential thinker and inventor of scientific method in the history of western civilization, spoke about the dual realities of "sensual perspective" and sexual appetite in the two of Plato's works most directly addressing homosexuality, *The Symposium* and *Phaedrus*.

In particular, in his second speech in *Phaedrus*, where the allegory of the charioteer and his two conflicting horses is presented, Socrates articulated what he called "the science of love."

The soul is composed of its winged charioteer and the two horses—one is good and one is not—that he describes as follows:

The first: "The horse that is harnessed on the senior side is upright and clean-limbed; he holds his neck high, and has a somewhat hooked nose; his color is white, with black eyes; his thirst for honor is tempered by restraint and modesty; he is a friend of genuine renown and needs no whip, but is driven simply by the word of command."

The second: "The other horse is crooked, lumbering, ill-made; stiff-necked, short-throated, snub-nosed; his coat is black and his eyes a bloodshot gray; wantonness and boastfulness are his companions, and he is hairy-eared and deaf, hardly controllable even with a whip and goad."

So, said Socrates, "When the charioteer sees the vision of the loved one, so that a sensation of warmth spreads from him over the whole soul and he begins to feel an itching and the stings of desire," the two horses act in an entirely different way. While the white horse and charioteer are "constrained by a sense of shame," the black horse "utterly heedless now of the driver's whip and goad, rushes forward, prancing, and to the great discomfiture of his yoke-fellow and the charioteer, drives them to approach the lad and make mention of the sweetness of physical love."

Socrates continued the allegory, "At first the two indignantly resist the idea of being forced into such a monstrous wrong-doing, but finally, when they can get no peace, they yield to the importunity of the bad horse and agree to what he bids.

"So, they draw near, and the vision of the beloved dazzles their eyes. When the driver beholds it the sight awakens in him the memory of absolute beauty...and in so doing inevitably tugs the reigns so violently that he brings both horses down upon their haunches; the good horse gives way willingly and does not struggle, but the lustful horse resists with all his strength."

Socrates demonstrated that by the charioteer's ability to restrain the "lustful horse," he was able to honor the beloved and his beauty with a true and enduring love.

Socrates was pointing toward the kind of "gay sensibility" I have identified, as he contrasted "excellence" to "pleasure" as the foundation of love.

The post-Stonewall gay movement has had the black horse as its core paradigm. The challenge for our future is in our ability to start consciously pulling on its reins.

Chapter 11

A "Sensual Perspective"
Beyond the Bedroom

For purposes of political expediency in arguments to extend equal legal rights to homosexuals, such as the December 2010 repeal of "Don't Ask, Don't Tell," it is clear why Rep. Barney Frank claimed that the only thing different about homosexuals from everyone else is what they do in the bedroom.

However, such a one dimensional definition of homosexuals leaves too many questions unanswered that are critical for a positive, and proper, homosexual self-identity. It leaves open, for example, the issue that, while acknowledged as equal under the law, homosexuals can still be understood as deficient or disabled, allowing for on-going negative attitudes, both externally and as internalized by many gays.

But by breaking down the term, "sexual orientation" to its historic corollary, "sensual perspective," puts a very different light on this discussion. All homosexuals in the history of humanity have harbored, by virtue of their orientation, a "sensual perspective" even if unable, as in the vast majority of cases, to act it out sexually.

The term, "homosexual," is a very recent invention, first coined by emerging legions of new social engineers in 1859. Minus that label, we homosexuals called ourselves by different names, if by any at all, and some associated our orientation within the grander design of things, such as the late 19th century term "Uranians" (Neil McKenna, *The Secret Life of Oscar Wilde*, 2005).

Before that era, "sodomites" were identified as those almost always among criminal outcast dregs of society, along with thieves and prostitutes, while the vast breadth of persons born as

"Uranians," shall we say, lived out their lives free of the "sodomite" label because they never acted out or got caught.

With the 19th century democratization pressures on Western cultures, in the context of the growth of easy transportation from rural to urban areas and ports of trade, and the rise of large industrial cities with their anonymity, an open, if narrow, discussion of a much wider set of options for sexual activity first began to emerge.

In Berlin in the Wiemar period of the 1920s, British writer Christopher Isherwood (of *Cabaret* fame) and poet W.H. Auden were free to act out their homosexuality, guided by new, radical theories of American psychologist Homer Lane and his protégé, John Layard. Lane's mantra was: "There is only one sin: disobedience to the inner law of our own nature" (Isherwood, *Christopher and His Kind*, 1976).

Still, as in the case of both of those, their primary identity was the literary and poetic sensibility that they contributed to the wider world in the form of their creative writing. Fleeing Berlin, their anti-fascist sentiments contributed to the forceful post-World War II moral sentiment in the U.S., also informed by the monumental creative contributions of homosexuals Eleanor Roosevelt and Isherwood's long-time friend, the playwright Tennessee Williams.

The World War II "greatest generation" of Americans had their ethics and ideals shaped by the towering contributions of homosexuals, who were far more committed to their creative work than their sexual identity.

The "gay sentiment" of these and many other figures, with its passion for honesty and social justice, helped to spark the civil rights movement in the U.S., and the growing power of labor unions fighting for livable working conditions and a brighter future for working people and their families.

A massive counteroffensive from the titans of the military-industrial complex, working through covert intelligence fronts, took shape beginning with the assassination of JFK in 1963, followed by the assassinations of Martin Luther King and Robert Kennedy in 1968, the provocation of inner city riots, and the launch of the "sex, drugs and rock and roll" hedonistic counterculture that escalated with the "Summer of Love" in 1967. That corresponded with the rise of an inward-directed "sensitivity training" movement out of California's Esalen Institute, the National Training Labs and other centers, and was coordinated with the CIA's domestic "MK-Ultra" operation that disseminated LSD and other drugs from forty college campuses and in urban ghettos (as revealed during the Church Committee hearings in the mid-1970s).

The "sensitivity training" movement was huge, causing a "drifting away" from scientific evidence and methods toward a "religiously-oriented social movement" (Kurt W. Back, *Beyond Words*, 1972).

While the earlier civil rights movement led to an inevitable surge for women's and gay liberation, the counter-forces steered them toward a noxious mix of radical hedonism and inward-focused "sensitivity" modes, such that the default definition of homosexuals became limited to personal sexual behavior, cut off from a wider social context, and nothing more.

Thus, Rep. Frank's characterization that the difference between gays and straights is limited to the bedroom is unchanged from what it came to be in the immediate post-Stonewall period forty years ago.

It overlooks what is the most important component of homosexual identity, the "gay sentiment," a product of the natural order of creation that, given its different "sensual perspective" empowers homosexuals with an uncommon ability to love, care for and speak passionately to the plight persons of their own sex in constructive, non-sexual ways.

Chapter 12

"Gay Sensibility" as A Gift of Nature

I have introduced two novel, reasonably-grounded concepts over the course of these columns, the notions of "gay sensibility" and "sensual perspective," that harbor the potential to elevate the gay movement beyond the tenacious clutches of sexual hedonism that has dogged it for forty years or more.

In the fall of 2010 YouTube video of White House staff members encouraging young gay and lesbian people that "It Gets Better," in the wake of last fall's spate of bully-driven student suicides, all of them testify about how they felt themselves to be "different" at very early stages in their lives, even before they were aware of how such differences should be defined.

This corresponds with my own childhood experience and those of countless other homosexuals I have talked with and read about over the years.

That "difference" is what I call a "gay sensibility," and it is more pervasive for one's personality than sexual orientation, usually preceding it. This, and not sexual orientation alone, is the central, defining feature of homosexuals.

From a scientific perspective, "gay sensibility" shows up routinely in human societies as dominant among a minority of persons. Indeed, it is an outgrowth of nature's creative process that has dissymmetry, not symmetry, as its core.

As symmetry, or equilibrium, leads to stasis, or idleness, it cannot account for the dynamic unfolding of creation. So, there must be a basic dissymmetric element to creation, which energizes a binary universe to grow, expand and develop. In philosophical terms, it is analogous to the active communicating component of a dialectic form of reasoning that advances knowledge.

The binary system of human species development is the distinction between its male (testosterone-based) and female (estrogen-based) components. But this system requires a dynamic bridge element to progress, and this element is comparable to the notion of "gay sentiment."

It is the component that tempers the otherwise stark distinction between the pure male and pure female parts, allowing for nurture and growth, fending off the extremes of dominance and submission otherwise inherent. It is a vital, indispensable component of creation itself.

Therefore, the person who finds him or herself to harbor a rich, defining portion of "gay sensibility" actually bears a special role in creation, and as such is the bearer of a special gift, not only in terms of one's own identity, but to society, as a whole.

"Gay sensibility" is a special gift. It is a gift that cannot be returned, as much as many may wish it could. It can be squandered, erased or almost destroyed, but remains a natural gift nonetheless.

We with a "gay sensibility" are not only capable of loving and caring for persons of our own gender in ways that those without it can't match, but we also have a unique capacity to love and care for persons of the opposite sex, because we do not measure such persons from the standpoint of dominion, procreation and society's structures for perpetuating these. "Gay sensibility" empowers us with a unique capacity to love all persons regardless of gender in a compassionate, empathetic way.

Naturally, such sentiments become co-mingled with the complex mysteries of erotic arousal, but for the self-actualized person, while these are powerful, legitimate and drive a longing for and pursual of reciprocal romantic relationships, they do not overwhelm a positive sense of personhood or fundamentally interfere with the creative vocations pursued to put a "gay sentiment" to best use in the world.

It was fitting that in his remarks on the occasion of signing the repeal of "Don't Ask, Don't Tell" into law on Dec. 22, 2010, President Obama cited the case of a gay World War II soldier's life-saving bravery.

During a firefight in the Battle of the Bulge, Obama recounted, "a private named Lloyd Corwin tumbled forty feet down the deep side of a ravine. Dazed and trapped, he was as good as dead. But one soldier, a friend, turned back. With shells landing around him, amid smoke and chaos and the screams of wounded men, this soldier, this friend, scaled down the icy slope, risking his own life to bring Private Corwin to safer ground."

Obama went on, "For the rest of his years, Lloyd credited this soldier, this friend, named Andy Lee, with saving his life, knowing he would never have made it out alone."

Forty years later, he added, Corwin learned that Andy Lee was gay. "Lloyd has no idea," he reported, "And he didn't much care. Lloyd knew what had kept him alive; what made it possible for him to come home and start a family and live the rest of his life. It was his friend."

This was a beautiful, real life account of "gay sensibility" in action. Clearly, it is not only those with that great gift who can perform such selfless acts of courage and love, but for us, it is our signature, it's why we're here.

Chapter 13

"Gay Sensibility" and Constructive Non-Conformity

With the December 2010 historic repeal of "Don't Ask, Don't Tell," the online *Box Turtle Bulletin*'s Timothy Kinkaid wrote a commentary entitled, "Trading in Our Sparkle and Our Freak."

His concern is for the pressure that advances in equality put on homosexuals to conform to dominant social expectations and norms. Are we running the risk of becoming "just like them?"

Surely, the pressure to conform exists for everyone in society, straight or gay, and gays have even more good reasons, apparently, to conform. The reasons range from keeping our orientation secret, to reassuring everyone we're just like them except in the bedroom and therefore non-threatening, to enjoying a sense of security that derives from conformity, and to the unresolved, residual "post traumatic stress syndrome" effects of the AIDS Dark Age.

But homosexuals are simply not wired for conformity.

All the empirical evidence suggests that homosexuality pertains to the whole psyche of the person, and not just to the narrow aspect associated with sexuality *per se*. An often-profound sense of differences in childhood, tied to different interests and desires, are normative and amplified as erotic arousal manifests itself to present two related, naturally-generated realities for homosexuals.

The first I have described as "gay sensibility," and the second as a different "sensual perspective."

These two factors operative in homosexuals establish that we look at the world in a fundamentally different way from non-homosexuals. Walking into a candy store, ninety percent of the people gravitate toward a certain favorite, and evaluate and prioritize everything in the store from that standpoint. The ten percent who prefer a different favorite accordingly look at everything in a different way.

Homosexuals can't be conformists without trying very hard, and are never quite up to the task. A passion to conform is almost as bad as being in the closet. It is just not natural.

What *is* natural is for homosexuals is what I call "constructive non-conformity." It could also be called "creative" or "compassionate" non-conformity, but "constructive" is preferred because it derives best from the notions of "gay sensibility" and "sensual perspective," and also defines natural gay non-conformity against corruptions of that concept.

To be specific, "constructive non-conformity" is definitely not the kind of anarchistic, self-obsessed, destructive and power-centered notions of non-conformity defined by the Beat Generation and related radical hedonist currents that hijacked the gay movement in the aftermath of Stonewall. It is not the postmodernist ugliness exemplified by the theories and mandates of the contemptible Michel Foucault. Nor is it the so-called "queer theory" current that worships Foucault as some sort of saint, and thereby embraces his jaded, angry and cynical perspective on reality and behavior.

No, "constructive non-conformity" reflects the enduring contributions of many homosexuals in history, and while they can be awesomely camp and outrageous, as in the likes of a Liberace, *Birdcage* heroes or figure skater Johnny Weir, such non-conformists are constructive, life-affirming givers of love and compassion, just as was the remarkably non-conformist life of Eleanor Roosevelt.

Imagine Eleanor Roosevelt breaking from every convention by simultaneously redefining the accepted definitions of both a "First Lady" and of a woman, in general. She guided her physically-disabled husband through the nation's most trying times of depression and war, and emerged after his death to champion the most progressive achievement of the modern era, the *Declaration of the International Rights of Man*. Most historians declared her husband, FDR, the Man of the Century for the 20th century. I give it to her, hands down the Person of the Century. And she was one of us.

Conformity is the bane of our, or any, age. In our times, young people are tracked almost like chattel into social expectations that lock them, with few variations, into routinely mundane and mediocre lives to reinforce the powers that be. Not a totalitarian system, this is the norm for our democracy, and it is done through our ruling class' vast resources of social engineering.

Boys play sports to ready themselves to fight and die in wars. Girls play with dolls and cheer boys on the sidelines of sporting events, groomed to comfort the fighting men and have their babies.

Alternatively, today's young are groomed to attend college, become steeped in student loan debt, to find a job to pay it off, afford marriage, buy a house and have children. By their early 20s, they're set in cement, locked in at an early age, with few inspired or motivated to buck the trend.

Televised sports, fantasy sports, sophomoric soap operas and other cultural drivel preoccupy them, leaving little time for anything original and creative. Meanwhile, American society drifts relentlessly to the right, toward indifference to the poor and paranoid about everything beyond its borders. So much for conformity.

It takes "constructive non-conformists" to alter such patterns for the betterment of us all, both by working individually with persons and with society as a whole. That means us.

Chapter 14

Constructive Non-Conformity
and Social Transformation

Those paying attention have seen that in these chapters a number of original notions have been derived from a wider examination of gay identity factors, especially as they have been extracted from captivity to the radical hedonism introduced into the gay movement the late 1960s and early 1970s.

The novelties here include identifying how radical hedonism, and its sinister roots, intervened into the gay movement, and by separating it out from the core homosexual experience.

By identifying and isolating that core, it became possible to glimpse at the notions of "gay sensibility" and alternative "sensual perspective" that have manifested themselves through human history as some of the most constructive currents in art, philosophy, science and progressive governance.

"Gay sensibility" precedes homosexuality, a term that didn't exist before 1859, because the vastest majority of persons in history who've experienced themselves drawn by erotic arousal to the same sex have never been able to act out those feelings.

Instead they focused on cultivating their creative capacity to express their alternative "sensibility," informed by the fact that they harbored an innate "sensual perspective" different from the norm. Such qualities inclined such persons toward a "constructive non-conformity" that has been decisive for moving societies toward more enlightened, democratic and compassionate forms.

It is in this context that an adequate accounting for the role of same-sex erotic arousal can be examined in a fresh and spectacular way.

The mysteries of same-sex erotic arousal take many forms and fluctuating degrees of intensity, involving a wide range objects, or triggers, for such arousal, well known in the gay community as extending from chubby bears to skinny twinks, from burly lumberjacks to preppies, from motorcycle gangstas to diva drag queens, all the shades in between and with their lesbian equivalents, as well.

The reality of such variety, by extension, accounts for bisexuality and the famous Kinsey scale, which was derived from the extensive compilation of interview data by Dr. Alfred Kinsey in the 1930s and 1940 that led to his groundbreaking published works, *Sexual Behavior of the Human Male* (1948) and *Sexual Behavior of the Human Female* (1953).

Kinsey's exhaustive research brought him to conclude that human sexual attraction is not confined to absolute "straight" or "gay," but exists on a continuum from 0 to 6, and that an individual's erotic attractions can move over time in one direction toward opposite sex attraction or toward the other, same-sex attraction.

Among other things, Kinsey's findings included the discovery that forty-six percent of males had "reacted" to the same sex and thirty-seven percent engaged in at least one homosexual encounter, percentages obviously far higher than most estimates of the percentage of the population that is self-identified as homosexual.

Such discoveries are a manifestation of what is actually an elastic quality of erotic arousal, as in a rise in the rate of homosexual arousal in environments of long-term same-sex confinement, including prisons and infamous British all-boy boarding schools ("On the basis of many confidential interviews, the author of a recent British study, *The Public School Phenomenon*, believes that an average of a quarter of the boys attending Britain's public-school system during the first decades of this century engaged in regular sexual contact. More than ninety percent owned up to 'fact or fantasy' love affairs with other boys," John Costello, *Mask of Treachery*, 1988, p. 64).

While all such examinations of erotic arousal are limited to sexual encounters, *per se*, what happens when they are applied to their broader dimensions of "gay sensibility" and alternative "sensual perspective?"

There are profound implications for positing a similar elasticity in these dimensions. It means the constructive non-conformity derived from "gay sensibility" and alternative "sensual perspective" harbors a great potential for profound social change. That is, the potential to tap into a similar sensibility that can be drawn out of a much wider population, even among those who do not associate such sensibility with erotic arousal at any given point.

Therefore, a passionate "gay sensibility" to apply constructive non-conformity to the struggle for civil rights and economic justice can spark an explosive response from a much larger segment of the overall population than just those who identify themselves as homosexuals.

The elasticity of such a sensibility allows it to spread throughout the public in a potentially "viral" fashion.

Therein lies the substance of our "gay sensibility's" fundamentally transformative nature. This realization accounts for the title of my essay in the 2009 collection of retrospectives on the post-Stonewall gay movement, *Smash the Church, Smash the State! The Early Years of Gay Liberation* (City Lights Books). My essay is entitled, "Berkeley and the Fight for an Effeminist, Socially Transformative Gay Identity" (p. 203).

In 1972, my friend, Jim Rankin, and I founded *The Effeminist*, a short-lived newspaper in Berkeley, Calif., dedicated to engineering such a transformation through a strategic alliance with feminism against society's dominant core paradigm of white male supremacy.

In short, we lost, and radical hedonism won, which brings us to now.

Chapter 15

Whitman's "Great Poets" and a New Gay Identity

"The attitude of great poets is to cheer up slaves and horrify despots"
—*Walt Whitman*, Leaves of Grass (1855).

This quote has been framed and posted on the wall in front of my computer in the *Falls Church News-Press* office since the late 1990s. It is the most succinct statement of everything I stand for and my newspaper is dedicated to I have ever come across.

That's little wonder when you consider the source. It is hardly irrelevant that the author, hailed as perhaps the greatest American poet ever, is "one of us."

In fact, I contend that, for a variety of reasons, Walt Whitman's notion of the "great poet" in his incredibly influential *Leaves of Grass*, first published in 1855, represents a high water mark for defining the positive notions of "gay sensibility," alternative "sensual perspective" and "constructive non-conformity" that I have articulated as platforms for a new "gay identity" in these chapters.

Whitman, who was gay, coined the term, "great poet" to describe sensibilities that are commensurate with the exercise of democracy in the young American republic and are entirely coherent with "gay sensibility" as I've described it, and as I've discovered most LGBT people to have experienced it in their own lives.

He coined the term at least fifteen years before social psychologists invented the word, "homosexual." Contrasted to existing labels laden with negative connotations in use in his time, Whitman carved out a universal notion of the "great poet" who stands staunchly for equality of all persons, on the side of the plight of the working poor and the oppressed, and for the merits of science, invention, beauty, sensuality, art and reason to lift humanity towards a better place.

Leaves of Grass, in its early editions, was condemned by many because it was considered immoral. Its sensual and homoerotic content leaped out from its pages, especially in its *Calamus poetry* section. But while many students of same-sex history view this as a precursor of an emerging homosexual subculture in the U.S., *Leaves of Grass* as a whole defies such narrow identity pigeon-holing. That was Whitman's point.

The "great poet" has command over the whole world by bringing the unique and passionate alternate perspective that drives a constructive non-conformity toward equality, democracy and justice. Thus, Whitman's twenty-seven-page *Leaves of Grass* introduction has a universal expression of "gay sensibility" dripping from its pages.

By this definition, the sensibility that precedes erotic arousal in homosexuals drives them toward an embrace of the talents and professions that correspond to Whitman's articulation of the "great poet."

That's really who we are. The same-sex part is a subordinate but defining component. It is a signpost that we are that element of nature which drives it from what was to what will be, from stagnation or regression toward progress defined by expanding democracy, science, education and art.

It is not defined by the inward-turning, narrow, calcified categorical thinking that sees reality in rigid terms of heterosexual and homosexual, and organizes humanity in defense of one or the other. When everyone is fighting for their own gains, and homosexuals become inclined to seek only their own "rights," all are thereby susceptible of becoming stingy and indifferent to the plight of others.

The "great poet" of Whitman inclines strongly for equal justice for all under the law, regardless of anything pertaining to orientations, sexual or otherwise. Therefore, striving for the full legal and cultural enfranchisement of homosexuals is a worthy and meritorious undertaking.

However, the "great poet" does not advocate this to the exclusion of the full enfranchisement of all persons, including the poorest and most needy.

While the massive influence of Whitman's *Leaves of Grass* on the psyche of all Americans in the latter half of the 19th century, through its many editions, additions and edits, until and beyond Whitman's death in 1892, its impact was especially profound in the burgeoning American cities, where the networks of creative and compassionate self-identified homosexuals grew quickly to something that persisted, through ebbs and flows, into the late 1960s, as described in George Chauncey's *Gay New York, 1890-1940* (1995), and Nan Alamilla Boyd's *Wide Open Town: A History of Queer San Francisco to 1965* (2003).

That was the world into which came still only the tiniest fraction of the seven percent of all humanity that inclines to homosexuality, and which took me twenty-four years to first discover in San Francisco in 1968.

But it was around that same time that a sea change occurred in the urban homosexual culture, simultaneously explosive, liberating and ominous. The notion of "great poets" eroded over time, the culture was not prepared for the level and intensity of radical hedonism that suddenly overwhelmed it in the early 1970s. I lived through that, and experienced the tumult that drove it toward the "valley of the shadow of death."

Chapter 16

Poet Vs. Tyrant: The Gay
Liberation Paradigm, Part One

America's greatest poet, the gay Walt Whitman, provided us with our our core gay identity one-hundred-and-fifty years ago with his notion of the "great poet," combining it with a passion to "cheer up slaves and horrify despots" and touting the virtues of democracy in his epochal work *Leaves of Grass*.

The "great poet" was inseparable from the felling of tyrants and the promotion of the disenfranchised through the promotion of mighty institutions of righteousness and democracy. This notion of "gay sensibility" is fully compatible with, indeed a very spirit of, our noble United States of America.

Sorry, right wingers, America is, at its core, very gay.

Dating back to the earliest times of recorded history, great poets and intimate same-sex affection have been associated with the conquest of tyrants and the establishment of virtuous governments. The first and most famous case is that of the young David who slew Goliath in the Old Testament.

David was more than just a prototypical underdog, he was destined to become one of the greatest poets in history (author of most of the Old Testament *Psalms*), the subject of the longest account of an intimate interpersonal relationship in the entire Bible, involving Jonathan for whom his love "passed the love of women," and the great king of a righteous people.

"Your love to me was wonderful, passing the love of women," David said of Jonathan at Jonathan's funeral (2 Samuel 1:27), following earlier Biblical accounts of the two exchanging clothing, embracing, weeping together, hugging and kissing each other.

Based on the notion of "gay sensibility" that I have earlier established, it is not necessary to prove the nature of this relationship by deducing that there must have been explicit sex between the two.

No, here is "gay sensibility" explicitly and deliberately reported by the author of 1 and 2 Samuel and preserved in the Old Testament, presented as a key element for understanding David, inclusive of his tyrant-slaying, poetry and nation building.

Sorry, right wingers, the Bible is, at its core, very gay.

As with the ancient Greek city-states, the correlation of "gay sensibility" with the construct of just, democratic institutions of government emerged again in the Renaissance when the image and spirit of David became the signature of Renaissance culture.

David, as the slayer of tyrants, was adopted by the Florentines as the patron and protector of their democracy. In fact, the first large free-standing statue in one-thousand years was of a bronze David crafted by Donatello.

With the head of Goliath under his boot and sword, in this famous statue, young David appears as a downright "flamer," sporting a fey hat and an angelic face. Later alternatives to Donatello's rendering by Verrocchio and Michelangelo (the most famous one) did away with the swish and presented a more conventional hero.

When America's Founding Fathers grappled with how to construct an enduring union based on certain "inalienable rights" extending to all persons, they had few precedents to rely upon but the works of the ancient Greeks, including the great homosexual Socrates and the extensive pro-homosexual symposiums and dialogues in which he took part.

One of the most eloquent apologists for Greek models of democracy, law and justice, author of at least fifty-one of the eighty-five Federalist Papers in the earliest days of the American republic, was Founding Father Alexander Hamilton.

It is well known to Hamiltonian scholars and historians the intense, intimate relationship between the young, brilliant

Hamilton and John Laurens (see Ron Chernow, *Alexander Hamilton*, 2004). "I wish, my Dear Laurens, it m(ight) be in my power, by action rather than words, (to) convince you that I love you," a young Hamilton (born in 1755 or 1757) wrote in one of many affectionate correspondences with his contemporary in George Washington's revolutionary army in the 1779-1782 period before Laurens' premature death in a military foray in August 1782.

Hamilton had it very rough being born and growing up in the British West Indies, his father deserting his mother and living branded as a bastard (all his life, actually), then becoming orphaned and a virtual street urchin at age fourteen.

An older patron recognized his brilliance, however, sponsored him and turned his life around. At seventeen, Hamilton, described as "bookish, delicate and frail," published his first poem in a newspaper in St. Croix. An articulate author and brilliant thinker, once in the colonies, he was recruited at age twenty by Washington to be his aide-de-camp in the revolution.

His relationship with Laurens, who was born to a high station in South Carolina, was based on their shared, passionate anti-slavery, abolitionist sentiments. For Hamilton, his sensibility for the downtrodden extended to the Jews, for whom he had the greatest admiration.

Little doubt why he and Laurens stood so firmly against the tyrant King George III, determined to topple him on behalf of universal human rights.

Chapter 17

Poet Vs. Tyrant: The Gay
Liberation Paradigm, Part 2

The progression in America's development from the gay sensibilities of Founding Father Alexander Hamilton to the next great gay American leader, Abraham Lincoln, is astonishing for the common vision and approach they took to advancing the cause to, in Whitman's words, "cheer up slaves and horrify despots."

Hamilton's profound, romantic affection for John Laurens has not awaited modern homosexual studies to be recognized. In her 1902 biography of Hamilton entitled, *The Conqueror: Being the True and Romantic Story of Alexander Hamilton*, Gertrude Atherton wrote that the bond between Hamilton and Laurens "was romantic and chivalrous. Each burned to prove the strength of his affection, to sacrifice himself for the other."

While Hamilton died at the hand of an assassin, technically in a duel with Aaron Burr, at age forty-seven, his indispensable achievements in the forging and providing for the sustainability of the great American experiment in Constitutional democracy were achieved against seemingly overwhelming parochial sentiments that would have made the young nation easy pickings for the British to rend it asunder with divide and conquer tactics.

Therefore, Hamilton's passionate desire to establish a strong central government, and a national bank to direct its defense and development, were born of his staunch determination to forge a lasting bulwark against tyranny.

Despite his premature death in 1804, his institutions and their merits outlived him, and were bridged to Lincoln by the great Whig leader Henry Clay. Clay's passion was also to prevent a dissolution of the union, and that mantle was passed to Lincoln, who then could only prevent its division by prosecuting the Civil War.

In his monumental study, *The Intimate World of Abraham Lincoln* (2005), the late C. A. Tripp surveyed four of Lincoln's adult same-sex relationships, beginning at age twenty-two with Billy Greene in New Salem, Illinois in 1831, and followed by one with Joshua Speed in Springfield beginning in 1837. He shared a bed with Speed for over four years. During Lincoln's presidency, he had intimate relations with Col. Elmer Ellsworth, "a flashy young drillmaster" who died in the early days of the war, and later, Capt. David Derickson, who in the words of his regiment's history published three decades later, "in Mrs. Lincoln's absence, he frequently spent the night at his cottage, sleeping in the same bed with him."

By contrast to these, Tripp studied Lincoln's special relations with three women, including Mrs. Lincoln, all of which were "problematic or distant."

Lincoln's untimely death in 1865, like Hamilton at the hand of an assassin, compelled his great admirer, the gay Walt Whitman, to pen his memorable poem *Oh Captain, My Captain*.

Beyond their common fates, the similarities in the exercise of their "gay sensibility" between Hamilton and Lincoln are astonishing. Although today's Republicans like to claim them both for their pantheon of heroes, their policies had far more in common, in fact, with the great Democratic presidents of the 20th century to the present, beginning with Franklin D. Roosevelt (whose conscience and sense of doing the right thing was aided immensely by his lesbian wife Eleanor) and his New Deal, empowerment of working people and war against one of the worst, most brutal tyrants in world history, Hitler.

Lincoln did not shy away from prosecuting a war against a Confederacy that was a proxy for the British, who relied for their textile industry on cotton from the southern U.S. states, and cynically perpetuated the institutions of slavery and exploitation against disadvantaged people worldwide.

Lincoln freed the slaves, realizing the dream of Hamilton and other Abolitionists, and set in place a set of policies that encouraged a half-century of unprecedented progress that absorbed and provided unprecedented opportunity for millions of immigrants. These policies included the Railroad Act, the Land Grant College Act, the Greenback Currency Act and the Homestead Act.

What "great poets" both Hamilton and Lincoln were! Their lives, their careers and their passions manifested full measures of their "gay sensibility," their unique "sensual perspective" and their "constructive non-conformity," the three gay attributes that I have identified in these chapters.

I remind readers that what is being presented here is unprecedented. This series marks the first effort to identify and develop the notion of gay attributes outside the limited realm of sexuality. It is a novel and original attempt to break out of the reductionist confinements imposed on us by the invention of the word, "homosexual," by social scientists in 1859, that has for the last one-hundred-and-forty years contained us within that category.

Rather than properly appreciating the homosexual impulse as a by-product, so to speak, of a more fundamental "gay sensibility" notion of person-hood, everything that has been written about us since the word "homosexual" was first invented has accepted that definition without question. All examinations of us have begun with the search for evidence of our sexual inclinations, when there is so much more, and fundamental, about us that is "different."

Chapter 18

Poet Vs. Tyrant: The Gay
Liberation Paradigm, Part 3

It makes total sense that, from a broad cosmological perspective, that which manifests the fundamental dissymmetry of the unfolding universe would be at the forefront of its progressive change and evolution.

In human development on this planet, cosmic dissymmetry is evidenced by a roughly seven-percent deviation from the norm, which accounts for such anomalies as left-handedness and primary same-sex orientation in persons.

While left-handedness is a physical phenomenon, same-sex orientation is a more-or-less mental one, one which reveals a predisposition to value reality and sensation from a different "vantage point," so to speak. It is not same-sex orientation which creates this predisposition, as is often thought, but the other way around.

That accounts for why most homosexual persons experience themselves as "different" in early childhood, long before sexual arousal is a factor in their lives, *per se*.

From this standpoint, it is clear that persons manifesting this alternative predisposition embody, as a general rule, the highest potential as vanguards in the universe's impulse for positive self-development.

They bring an alternative sensibility, an alternative perspective and a natural constructive non-conformity to everything they experience and impact, and it is just those features that constantly presses humanity to break out from its *status quo* at any given moment to progress to greater enlightenment, self-consciousness and the extension of progress to the entire species.

Such progress is in the direction of, in human social terms, universal rights and democratic values and therefore, at any stage, it presses against the normative social organization based on "social Darwinist" or "might makes right" paradigms.

Thus we have, since the first emergence of human society, the struggle of the "poet," the manifestation of dissymmetry and progress, against the tyrant, the "king of the hill" at any given moment, ruling with an iron fist as the dominant male.

In the last century or so, the notion of "revolution" has had a bad connotation because it has been associated with developments in Russia and China, for example. But those did not produce progressive change, despite claims to the contrary, and were in fact merely the succession of one form of tyranny over another.

The last major example of a real "revolution" advancing humanity was that which resulted in the founding of the United States of America. It was egalitarian, it advanced democracy rooted in core concepts of the inalienable rights of all persons. Since the founding of the republic and its Constitution, it was progressed toward the fuller realization of those core values by eliminating slavery, granting suffrage to women, outlawing child labor, empowering workers and spreading such values abroad.

So, there is little doubt why evidence shows the seminal role of same-sex oriented persons in the development of the U.S., from her spiritual forebears in the Old Testament David, to Socrates and the Greek republican model, to the pillars of the Renaissance and the emergence of modern scientific method, to Founding Father Alexander Hamilton, national poet Walt Whitman (who coined the term, "Great Poets," to apply to us), preserver of the union and freer of slaves Abraham Lincoln, and to Eleanor Roosevelt, the shepherd of the nation through its Great Depression, its global leadership in vanquishing genocidal fascism and extending the notion of American core values through the United Nations' *International Declaration of the Rights of Man.*

Through all this, tyrants that have resisted these constructive developments have fought against them bitterly. Is there any doubt why they, and the social systems that prop them up, train their young to bully and beat up "young poets" on the nation's playgrounds, and to bash, marginalize and drive them to suicide whenever they can?

But by the late 1960s, in fact, the tyrant paradigm was on the ropes as never before in history. Its slavery was gone, its male-exclusive right to vote was gone, its structural institutions of domination—racism, sexism and anti-labor thuggery—were crumbling like never before. Progress against it had led right into their homes, turning their own chattel, their wives and children, against them.

"Gay liberation" was poised to be a death blow, freeing countless of the tyrants' own children to fully actualize their constructive non-conformist revolutionary potential through the process of "coming out" boldly against any arbitrary social constraints set up to deter them. The fullest liberation of all persons on the planet, to be led by this vanguard, was closer to realization than ever.

The tyrants did not take this lying down. They unleashed a massive counteroffensive.

As their hands were tied by institutional gains in justice and the force of law, the more clever among them fought back with a three-part counterpunch, the cornerstones of enlightened counterinsurgency, the full deployment of the infamous "Three C's:" containment, conflict and cooptation. "Containment" aimed to circumscribe the target population, to cordon it off, to separate it from the rest of society. This involved the invention of the term, "homosexual."

Chapter 19

What Led Up to Sparking
That "Stonewall Moment"

While the Stonewall riots of June 1969 are considered the storied launch of the modern gay movement, they were but one inflection point in the gradual progress of self-esteem and empowerment of same-sex oriented persons in the U.S., a progress which accelerated fiercely in the context of the pro-civil rights and anti-Vietnam War ferment of the late 1960s.

That progress was integrally tied to notions of human dignity and moral fortitude applied to the struggle for justice and peace for all persons. Regrettably, it was not long after that Stonewall moment that for the gay movement, a descent in the early 1970s toward inward-directed hedonistic excess overtook it, and the demand for "rights" became little more than a demand to perpetuate such excesses without interference.

Recognized accurately, homosexuality and its inherent humanistic sensibility and constructive non-conformity was both a driver and derivation of the universal notion of gay poet Walt Whitman's "great poet," as presented in his epochal *Leaves of Grass*, advancing progress, evolution and enlightenment against tyrants and despots since the beginning of time.

History is as a fugue of these hostile contenders—tyrants fighting a desperate battle against the aspirations of "great poets" for justice, beauty and the empowerment of all persons—on the grand panorama of centuries and in the intimate struggles of individuals in their households and private settings.

In Western Civilization, tyrants have grudgingly given ground to "great poets" since the Renaissance, when access to the great intellectual and poetic contributions of the gay Socrates and other brilliant ancient Greeks and the invention of movable type combined to unleash, in a manner similar to the ways modern forms of Internet social networking are changing the face of the Middle East today, the dignity and aspirations of individuals against brutal, superstition-enforced religious and political tyrannies.

Thus came the American Revolution carried out by the seminal roles of our same-sex oriented "great poet" forefathers Hamilton, Lincoln, Whitman and many more.

Still, in the manner of a fugue, the tyrants have fought back, reasserting their claim to dominion through force and every divisive trick in the books, making their final and most resolute stand on a bedrock of an imperialist, patriarchal, male supremacist social order.

In the U.S., they were forced to abandon slavery, child labor and a propertied male-only right to the vote as legions of racial minorities, working poor and women struggled for their freedom and enfranchisement. This has not unfolded overnight, and the effort is far from over.

But with every advance, in one form or another "great poets" inspired downtrodden and oppressed people to, as the Rev. Martin Luther King expounded, "Stand up straight, because it's only if you're bent over that oppressors can hold you down."

Those great words of fortitude by Dr. King, as he echoed them at a rally of Memphis sanitation workers just before his assassination in 1968, were at the heart of all struggles for freedom and equality, a struggle that does not end until that imperialist, might-makes-right patriarchal, white male chauvinist tyrant paradigm is finally vanquished once and for all.

In 1968, those of us who knew ourselves to be gay, myself being a seminary student at the time, stood with Dr. King in the framework of centuries of "great poet" struggles, taking his words to heart on behalf not only of all peoples, but on behalf of ourselves as homosexuals, as well.

This is what sparked the rise of the modern gay liberation movement. With pioneers like Frank Kameny, Lilli Vincenz and others igniting the flame in the mid-1960s, following the assassinations of Dr. King and Bobby Kennedy in 1968, it became no longer possible for millions of us who were secretly gay to do anything but stand up straight, in response to Dr. King's admonitions, ourselves.

We claimed the moral integrity and personal liberation associated with Dr King's call by "coming out proud and fighting," standing tall by claiming our gayness not only for ourselves, but as a beacon of hope to all others—gays, women, minorities, children—laboring under the burden of white male domination and oppression.

We would no longer allow society to force us to compromise our personal integrity and dignity. Living "in the closet" was living a lie, a structural internalization of a duplicity of spirit and character that led to deceit and self-destruction. Once we "came out" in that context, nothing mattered more than claiming the personal integrity we felt from such a defiant act, despite the hostility encountered not only in the wider society, but in countless individual households.

On all levels, the tyrant paradigm lurched in anger and horror. Combined with the mobilized aspirations of women, minorities and youth, aroused for civil rights and against the war, the rise of gay liberation from among society's "great poets," its most creative artists, educators, scientists and humanitarians, shook the foundations of that paradigm's very existence.

Chapter 20

The Original "Love Anthem" For Our Role in Society

Western civilization's struggle to emerge from a thousand-year Dark Age brought on by corruption and decadence that fed the decline and fall of the Roman Empire was achieved by the courageous efforts of those who fomented a rethinking and redefinition of what it means to be human from a higher standpoint, that of the universal values of virtue and a dedication to the dissemination of principles of knowledge, science, beauty and social justice.

Such an arduous, dedicated effort defines the challenge today not only to our wider society, pressed by a forceful inertia of greed and consumerist indifference in the direction of perhaps a new dark age, but for the LGBT community, more specifically, as well. It has lived through its own descent into the hell of radical hedonism, as the wheels came off the progressive gay liberation movement in the years immediately following Stonewall, leading swiftly to its hideous AIDS Dark Age.

Lacking models and guidelines to meet that challenge since, the LGBT community has largely resorted to a "post-traumatic stress" copycatting the dominant society's patterns of descent into myopic selfishness, stifling "gay sensibility" and perpetuating some underlying behaviors that could cause another AIDS-like scourge to burst forth.

For those willing to look truth in the face, rather than a self-serving illusion, this is an overdue and essential undertaking.

There is no doubt, none at all, that the phenomenon we have come to call homosexuality is a derivative of a natural impulse among a certain consistent percentage of the population of all human cultures over time to manifest a heightened empathy toward persons of their own sex.

In the natural order of things, this is for the essential purpose of bucking the prevailing trend toward fixed social roles for the sexes that subordinate them to male-dominated procreative roles and functions, which include the preparation of males for war and conflict, and females for slavish obedience to men and the perpetuation of the social paradigm through child rearing.

As a natural function of creation, what we call homosexuality inclines a proportion of the dominant population away from total, slavish adherence to this paradigm, and to the direction of its progress through enlightenment, empowerment of individual creative potential, universal beauty and social and governmental institutions that affirm and protect all persons.

This is done through a form of same-sex loving that is not a subordinated function of the dominant social paradigm, but which defies and baffles it, tending to nurture and inspire a wider population to break from brutish, male-dominated behaviors toward others to acknowledge and inspire what Lincoln called "the higher angels of our nature."

In this, those of us called homosexuals are called to "love that to which we are inclined," and to affirm, in the Biblical sense, "By the grace of God, I am what I am," by loving the objects of our natural affection, and not by exploiting, denigrating or diminishing them.

In the many modern histories of "homosexuality" (that term was invented in 1859 and never used outside of narrow social science contexts until 1953), the studies all document evidences of same-sex sexual behavior, dating back to the boundaries of pre-history, without making serious distinctions between same-sex relations defined by faithfulness and commitment to common virtues, and those which were exploitative, depersonalizing, predatory and destructive.

For example, in ancient Rome, the widely-accepted practice of male prostitution, on the streets and in the temples, legal and taxed by the state until the sixth century A.D., is reported in the same value-neutral breath as citations of sustained commitments to mentoring involving older-younger pairings, or long-term relations among equals.

It can be argued that the entire Judeo-Christian tradition, and among certain currents of most other major religions, it is the contrast between love, nurturing and the shared values of virtue, respect for persons and justice, on the one hand, and against brute force, lust, rape and might-makes-right behaviors, on the other hand, which is at the core of their ethical structures.

Taken in this light with regard to same-sex relations, the Judeo-Christian tradition condemns the behavior of the rapists of Sodom and Gomorrah, and the lustful practice of male prostitution in the Roman Empire (the *Book of Romans*), on the one hand, and yet holds up as exemplary a long-standing love affair between two males, David and Jonathan, as virtuous and worthy not only of being recorded, but maintained in the Biblical canon over eons (the *Books of Samuel*).

In like manner, it can be argued that the entire tradition is built around the essential content in the famous "prose poem" of the Apostle Paul, I Corinthians 13, expounding on the qualities of love. With no reference to deity or doctrine, this chapter stands alone, a mirror of similar praises of love in Plato's *Symposium*, above gender and sex and their traditional roles in patriarchal society, as if the original anthem for those of us "homosexuals," if you will, who are called to liberate and advance societies beyond their myriad forms of slavery and barbarism.

Chapter 21

The Greatest Gay Film Ever:
A Streetcar Named Desire

March 2011 marks the 100th anniversary of the birth of Tennessee Williams, a blazing star in the galaxy of great gay contributors to the progress of human civilization as America's greatest playwright.

His most poignant among his many enormous achievements was his second great play, *A Streetcar Named Desire*, first presented in 1947, a smash hit on Broadway and then as a compelling film in the early 1950s.

That film version of *A Streetcar Named Desire* could qualify as the greatest gay movie of all time, a claim that may confound many who think that gay matters involve only players that wear the word "gay" emblazoned on their chests.

Every creation by someone who is homosexual is by its very nature gay, including every great work of, in the modern era, Williams, Walt Whitman, Oscar Wilde, Christopher Isherwood, Cole Porter and the list goes on.

In her book, *How the Homosexuals Saved Civilization* (2004), Cathy Crimmins wrote, "Looking back, I can see how America fought hard to ignore the gay undertow of our culture from the fifties well into the eighties. There were so many unanswered questions. Why was Paul Lynde the funniest guy on *Hollywood Squares*? Why were Liberace's clothes and jewels the most fabulous? Why were Johnny Mathis ballads the favorite make-out music for heterosexual couples in the sixties? Why were many of the greatest playwrights of the last half of the twentieth century—Tennessee Williams, Lanford Wilson, Terrence McNally, Edward Albee—all gay men writing for straight audiences? Why are Cole Porter's love songs the cleverest and most poignant?"

She names many more creative and accomplished persons in her volume (limited to gay men), from James Beard to Peter Tchaikovsky, Elton John, Noel Coward, W. H. Auden, Tab Hunter, Truman Capote, Nathan Lane, Carson Kressley, David Sedaris, Malcolm Forbes, Harvey Fierstein, Jerome Robbins, Barney Frank, Augusten Burroughs, Craig Clairborne, Leonard Bernstein, Stephen Sondheim, Montgomery Clift, Authur Laurents, Tony Kushner, Rufus Wainwright, Gore Vidal, Thornton Wilder, Jerry Herman, William Inge, John Waters, Freddie Mercury, George Michael, Boy George, Clay Aiken, the Village People, David Bowie, James Dean, Ray Davies, Andy Warhol, Pete Townsend, Little Richard, Dick Sargent, Rip Taylor, Charles Nelson Reilly, Rock Hudson, Cary Grant, James Dean, Dirk Bogarde, Anthony Perkins, John Gielgud, George Cukor, Raymond Burr, Richard Chamberlain, Rudolph Valentino, Charles Laughton, Tyrone Power, Sal Mineo, Todd Haynes, Ian McKellen, James Whale, Franco Zeffirelli, Michael York, Isaac Mizrahi, Liberace and more.

While Crimmins acknowledges a "gay sensibility" factor linking gayness and creativity, I differ on the core matter of causality. Are they creative because they're gay, as she suggests, or are they gay because they were born with what I've described as an inherent "gay sensibility," involving a different sensual perspective and a necessarily constructive non-conformity that are indispensable components of social progress?

A Streetcar Named Desire was not the clarion call of the new wave of social progress that led into the 1960s, but it was its awakening. Followed by more biting Williams plays, it set the stage for the civil rights, women's rights and gay liberation struggles that followed over the subsequent twenty years.

The vulnerable Blanche in *Streetcar* embraces the archetypal gay sensibility. She describes herself as, "A cultivated woman, a woman of intelligence and breeding can enrich a man's life— immeasurably! I have those things to offer, and this doesn't take them away. Physical beauty is passing. A transitory possession. But beauty of the mind and richness of the spirit and tenderness of the heart—and I have all those things—aren't taken away, but grow! Increase with the years! How strange that I should be called a destitute woman! When I have all the these treasures locked in my heart."

She is confronted and dissembled by the boorish Stanley and his slavish wife, Blanche's sister Stella, archetypes both in their respective roles and in their relationship of brutal white male-dominated society. The profound injustice portrayed so poignantly by Williams spoke directly to the oppression of women and gays, in particular, and sparked a consciousness in relevant circles, including and on college campuses, across the land.

It changed the terms of the gay invisibility of the previous fifty years, since Oscar Wilde was publicly ruined for his "love that dare not speak its name" by the brutish father of his erstwhile lover, Bosie.

Only some heavily-coded references by gays and their allies made their way to a wider social consciousness in the decades that followed, one example being the extraordinary rendering by artist Norman Rockwell on the cover of the April 8, 1933 *Saturday Evening Post*. It showed a farm boy standing in a field listening intently as a life-sized fairy in a green dress whispers in his ear, the artist's stealth affirmation of a boy's gay awakening.

That awakening, and *Streetcar*'s, were indispensable precursors to the late 1960's eruption of the modern gay movement.

Chapter 22

Breaking the Silence About
Those "Friends of Dorothy"

In fairness, it can be argued that the great American illustrator Norman Rockwell's cover art for the April 3, 1933 edition of the *Saturday Evening Post*, entitled "Springtime," was not as deliberately a coded affirmation of a "gay awakening" as some might presume.

The magnificently tender rendering of a young adolescent boy in a field listening intently as a tall, feminine green fairy whispers in his ear could have been meant to reflect an awakening of a more general nature associated with the onset of spring.

But since his death in 1978, there has been a growing awareness of Rockwell's social consciousness and the often subtle ways it manifested itself in the three-hundred-and-twenty-two separate *Saturday Evening Post* covers, and other works he drew over many decades.

That social consciousness, combined with the overwhelmingly dominant social definition of "fairy" in the American vernacular of that era being an effeminate homosexual, and the clear need for any conversation about homosexuality to be heavily coded and invisible to the untrained eye until the late 1960s, make the case for the Rockwell "Springtime" illustration to be perhaps one of the most important representations of gay identity ever, along with Donatello's bronze statue of an effete, Goliath-slaying David, *circa* 1440.

But the persisting, perhaps eternally-destined ambiguity about the Rockwell work underscores the hidden nature of gay culture until recently. Growing up as a gay lad in the post-World War II period, I never met a self-identified gay person until I was in my mid-twenties. Liberace notwithstanding, I'd never knowingly seen one on TV or in a magazine, either.

I grew up in a California coastal town of 50,000 north of Los Angeles. My "gay awakening" came more than two decades after Rockwell's representation. I knew I was "different" from my earliest days as my interests took me to places totally unfamiliar to my family: my interest in newspapers, in the U.S. presidents whose names I memorized, in classical music and my special empathy toward my struggling, abused mother.

At the onset of my adolescence, I developed a special relationship with another boy my age. For a year-and-a-half, we were famously inseparable, taking long bike rides, founding a junior high newspaper (that I recruited him into) and sleeping over at each other's homes.

As a result of the Kinsey reports about sexuality published in the late 1940s, the term "homosexual" began in the 1950s being used outside professional circles for the first time. One night my brother asked about the term at our dinner table, and I felt my face burn with an intense blush. The same thing happened later in a college classroom when someone asked about the movie version of Tennessee Williams' play *Suddenly Last Summer*, and our teacher made a disparaging comment about homosexuals.

I loathed my gayness. Whenever the notion was suggested, it was in an overwhelmingly negative way. Acting it out was simply not an option. I vowed to take my secret to the grave.

If five or seven percent of the species is naturally born with a gay sensibility, then from the dawn of civilization, and all around the globe, imagine how many have faced similar conditions as mine in my youth, but for their entire lives.

The silence began to be broken very slowly with the emergence of modern electronic mass media: radio, the movies and TV.

Coded representations were permitted rarely, allegories usually involving spunky misfits battling tyranny. J.M. Barrie's *Peter Pan* smashed stuffy British convention with the depiction of a leader among homeless boys, aided by a fairy. Barrie's Peter maintained his youth and puckishness by contrast to the "normal" boys he rescued, who in the final chapter are followed into their boring, mediocre, "normal" adulthoods.

Misfits also conquered evil in the classic, *The Wizard of Oz*, with Dorothy played by a young Judy Garland. She later became a wounded misfit in her own right, thereby a gay icon. Gays adopted the term, "Friends of Dorothy" as a coded reference to their own kind.

Women in the movies and on TV who struggled to break the mold of straight, white male-dominated culture, resisting conventionality with their own strength and suffering as a consequence, became champions to those of gay sensibility, the likes of Bette Davis, Joan Crawford, Marilyn Monroe, Katharine Hepburn and Lucille Ball.

Little did I know as an adolescent gay boy that I was swooning to the songs of a gay Tab Hunter and a gay Johnny Mathis and drawn to the young star my age in "Old Yeller," a gay Tommy Kirk, to a pajama-gaming gay Rock Hudson and causeless rebels gay James Dean and gay Sal Mineo. Little did I know, and not find out for many years, that two hours away, my aunt was renting her house to the creator of *Cabaret*, the famous gay writer Christopher Isherwood and his young gay partner, Don Bachardy.

Chapter 23

Breaking the Silence About Those "Uranians"

The biggest plus from the late 1960s rise of the gay liberation movement was the incredible benefit to homosexuals that being "out and proud" provided. It allowed gay people for the first time to enjoy a level of personal integrity within the larger society that "living a lie" had denied them for eons.

A second key development was the ability to talk, depict and debate same-sex relations openly in literature, in the media, in films, classrooms, open forums and in every conceivable manner, including more recently via the Internet, such that the great silence on the subject throughout most of history was broken at last.

This included the rise of gay-themed newspapers in major cities across the U.S., including the Gay *Sunshine* in the San Francisco Bay Area, where I wrote its first editorial and became a prolific writer on gay liberation themes in other area counterculture print media, as well, including the *Berkeley Barb, Berkekey Tribe*, the *San Francisco Kalendar*, and my own *The Effeminist* between 1970 and 1973.

At the same time, a ton of research on gay history was unleashed, resulting in large volumes including Colin Spencer's *Homosexuality in History* (1995), K. J. Dover's *Greek Homosexuality* (1978), Daniel H. Garrison's *Sexual Culture in Ancient Greece* (2000), Louis Compton's *Homosexuality and Civilization* (2003), Francis Mark Mondimore's *A Natural History of Homosexuality* (1996), Vittorio Linardi's *Men in Love: Homosexualities from Ganymede to Batman* (2002), Paul Russell's *The Gay 100* (1995), Thomas Hubbard's *Homosexuality in Greece and Rome* (2003), John Boswell's *Christianity, Social Tolerance and Homosexuality* (1980), Jonathan Katz' *Gay American History* (1992),

Robert Aldrich's *Gay Life and Culture: A World History* (2006), Martin Duberman, Martha Vicinis and George Chauney, Jr.'s *Hidden from History: Reclaiming the Gay and Lesbian Past* (1989), Kenneth Stern's *Queers in History* (2009) and more.

All this had not been available before except to the serious scholar. All were written from a value-neutral standpoint, with simply same-sex sexual relations as their common parameters.

Still, they include a continuity of important thinkers on gay origins and purpose from Walt Whitman (1819-1892) into the 1970s works of Tennessee Williams (1911-1983) and Christopher Isherwood (1904-1986). It flowed from Karl Heinrich Ulrichs (1825-1895) to Mangus Hirschfeld (1868-1935), to Edward Carpenter (1844-1929), to E. M. Forster (1879-1970), to Isherwood and Williams.

This was matched on the lesbian side by women's rights and suffrage pioneers including Mary Wollstonecraft (1759-1797), Susan B. Anthony (1820-1906) and Gertrude Stein (1874-1946).

It was Ulrichs who first attempted to integrate gays into a positive wider notion of universal reality, as I have sought to do in these installments, more explicitly than Walt Whitman's idea of "great poets."

In 1864, under a pseudonym, Ulrichs wrote a series of five booklets called *Researches Into the Riddle of Love Between Men*. In it, he expounded a theory of the origins and nature of same-sex erotic attraction, which he attributed to the notion of a female soul trapped in a male body, making for a third sex. He coined the term, "urning," or "uranian," derived from a reference in Plato's *Symposium* to love between men as "the beautiful love, the heavenly love, the love belonging to the heavenly muse Urania."

In 1865, Ulrichs founded the first gay organization ever known, the Uranian Union, and despite his arrest in 1867, he persisted as a self-proclaimed "uranian" to fight for the repeal of anti-sodomy laws.

But it was Carpenter who did the most to advance constructive theories about a universal purpose behind same-sex attraction. In his tract, *The Intermediate Sex* (1908), he coined the term, "homogenic love" (preferring it to the term, homosexual), Carpenter built on the theories of Ulrichs, adding that, because of their "doubleness," "homogenic lovers" have "special work to do as reconcilers and interpreters of the two sexes to each other." He added that "homogenic love" is a "spiritualized and altruistic comrade attachment" derived from Plato and Whitman's notion of "fervid relationships."

He saw same-sex erotic attraction and comradeship as an integral stage in human evolution, an "indication of some important change actually in progress," adding that "certain new types of human kind may be emerging, which will have an important part to play in the societies of the future, even though for the moment their appearance is attended by a good deal of confusion and misapprehension."

It was while visiting Carpenter that the already-famous author E.M. Forster wrote that he experienced his own "gay awakening," derived from something as simple as Carpenter's young partner, George Merrill, affectionately patting him on his rear.

That resulted in Forster's great novel of gay love, *Maurice*, based on Carpenter's and Merrill's relationship, which though written in 1914, could not be published (or subsequently made into a motion picture) for general circulation until after Stonewall in 1971.

Chapter 24

The "Uranian" View of
Gay Identity and Mine

As pioneering gay activist Edward Carpenter wrote in 1908, Karl Heinrich Ulrichs posited a notion of gay identity apart from sexual orientation *per se* and remains to this day one of the very few equal rights advocates to do this. In Carpenter's *The Intermediate Sex* (1908), he summarized Ulrichs' theory about the male "uranian" as follows (as taken from Paul Russell's work):

"He's a man who, while possessing thoroughly masculine powers of mind and body, combines with them the tenderer and more emotional soul-nature of the woman—and sometimes to a remarkable degree...Emotionally they are extremely complex, tender, sensitive, pitiful and loving, 'full of storm and stress, of ferment and fluctuation' of the heart: the logical faculty may or may not, in their case, be well-developed, but intuition is always strong; like women they read characters at a glance, and know, without knowing how, what is passing in the minds of others; for nursing and waiting on the needs of others they have often a peculiar gift; at the bottom lies the artist-nature, with the artist's sensibility and perception. Such an one is often a dreamer, of brooding, reserved habits, often a musician, or a man of culture courted in society, which nevertheless does not understand him."

For the female "uranian," he provides the following:

"The inner nature is to a great extent masculine; a temperament active, brave and originative, somewhat decisive, not too emotional; fond of outdoor life, of games and sports, of science, politics or even business; good at organization, and well-pleased with positions of responsibility, sometimes making an excellent and generous leader. Such a woman, it is easily seen, from her social combination of qualities, is often fitted for remarkable work, in professional life, or as manageress of institutions, or even as a ruler of a country...Many a Santa Clara, or abbess-founder of religious houses, has probably been a woman of this type; and in all times such women—not being bound to men by the ordinary ties—have been able to work the more freely for the interests of their sex, a cause to which their own temperament impels them to devote themselves *con amore*."

This represents the otherwise-almost-non-existent attempt to identify "uranians" in terms of personality type above and preceding sexual orientation, and as such to develop a notion of a gay, or "uranian," identity beyond the domain of sexuality.

In the early days of the post-Stonewall movement, I suggested a similar approach to gay identity in the editorial I wrote for the first-ever edition of the *Gay Sunshine* newspaper in 1970.

Seeing the gay liberation struggle as an extension of the torrid 1960s civil rights, feminist and anti-war movements up to that point, I wrote that the new *Gay Sunshine* newspaper should be "a newspaper that will represent those who understand themselves as oppressed—politically oppressed by an oppressor that not only is down on homosexuality, but equally down on all things that are not white, straight, middle class, pro-establishment...It should harken to a greater causes—the cause of human liberation, of which homosexual liberation is just one aspect—and on that level make its stand."

Thus, the proposition was that gay identity is rooted not primarily in sexual orientation, but in a common "political oppression" with others, and is thus susceptible to "harken to a higher cause—the cause of human liberation."

My San Francisco Bay Area circle and I continued with this approach to gay identity, going on to produce *The Effeminist* newspaper, among other things, seeking to assert gay identity as subsumed in the feminist struggle. However, we were overwhelmed, as by a tsunami, by currents preoccupied with a hedonistic "sexual freedom," and for whom the movement was nothing more than to realize that as fully as possible, and to underscore, therefore, that there was nothing more to being gay than craving sex with the same sex.

I have come now to refine a concept of gay identity that differs from the Ulrichs-Carpenter "uranian" notion primarily by utilizing the more general concepts, based on the unprecedented idea of a natural and important universal role for gays, or "uranians," whose "gay sensibility," "alternative perspective" and "constructive non-conformity" actually precede sexual orientation. Unlike Carpenter's British aristocratic perspective, mine draws from the more red-blooded American revolutionary identity inherent in Walt Whitman's "great poet" notion in his *Leaves of Grass*, especially in terms of a disposition for "horrifying despots."

We are the people who as nature's essential seven percent, are not bound by a conventional sensibility, who bring a different, "gay" sensibility, and an alternative perspective on reality, necessarily resulting in a penchant for a constructive non-conformity that compels human progress. For that tiny portion of our seven percent that finds itself in the right circumstances, we experience our identity in terms of same-sex attraction.

Chapter 25

Shining New Light on
Corners of Gay History

With the floodgates open at last in the wake of the June 1969 Stonewall riots, tons of material began being compiled and disseminated on all things homosexual for as far as history would go. It was as if a light switch was suddenly flipped to "on."

Of the many, many things that issued forth, the most prominent, not surprisingly, was evidence of the institutional repression, hatred and cruelty perpetrated against anyone who was either caught in a homosexual embrace, or who even looked like a sissy or fairy.

Throughout history, for example, it was the sissies who were the first to be deployed into quasi-suicidal missions in military campaigns, because they were seen as the most expendable and devalued. The death penalty for sodomy was common, notwithstanding specific exceptions, such as the ancient Greeks and Romans.

Prior to 1969, the public's awareness of homosexuality in culture had been generally limited to some vague awareness of those degenerate ancient Greeks, the Biblical condemnations (overlooking the David-Jonathan relationship reported in the *Books of Samuel*) and the cruel fate imposed on Oscar Wilde for being convicted of "the love that dare not speak its name" with his erstwhile lover Alfred Douglas ("Bosie") in 1895.

All references to homosexuality by great gay poets and playwrights like Shakespeare and Walt Whitman were interpreted as something else, and Thomas Mann's *Death in Venice* 1912 novella was understood as the pursuit of ideal beauty, not in terms of a same-sex orientation (in post-Stonewall 1971, Luchino Visconti made a beautiful film version of starring Dirk Bogarde and Bjorn Andresen).

Great homosexual literary giants like Tennessee Williams, Christopher Isherwood and E. M. Forster faced the same need to mask the true meaning of many of their works, although in 1947 Williams slipped a homosexual reference into *A Streetcar Named Desire*, concerning Blanche's recollection of her young husband, a reference that was edited out of the famous film version.

Isherwood also sidestepped the hugely homosexual contexts of his *Goodbye to Berlin* and *I Am a Camera* works that later morphed into the stage and film productions of *Cabaret*.

Forster wrote the gay-themed *Maurice* in 1913, but couldn't have it published until after his death in post-Stonewall 1971. It also became a beautiful movie after that.

Only after 1969 did both Williams and Isherwood unveil their own homosexuality and the veiled homosexual themes in much of their best work. Williams, who "came out" in an interview with David Frost in January 1970 with his famous quote, "I've covered the waterfront," wrote his first overtly homosexual-themed play, *Small Craft Warnings* in 1972, at the same time he began his *Memoirs* that brought out the central role homosexuality played in his life. By 1976, Isherwood followed suit with an autobiographical work, *Christopher and His Kind,* that put the thoroughgoing homosexual content into his Berlin stories.

Eventually, both Williams and Isherwood, who were friends, published their tell-all extensive diaries and notebooks, with Isherwood's from the 1960s period coming out only last fall. Williams did not hold back describing his cavorting among sailors on the palisades above Santa Monica during the nightly blackouts in 1943, for example.

Before 1969, the portrayal of "fairies" in the movies were harshly prohibited by the Hays Code, adopted in 1934 to censor American films for morality and in effect until 1968. While gays were a major force in all the arts throughout that era, they were completely hidden from public view. There were tragic outcomes, such as the suicide of a young, handsome leading man, Ross Alexander, in 1937. Starring in 1935 with Errol Flynn and Olivia DeHavilland in the swashbucking *Captain Blood*, Alexander's homosexuality was well known in inner Hollywood circles, but as with so many gays, he married a woman. His double life drove his wife into depression resulting in her suicide a year before Alexander then took his own life.

Double lives under the threat of exposure and ruin characterized the lives of many in the pre-Stonewall era. The only portrayals that made the screen were *The Children's Hour* and *Victim*, both in 1961 when the first cautious steps to open the subject up were taken. Both films, however, presented a very troubled and painful view of homosexuality, leading to ruin, blackmail and suicide. *Victim*, a British film starring Dirk Bogarde, was intended as a compassionate argument for ending the laws against sodomy.

Shining the light on the recorded history of homosexuality also showed that from the beginning, same-sex relations were often based on inequalities in age and station, with few cases of long-term sustainability. The earliest case, after all, was an abduction by the greatest of the Greek gods, Zeus, of the prettiest boy among mortals, Ganymede. At least Zeus arranged a good job for Ganymede as the cup bearer of the gods and later honored him by positioning him in the heavens as the constellation Aquarius.

Chapter 26

Ganymede and the Three Greek Terms for Love

The earliest ancient Greek myth with an explicitly homosexual theme is the story of the abduction of Ganymede, the most beautiful among mortal boys who is abducted by no less than Zeus himself, the god of the gods. Zeus espied the beautiful young mortal, swept down in the form of an eagle to kidnap him and brought him to Mt. Olympus, where he was assigned "cup bearer for the gods," and was ultimately honored by Zeus by being transformed into the starry constellation of Aquarius.

The myth reflected the most common form of homosexual relations documented in ancient Greek and Roman cultures covering over 1,000 years, that involving older men and younger boys who'd reached their "full height," as in their upper teens (citing K.D. Dover, *Greek Homosexuality*, 1978).

According to the historical record, almost all identified homosexual relations, at least up until the modern era, involved inequalities of age and station in society, the paradigm being the Greek-Roman model of an older man of wealth seeking liaison with a younger lad, commonly in search of the older's money, gifts and pathways to success in later life. Record of such trysts ranged from more acceptable ones among free men to less savory encounters involving slaves and prostitutes.

While such disparities are disquieting to modern sensibilities, if not illegal, in the ebbs and flows of history in the West, higher regard for the potentially virtuous nature of such relations was held in times that roughly correlated to eras of great cultural, scientific and political advance, such as in the fourth and fifth centuries B.C.

in Greece, and the height of the Italian Renaissance in the fifteenth and early sixteenth centuries A.D.

In both those periods, the writings of Plato, especially those dealing explicitly with homosexual relations, *The Symposium* and *Phaedrus*, were models for discourses on the role of ethics and morality in those relations. Arguments ranged from, among others, (1) limiting expectations to purely non-abusive pleasure-seeking, to (2) considering the younger participant's well being psychologically and over the long haul, and (3) Plato's and Socrates' case for restraining from sex, but to use the erotic impulse as a driver to introduce higher notions of love, of friendship and of love for beauty and truth, into the relationship.

In that order, the three Greek words for love—*eros* as sexual desire, *philia* as friendship and *agape* as divine or universal love—are summoned as applied to the three stages of the Plato/Socrates option, and they all are deployed in that fashion as well in the myth of Ganymede.

First concerning that myth, it should be noted that, insofar as it was Zeus, the highest of the gods, who initiated the relationship, it signals that in the ultimate order of things there is a proper and sanctified role for same-sex passion. While most of Zeus' appetite was for women, his Ganymede caper showed that a role for homosexuality in the eyes and desires of the top god was OK.

Second, the disparity in ages and rank not only reflected the prevailing cultural norm (Dover's researches indicate in that era there was no record of any other kind of homosexual relations, at least that were sanctioned or reported) but was symbolic of the kind of inequality that is, on a personal level, endemic to most relationships: one party usually having some, even nuanced, role difference from the other (one more active than passive, for example) that belies the exact notion of equality as a political and legal term. As terms best to describe interpersonal relations, "complementarity" and "reciprocity" are better choices.

In the disparity of roles, the issue lies in what each party brings to the other and whether it is "net zero sum" in nature, a reciprocity that fulfills the expectations, goals and gratifications of both. Of course, all unequal interactions bear an acute potential for abuse and cruelty, such as especially when one lacks the maturity for discerning powers of free choice, which is why the matter of the true meaning of love, versus abuse and exploitation, is always so important.

In the Ganymede myth, Zeus, synonymous among the Greeks with our notion of God as the creative force of the universe, embraces Ganymede, the archetypal representation of same-sex passion, brings him to a heavenly purpose as servant to the oversight of human affairs (the gods on Olympus). Then finally he elevates and sanctifies him, lifting him to the status among the twelve gears of the universe in the sky as the constellation Aquarius in the Zodiac, by which the entire universe is governed and unfolds, and from whence the very notions of beauty and truth are derived.

Ganymede is transported by Zeus through the three powers of love, in its *eros, philia* and *agape* manifestations, for purposes of aligning human behavior in accordance with the divine purpose present in the homosexual impulse.

Chapter 27

Gay Love: Procreation
Of the Spirit of Love

The problem is this: We post-Stonewall gays are collectively as if an entirely new species, being fully open and "here" for the first time in the history of the species. Yet we have yet to define ourselves to ourselves.

Instead, we are defined by default by an era of hedonistic excess and reductionist categorization.

Indicative of this problem is the inability of any of the post-Stonewall historians, who have worked so diligently to fill in the cavernous silences on matters of same-sex relations over the centuries, to describe same-sex desires and practices in any terms other than the pursuit of pleasure.

Even in the rare cases where efforts at sustainable relationships are found in the record, the homosexual act is understood in terms solely of the pleasure derived from it.

This is not surprising, since the sexual act in the heterosexual context is clearly geared to procreation, to reproducing the species. There is no such procreative element to a same-sex encounter, so, they argue, it can be explained only by the pleasurable experience it brings.

However, the claim that there is nothing to gay sex but the experience of pleasure is a fallacy perpetrated by the false prophets of postmodernism such as Michel Foucault and his predecessors, the socially-engineered "sexual freedom" movement of the 1960s, the scions of the "Beat generation," and the benefactors of Nietzschean, proto-fascist doctrine that "might (and pleasures that derive from it) makes right."

This is the regrettable legacy that, by default, has persisted in the post-Stonewall gay movement to this day, as "gay liberation" has come to be understood simply as "liberation" from restraints, either in the outside society or in one's own psyche.

Yet, an alternative interpretation of the meaning of gay sex, in the context of the nature of things, has been here all along, one that does not deny the procreative role of sex, but embraces it fully and gives gay sexual desire a special role in creation.

In mythic-poetic form, it is contained in the ancient Greek myth of Ganymede, and it is spelled out more explicitly by the aged female prophet Diotima in *The Symposium* by Plato (427-347 B.C.).

Erotic attraction for purposes of reproduction is one of the two greatest driving forces of life. It and the mother's protection of her young account for the perpetuation and survival of the species, and nothing is more important to Mother Nature than this.

When the same powerful erotic attraction is found to be directed in the case of some (the ancient Greek Zodiac has it at one, Ganymede/Aquarius, in twelve, a plausible proportion) to the same, not opposite sex, then it is also designed to perpetuate the species. But it goes beyond the simple physical acts of reproduction and protection, which do nothing to account for the progress of the species, but only its survival.

Erotic attraction (which Diotima says is itself a "spirit") to the same sex provides the passionate ground for the cultivation of beauty and truth in both parties.

"When a man, starting from this sensible world and making his way upward by right use of his feeling of love for young men, begins to catch sight of that beauty... This is the right way of approaching or being initiated into the mysteries of love, to begin with examples of beauty in this world, and using them as steps to ascend continually with that absolute beauty as one's aim...from physical beauty to moral beauty, and from moral beauty to the beauty of knowledge, until from knowledge of various kinds one arrives at the supreme knowledge whose sole object is that absolute beauty, and knows at last what absolute beauty is," Diotima says.

The most passionate of erotic attractions and of sexual desire, when drawn from attraction to one of the same sex, is present in creation not simply to devour pleasure, but to be the compelling force that directs both the lover and loved toward a higher and higher appreciations of beauty and knowledge, which leads to universal justice:

"There are some (gays—ed.) whose creative desire is of the soul, and who long to beget spiritually, not physically, the progeny which it is the nature of the soul to create and bring to birth. If you ask what that progeny is, it is wisdom and virtue in general; of this all poets and such craftsmen as have found out some new thing may be said to be begetters; but far the greatest and fairest branch of wisdom is that which is concerned with the due ordering of states and families, whose name is moderation and justice," Diotima proclaims.

With Stonewall, for the first time since this was written 2,500 years ago, we come onto the scene of history capable of fully embracing and advancing such a potent force of the universe. That notion, that level of personal fulfillment, must not longer be sidetracked by the dogs of shallow hedonism.

Chapter 28

History's Record of Variables
In Homosexual Identity

Reviewing the long historical record of matters concerning same-sex erotic attraction in the West that's come to light in the years since Stonewall, there are two important overarching summary points to be made.

The first is the pervasive way in which homosexual identity shapes every aspect of a gay person's life, expressed through the qualities I've identified as "gay sensibility," "alternative perspective" and "constructive non-conformity," whether they are "openly gay" or not.

The second is the historical divergence between expressions of same-sex erotic attraction. On the one hand—amid the silence and darkness of civilizations since the ancient Greeks, with no mass media, no investigations exposing patterns of abuse within the corridors of power and silence—the attraction is expressed through dangerous, marginalized and only sometimes sanctioned sexual acts. On the other hand, it is expressed in the myth of Ganymede and the writings of Plato on the subject, with homosexual passions directed to the care, uplifting and cultivation of the creative powers of the subjects of such love.

On both points, I defer to our great Patron Saint, Tennessee Williams, to comment through his writings.

On the subject of homosexual identity, he remarks through a soliloquy by his character, Mrs. Venable, in the opening section of *Suddenly Last Summer,* speaking about her late homosexual son, Sebastian:

"It still shocks me a little to realize that Sebastian Venable the poet is still unknown outside of a small coterie of friends, including his mother. You see, strictly speaking, his life was his occupation... Sebastian was a poet! That's what I meant when I said his life was his work because the work of a poet is the life of a poet, and vice-versa, the life of a poet is the work of a poet. I mean you can't separate them...

"I mean—well, for instance, a salesman's work is one thing and his life is another—or can be. The same thing's true of—doctor, lawyer, merchant, thief!—But the poet's life is his work and his work is his life in a special sense."

In this 1958 play, Williams still identifies homosexuals with "poets," just as the great gay poet Walt Whitman did in the 1800s, and also the seminal influence on Williams, the brilliant but tragic gay poet Hart Crane. Williams, in fact, thought of himself primarily as a poet, growing up writing poetry and in what he called his "nomadic period," prior to his breakthroughs into greatness, there was an entire time when the only book he carried in his possession contained only Crane's works.

When he died accidentally in February 1983, Williams had prepared a speech for delivery to students in New York in which he reiterated that he would want, primarily, to be remembered as a poet.

The identity of the poet, *a.k.a.* homosexual in Williams' meaning, is permeated through and through him or her, coloring everything about one's internal soul and sensibility, and every creative contribution one makes to the world.

On the subject of the historical divergence of same-sex erotic behaviors, there is considerable evidence of abusive, transient, fleeting, depersonalized and dangerous encounters, ranging from systematic rape by persons in power, including Roman emperors and clerical and other potentates, military leaders, prison guards and slave owners, to the hundreds of years of legal male prostitution in Roman religious temples and on street corners, exploiting differences in power and wealth, and leaving the exploited in the dust, at best.

But on the other hand, while there is no clear evidence of those homosexuals who followed the guidance of Socrates, Plato and Diotima, it can be imagined they became a dominant, if closeted, influence in the shaping of Western Civilization.

While permeated with the soul of the "poet" defining everything about them, homosexuals focused their lives and passions on elevating the objects of their attraction to higher domains of social sensibility and behavior. The pursuit of the "good" in the Platonic sense was described by Tennessee Williams in a more modern, vernacular sense.

Writing in 1947, he said, "Then what is good? The obsessive interest in human affairs, plus a certain amount of compassion, and moral conviction, that first made the experience of living something that must be translated into pigment or music or bodily movement or poetry or prose or anything that's dynamic and expressive—that's what's good for you if you're at all serious in your aims."

The "good" to Williams, just as with Plato, lies in the cultivation of compassionate, creative potential for the general good, based on an "obsessive interest in human affairs."

In the silence of history, a preponderance of homosexuals channeled their passions to such objectives, especially in the context of the patterns of brutal abuses that characterized common society. We see these sisters and brothers in the forging and maintenance of institutions and practices of compassion, morality and purpose.

Chapter 29

A Recapitulation of
My Argument

My argument in these installments is to establish that what primarily defines what society calls us as "homosexuals" lies beyond, or prior to, the domain or erotic same-sex attraction and behaviors *per se*, and is found in those ubiquitous evidences in the chronicles of Western civilization as a unique "gay sensibility," an alternate perspective and a constructive non-conformity.

It is in the areas of creative contributions to all the arts and sciences, including the art of politics, that this unique identity's stamp is seen most clearly.

It is also my argument, in this context, that "homosexuality" is not an aberration or chance of nature, but that it is built into the very fabric of the unfolding of the universe. It is a dissymmetry whose role is to shatter an inertia derived of the simple, dominant binary male-female-reproduction-survival nature of things in favor of not merely the survival, but the progress and advance of the species.

In other words, "homosexual" passion is directed toward a different kind of procreation, one which advances the pursuit of beauty, justice, knowledge and truth, which are different facets of the same thing.

The "poetic principle" at the core of this special role is reflected in Plato's assertion, "Poetry is nearer to vital truth than history."

Insofar as it is the inherent role of "homosexuals" to shatter the cultural *status quo* wherever their influence can be felt, they become easy targets of angry, brutal repression and isolation, especially when the *status quo* is a male dominated cultural model.

That's because, among other things, to the extent it is the natural inclination of "homosexuals" to manifest thirst for justice and to affirm the essential humanity of all, they tend to side with the oppressed, including women, orphans and the downtrodden, those whose exploitation males in male domination cultures feed upon to buoy their social roles.

Therefore, just as "homosexuals" are defined by their DNA, so to speak, it is also true that heterosexual males defined in terms of domination over women and military enemies, have it built into their biological memories, their DNA, to hate and seek to hurt "homosexuals."

Ultimately, the only way for "homosexuals" to be freed from this oppression, therefore, is for their influence to be felt in society, along with women and other oppressed groups, so strongly that the paradigm of male domination is overthrown in the culture once and for all.

It is not by receiving "equal rights" that this is accomplished, although gains on that front may reflect progress toward the ultimate liberation of "homosexuals" and all persons from the repressive male chauvinist social paradigm.

"Equal rights" and attitudes of "tolerance" can be reversed swiftly in any situation where male dominion still rules, and the most unfortunate approach "homosexuals" can take overall is to attempt assimilation and accommodation to that dominant culture by announcing things such as, "We're just like you, except for who we sleep with."

This is why, from the beginning of the modern gay liberation movement in the developments that surrounded the Stonewall Riots of 1969, I and others with me in the San Francisco area fought to forge alliances with *avant garde* feminist and civil rights activists to take on "The Man," the culture that was resisting gains so ferociously of minority, labor, women's and gay rights, and was sending its own young (mostly) sons to jungles halfway around the world where over 50,000 of them died for oil.

I lost two friends in Vietnam. I "came out" as a "homosexual" in part for that reason. Awakening to the consummate evil of militaristic male dominated culture marked the single most important event in my life.

With the veil of secrecy lifted away from "homosexuals," removing the crippling duplicity we were forced to internalize, liberated an internal integrity in us all and sprung a heretofore never-experienced potential for a full, unrestrained explosion of "gay sensibility" on society.

Unfortunately, that potential has not yet been realized. While the indestructible creative spirit of "homosexuals" has continued to stumble forward, an unabated descent into radical hedonistic behavior overwhelmed our infant liberation, diverting attention away from the many salutary ways in which "homosexuals" were better poised than ever to transform society, and instead causing careers and aspirations to be cast overboard in favor of gratuitous excesses of sex.

But as Oscar Wilde's hedonistic character Dorian Gray came to learn, "Pleasure and happiness are not the same thing."

The consequence of the wanton abandonment to sex was, unfortunately, the AIDS epidemic and the deaths of over 600,000 in the U.S. so far, and globally more like 33 million. The epidemic, and the rising death tolls, are far from over, here or abroad.

So, the "homosexual" cause still awaits a definition and call grounded in the unique gay sensibility, perspective and constructive non-conformity that are at the core of our being.

Chapter 30

Eros' Corruptions Vs.
Shakespeare in Love

My view of gay identity is premised on two affirmations: 1. that there is an underlying order and purpose to the universe (propelled by a self-developing negative-entropic scientific lawfulness that appears in nature; some may credit God for it) and, 2. within that, same-sex erotic attraction plays a positive, meaningful role. Everything in my explorations is derived from these.

In my argument, the role of same-sex erotic attraction as a dissymmetric tendency in the universe unfolds in human history in an uneven and bumpy way. Mother Nature is far from precise, especially in perpetuating an embedded, necessary alternative to the norm that is subject, for that reason, to repression and brutality.

Thus, an empirical examination of same-sex erotic attraction and behavior runs the gamut from the most abusive to the most loving—from viewing desired persons as "meat," on the one hand, to "beautiful souls," on the other. Homosexuality's marginal status has made it susceptible to abuse, even as its uncorrupted natural impulse weds erotic attraction and the pursuit of beauty, art, science and "the good."

So the history of homosexuality is far from uniform. There are many forms that are cruel and exploitative. There's the socially-accepted ritual abuse of prepubescent boys by older men in certain tribes of New Guinea, ancient Cretan pederastic abduction rituals, Spartan-like militaristic cults, present-day practices by tribal leaders in Northern Afghanistan, examined in PBS' 2010 *Frontline* documentary, *The Dancing Boys of Afghanistan*, where homeless boys are dressed up like girls to dance and be sexually abused by gatherings of powerful men.

For thousands of years, rape and abuse by the rich and/or powerful in political, religious or other institutions has undoubtedly occurred under cloaks of silence.

Still, it is not homosexuality which is to blame. It is man's inhumanity to man, and for most of history, women have seldom fared any better, either.

But by contrast are examples of uplifting and progressive forms of same-sex erotic expression, which elevate beauty and the enduring and loving nurture of the subjects of same-sex love.

Over the course of history, the vast, vast majority of same-sex oriented persons remained invisible, largely because they did not do anything to draw attention, but also because so many deigned to follow the humane and empathetic model of Plato and Socrates and their followers, focusing their same-sex erotic attractions and loves toward advancing notions of beauty, art, learning and institutions of compassion. Thus, they lived the creative and progressive lives that nature had intended for them.

Few homosexual "love letters" have persevered through all the years, though gay historian Rictor Norton assembled a bunch in his *My Dear Boy: Gay Love Letters Through the Centuries* (1998). But there is no case that has matched the Sonnets of the English language's greatest pen, William Shakespeare. His *Sonnets* were published without his approval (thus "outing" him) in 1609 only a few years before his death, and they resonate with the highest expression of same-sex love.

There is no mistaking that 126 of the 154 total Sonnets were written as love letters to a young man, the mysterious "Mr. W.H" to which they were all dedicated.

In 1766, a scholar named Thomas Tyrwhitt theorized that "Mr. W.H." was an Elizabethan boy actor, Willie Hughes. That theory was based in part on the use of a pun in Sonnet 20, referring to, "A man in Hew, all Hews in controlling." That sonnet, considered the first by some scholars, began, "A woman's face with Nature's own hand painted, hast thou, the master-mistress of my passion."

In 1889, gay writer Oscar Wilde wrote a short piece of fiction entitled, *The Portrait of Mr. W.H.* about this object of Shakespeare's passionate affection.

The passion expressed in Shakespeare's *Sonnets* is breathtaking, revealing a depth of emotion that remind us all of our most intensely desired subjects of love. Shakespeare wrote of the "desire of perfect'st love being made" in *Sonnet 51*, and proclaimed, "So are you to my thoughts as food to life, or as sweet-season'd showers are to the ground" (*Sonnet 75*).

Shakespeare sung of "the beauty of your eyes and in fresh numbers number all our graces" (*Sonnet 17*), and in the famous *Sonnet 116*, he proclaimed the eternal nature of such passionate love:

"Love is not love which alters when it alteration finds, or bends with the remover to remove: O no! It is an ever-fixed mark that looks on tempests and is never shaken; it is the star to every wandering bark, whose worth's unknown, although his height be taken. Love's not time's fool, though rosy lips and cheeks within his bending sickle's compass come; love alters not with his brief hours and weeks, but bears it down even to the edge of doom."

The physical beauty of the present is extended to the eternal beauty of the soul forever, the greatest ever expression of same sex passion.

Chapter 31

What Accounts for Us, Other Than Sex?

The approach I am taking in these chapters is to examine the prospect that there is something unique and defining that underlies the fact that a certain number of us turn out to be homosexual, and not heterosexual. In other words, where does homosexual orientation come from? If it is not from a deficiency, or sheer randomness, then what?

By "unique," I don't mean superior. But gays (shorthand for LGBT people) are different from straight people, and therefore by that obvious fact "unique." What is at the core of that? If it can be found, wouldn't that help to define a positive identity for gay people, generally?

So when I suggest that three aspects help to define gay identity—notions of sensibility, alternative perspective and constructive non-conformity—I do not mean that these qualities are unique to gays. On the contrary. But what *is* unique is *gay* sensibility, *gay* alternative perspective and *gay* constructive non-conformity.

I do not claim to impose an identity onto gays, obviously I couldn't if I wanted to. But I strive to raise questions and propose hypotheses out of which a more universal sense of gay identity may emerge, if not immediately, perhaps over decades or longer.

At present, that identity is not defined. Society's definition of "homosexuals" as a *class of persons* is barely a 150 years old, although there is an abundance of documentation of same-sex relations going back as far as historical records have existed. Up until the word, "homosexual" was first coined in 1859, persons in same-sex relations were defined individually by their behavior, solely, either punished, reviled or in some rare cases, grudgingly tolerated.

"Homosexuals" as a class of persons is a very new concept, emerging with the rise of urban cities and the transport and communication means for their explosive growth during and following the Industrial Revolution. The notion of a gay "community" became possible for the first time as, in particular, the telephone had the same revolutionary effect on urban culture 100 years ago as the Internet has now.

Means for social outcasts to connect privately by telephone to meet one another, and assemble in designated secret locations led to the formation of tiny urban "communities" of self-identified homosexuals during the 20th century.

While homosexuals had no way to define themselves, other than by their sexual orientation, there were efforts in the early days of the modern era. While "homosexual" was a term imposed by straight society, from within fledgling gay communities efforts at defining what was called a "Uranian" sensibility evolved up until World War I. But then that terrible global massacre wiped out the credibility of anything from the softer age of *Art Nouveau*, optimism and romanticism before it.

But then, while managing the ebbs and flows of greater and lesser periods of repression and hate, with the emergence of radio and film, gays began to make enormous achievements in the creative arts and other fields, while remaining closeted to all but their most intimate circles of friends.

The socially-mandated duplicity that gays were compelled to internalize as they became more visible to the general public via their creative contributions and the emerging mass media, caused them to psychologically bifurcate their creative work from their personal sexual desires. The two, like the double lives they were forced to live, were made to seem unrelated to each other.

Following World War II in the U.S., one of the most remarkable windows of generosity of spirit involving an entire nation unfolded. Having defeated tyrants to the east and to the west,

America came out of the war with a new confidence and faith in its own institutions of justice and mercy. Rather than retribution, it greeted the post-war period by founding the United Nations and launching the reconstruction of Japan and Europe. In 1947, Eleanor Roosevelt led the development remarkably progressive and visionary *U.N. Universal Declaration of Human Rights.*

This context, also shaped by the amazing works of Tennessee Williams, led to the advancement of civil rights. It was in this environment that urban homosexuals began looking at themselves in a new way, as not misfits, ingrates or sinners, but as human beings. By the mid-1960s, a nascent homosexual rights movement became visible.

But a tsunami of drug-infused radical hedonism was unleashed in the same decade from a "counterculture" synthetically created by a domestic CIA covert operations, known as Operation MK-ULTRA, that swept up civil rights, anti-Vietnam War, feminist and gay activists in a tide of self-indulgent excess that came to define, in particular, the gay movement of the 1970s.

That led to AIDS, and in the years since gays have still lacked a cogent self-identity apart from this.

In my view it can be found by achieving what was denied us earlier, overcoming the bifurcation of our lives through the integration of our "unique" creative potentials and achievements with the sexual components of our identity.

Chapter 32

Toward a Genuine
Gay Morality, Part 1

*"The liberation of sexuality from the bonds of moralism has
left in its wake a crying need for principled, intelligent, vigorous
explorations of how a genuine morality can be introduced into
our newly minted freedom"*
— Tony Kushner in an introductory comment to the
2000 reprint of Larry Kramer's 1978 novel *Faggots.*

This succinct statement by the great contemporary playwright
who brought us *Angels in America* in 1993, and a new play that
opened in New York in the Spring of 2011, sums up precisely my
intent through the course of these *Gay Science* installments.

"Morality" is one of the most highly-charged words in our
language, one of the most abused and feared. But that a "genuine
morality" is important is without question. There is a crying need
for it, with the emphasis equally on both words, and that's why it
is conditional upon three other words—principled, intelligent and
vigorous. From what I can see, for homosexuals it has never been
systematically attempted.

"Gay liberation" 'morality,' such as it is, has persisted as little
more than freedom of homosexuals from discrimination, without
attention to how homosexuals treat each other and themselves.
For homosexuals, unlike for straight people, there are no inherent
societal or cultural rules or expectations for guidance, and in fact
resisting any such perceived impositions is thought of by many as
essential to freedom.

My efforts at exploring a "genuine gay morality" have centered on identifying qualities of gay sensibility and creative, constructive non-conformist potential linked to erotic same-sex attraction as a starting point, and examining the implications of that from different perspectives.

Since Stonewall, only New York playwright Larry Kramer has stood out for also taking up this "morality" challenge, though not systematically. The messages in his novel, *Faggots*, and his play, *The Normal Heart*, in the Summer of 2011 a Tony-nominated revival on Broadway, assert that "having too much sex makes finding love impossible" (echoing from the corridors of real life the observation by Oscar Wilde in *The Picture of Dorian Gray* that "pleasure and happiness are not the same thing"), and that gays should stop killing each other by continuing to have unprotected sex in the midst of the AIDS crisis ("Being defined by our cocks is literally killing us. Must we all be reduced to becoming our own murderers?" the character Ned says in *The Normal Heart*).

Moreover, Kramer was far ahead of anyone with his passionate response to the AIDS epidemic once it hit, forming activist institutions, the Gay Men's Health Crisis and ACT UP, to mitigate its impact. Still, all these efforts earned him the angry enmity of the gay "establishment," beginning with its reaction to his *Faggots*.

Kramer made many enemies with that book, released as if an ominous Old Testament prophecy, on the eve of the outbreak of AIDS. Then, the excesses of extreme hedonism had swept over the lifestyles of tens of thousands in major cities, as chronicled in Kramer's 2006 film documentary, *Gay Sex in the 70s*.

"Why can't I get out of this lifestyle that is going crazier and more out of control and more mad and legitimized," a character in *Faggots* lamented.

Kramer's enemies resulting from that book turned out to be many of the same who fought against efforts to prevent the spread of the AIDS virus in the early 1980s, including profiteering bath house owners, their friends and political radicals who equated frequent and impersonal bathhouse sex with the very essence of gay liberation (Randy Shilts, *And the Band Played On*, 1987).

The spring of 2011, the first documentary has appeared taking a hard look into the pained, emaciated and wounded faces of the AIDS epidemic in the U.S. *We Were Here*, which made the rounds of film festivals before a general release later that year, looks at how the crisis impacted San Francisco.

While it marks a breakthrough for facing down the crisis (after years of denial and post-traumatic stress), it nonetheless adopts an "upbeat" focus on the gay community's caring and compassionate response to the epidemic, sidestepping any consideration for what brought it on in the first place.

In another 2011 film documentary, *Making the Boys*, about the making of the 1968 Broadway play and movie, *The Boys in the Band*, Larry Kramer is shown commenting to the effect that gay people "killed thousands of their friends" by their sexual behavior in the early days of the AIDS crisis, adding, "And we really haven't come to grips with that fact."

Following a screening of *We Were Here* at the Baltimore Film Festival, I asked its producer-director David Weissman to respond to Kramer's comment, and I was disappointed to once again hear his reaction come in the form of an indictment of Kramer for his "anger issues."

Kramer's "anger issues," it seems to me, are in fact his overwhelming compassion for his fellow homosexuals translated into urgent calls for them to change their destructive behaviors.

Chapter 33

Toward a Genuine
Gay Morality, Part 2

The death at age 100 in May 2011 of renowned atomic physicist Maurice Goldhaber has helped to bring to light, through lengthy obituaries, his work in the discovery of a fundamental "left-handed" component to the elemental, sub-atomic structure of physical reality.

This discovery about particles known as "neutrinos," which according to the obituary by the *New York Times'* Kenneth Chang, "violate mirror symmetry" of the universe, brought to light something "odd and unexpected" about physical space, contradicting Newton's law of motion. A critical experiment by Goldhaber showed that, unlike the illustrative case of arrows whose rotation one way is, if reflected in a mirror, seen moving in an opposite rotation, neutrinos always rotate in one direction (counterclockwise) and never the other.

Already in over my head on this subject, I raise it claiming nothing other than to show there is evidence in physics of what I've contended about a lawful "dissymmetry" built into the fabric of a universe that, among other things, accounts for homosexuality.

"Dissymmetry" propels the universe's motion away from a static equilibrium to "negentropic" development, and manifests itself in the human social sciences in lawfully "off beat" epiphenomena such as left-handedness, right-brain domination and homosexuality, among other things.

These are essential core components of the universe, not accidents, random deviations, corruptions or perversions. They are by-products of the universe's essential drive to self-develop, the drive from which the human mind has evolved.

By a preponderant natural affinity towards more global perspectives and of artistic, poetic and other forms of the idealization of beauty and knowledge, those of us with an erotic passion that extends outside the process of species reproduction are essential to help drive the development of the individual, civilization, and therefore the universe, forward.

This is not to say these affinities are exclusive to homosexuals, but that such qualities can be found more naturally and acutely among those who find themselves not driven to species reproduction but instead to prefer love of the species itself. Thus, homosexuals.

Granted, the leap from "left-handed" neutrinos in sub-atomic physics to homosexuals in social science may seem great, wild and preposterous. But there is definitely something to it.

As such, in the discussion of a new "genuine morality" for homosexuals, I contend that it has been there all along, and remnants of recorded history show it has always been contained in the Platonic concept of focusing passionate and erotic same-sex attraction toward the elevation of the character, soul and talents of the beloved.

There has been a tension existing all along between the impulse to short-circuit erotic love in the pursuit of instant sexual gratification and the passionately-driven cultivation of love for the beloved.

After Plato, after the myth of Ganymede, that tension appears in the Old and New Testaments, and in St. Augustine's *Confessions*, in Dante's *Divine Comedy*, in Shakespeare's plays and sonnets. In more modern times, it is seen in the struggles over relationships, including those of Oscar Wilde with Bosie in his *The Picture of Dorian Gray* and *De Profundis*, of Tennessee Williams in his striving to maintain his creative sensibilities, in the 1968 play / movie *The Boys in the Band* and in the diaries of writer Christopher Isherwood that informed the 2007 film documentary, *Chris and Don, a Love Story*, chronicling the decades-long relationship between Isherwood and his young companion, my friend Don Bachardy, among many more.

Indeed, wrestling with that tension all throughout history has been at the core of a homosexual "genuine morality" experienced in ways more acute and painful than for those of the dominant heterosexual culture: It occurred, almost exclusively, in isolation and dread, and without solid social guidelines and reinforcements, burdening the homosexual with an overwhelming level of personal responsibility for his or her behaviors.

Perceived shortcomings under such conditions accounted for a lot of self-loathing among homosexuals, more than the orientation, itself. No wonder so many sought closeted refuge in institutions like the church, in heterosexual marriage, and eventually for a tiny few, in small urban gay communities. There, such struggles could be shared with other gays with a modicum of empathy, companionship and courageous humor.

With the Stonewall revolution, the opportunity arose for homosexuals for the first time ever to experience the salutary effects of a personal self-integration, an end to double lives and lonely struggles with uncontrollable obsessions. However, it did not end the challenge of a genuine homosexual morality. Instead, it opened it up to infinite new possibilities for self and social fulfillment.

But the revolution was quickly hijacked by radical hedonists, crawling out of the dregs of a reactionary, socially-engineered "counterculture," who insisted the enemy of the revolution was morality itself. Restraint was condemned, as was anything but a relentless extraction of pleasure from as many anonymous sexual objects as stamina permitted.

They won the day. Thus, they won us the sexual excesses of the 1970s and AIDS. Their worldview still dominates the gay community.

Chapter 34

How I Know What I Know, My Gay Pioneer Days

I was deeply involved in the early days of the modern gay liberation movement in the San Francisco Bay Area between 1969 and 1973. A graduate seminary student in Berkeley, I witnessed events in the Bay Area beginning in 1966 which lead up to and followed the Stonewall Riots in faraway New York in June 1969.

Soon after earning a Masters with honors that same year, I became the co-founder of the Berkeley, Calif., chapter of the Gay Liberation Front, wrote the editorial for the first-ever edition of the *Gay Sunshine* newspaper, was selected by my gay colleagues to become the first-ever officially-invited gay movement representative to speak at a major anti-war rally, and became the most prolific and high-profile writer on the gay movement in the area, contributing almost weekly to the *Berkeley Barb*, the *Berkeley Tribe*, *Gay Sunshine* and the *San Francisco Kalendar*. I also did my own newspaper, *The Effeminist*.

I knew and interacted with all the Bay Area region's gay activists of that turbulent era, including Larry Littlejohn, George Mendenhall, Phyllis Lyon, Del Martin, Konstantin Berlandt, Leo Lawrence, Gary Alinder, Carl Whitman, Mike Silverstein, Michael Itkin, Winston Leyland, Smedley Ambler, Jim "Elijah" Rankin, Don Jackson, Rick Stokes, Ray Broshears, Jim Kepner, Allen Ginsberg, Jim Foster, Harvey Milk (somewhat later) and many more. The same went for non-gay allies like Max Scherr, Willie Brown and Cecil Williams.

I brought to my efforts a unique vantage point as a graduate seminarian, steeped in the study of social, moral and philosophical currents historically and of those days. One of my first major gay writings was a tract entitled, *God and My Gay Soul* (1970).

Among other things, my perspective enabled me to identify divergent social forces of that era. There were three, each with a radically different view of morality:

First, the raw right-wing "military industrial complex" establishment reactionaries, who defined morality as obedience to the *status quo* as they defined it, a white male dominated paradigm which included the systematic suppression of women and minorities, including gays.

Second, an increasingly muscular and effective student-racial minority-feminist-labor movement inspired by Dr. Martin Luther King with enormous contributions from gay giants Eleanor Roosevelt and Tennessee Williams. I identified strongly with that. For it, morality was associated with social and economic justice and fairness. Riding this current in the 1960s was the early gay movement, led by pioneers like my current friends Frank Kameny, Lilli Vincenz and Nancy Davis.

Third, a "third way" which, as it later was revealed in Congressional investigations, was a covert flank of the right-wing establishment, posed as a radical, hedonistic "drugs, sex and rock-and-roll" counterculture. It was disguised to infiltrate and misguide the progressive movement, and it had a particularly profound impact on gay liberation efforts. The morality of that current was "anti-morality." Anything that imposed itself as a burden of responsibility or obligation to others was seen as the enemy of unbridled pleasure-seeking.

That "third way" soon swept over the gay movement like a tsunami, dominating the 1970s as major urban centers became like cesspools for indiscriminate sex, spreading venereal disease and creating a context for the spread of the HIV virus beginning in the mid-1970s.

In particular, students coming back to their colleges and universities in the fall of 1971 seemed to have been overtaken by this trend that summer, with everybody suddenly deciding to be gay whether they actually were or not, and frequent, indiscriminate sex becoming the norm, not the exception.

By 1973, all this drove me out of the gay movement. As one of the highest-profile champions of the cause in the region, I "resigned," so to speak, in an article entitled, *Homosexuality Vs. Socialism*, contending that the gay movement had come under the sway of such mindless hedonism and commodity-modeled exploitation of human flesh that I would follow a socialist path, as best I could, instead.

My parting shot was a tract I wrote, still available on Amazon, entitled, *Sexism, Racism and White Faggots in Sodomist Amerika* (1972). Re-reading a copy almost 30 years later, I was surprised how, though matured through on-going study and insights, my views remain much the same after all this time, even if my language now is less radical and angry.

Still, my work came years before Larry Kramer's prophetic *Faggots* (1978) and the beginning realization of the AIDS epidemic (1981).

To this day, the "third way" current continues to heavily influence the gay movement, including through the influences of Ayn Rand, Michel Foucault, the Koch Brothers' Cato Institute and the radical libertarians of the Tea Party and more.

As for myself, upon taking up a socialist cause in 1974—as ineffectual and misguided in its own way as it may have been—I was abruptly written out of the gay movement and its history. By 1978, a second edition of the Ramparts Press' *Gay Liberation Book* had removed all three of my articles (I had more than any other contributor in the first edition).

Chapter 35

How the Right Unleashed
60's Radical Hedonism

"Kings are interested not in the morality but the docility of their subjects"
— St. Augustine, City of God, Book 2, Chap. 20.

This subject concerns what happened to American society in general, and is of specific relevance to the post-Stonewall gay movement and its values and behaviors from the 1970s to the present.

With the Industrial Revolution, a natural tension developed between the captains of industry and their burgeoning work forces. From the mid-19th century on, industrialists and their monied associates devised strategies to blunt efforts of workers to organize and utilize collective action to achieve economic and social justice.

Tyrants, the industrialists understood, are beneficiaries of a radical individualism that undermines collective organization, as Plato expounded in *The Republic*. Therefore they promoted the ideologies of nihilists, anarchists, the likes of Nietszche, and "might makes right" forms of "social Darwinism" against the growing organization of labor.

These ruling class capitalists, champions of the political right wing, saw emerging urban communities of homosexuals as hostile to their efforts, because of their general disregard for authority and predisposition to identify with the plight of the underdog.

The 1960s quasi-Marxist theory that homosexuals were repressed by capitalists because they undermined the production of stable, obedient households of workers (e.g. Herbert Marcuse,

Eros and Civilization, 1962) was only partly true. Additionally, gays were seen as actively politically dangerous, a genuine threat to the ruling class agenda.

In Nazi Germany, while homosexuals were tolerated in the ranks of the socially-amorphous Brownshirts to help Hilter overthrow the existing order, they were turned on by the militant Blackshirts during the infamous "Night of the Long Knives" in the summer of 1934. Subsequently, the Nazis systematically rounded up homosexuals along with Jews and gypsies and sent them to death camps.

Urban homosexuals had been supporters of progressive Social Democratic regimes in Germany prior to Hitler's takeover, and in England and the U.S. In America, the nation's emerging greatest playwright, the homosexual Tennessee Williams, voted for the Socialist presidential candidate Norman Thomas in 1932.

Meanwhile, when thousands of World War I veterans assembled in Washington, D.C., known as the "Bonus Army," in the Great Depression's dismal summer of 1932 to demand their pensions, Republican President Herbert Hoover called out the U.S. Army against them. Later, after President Franklin D. Roosevelt was elected, many of the same who'd backed the use of the Army against U.S. citizens plotted a military coup against Roosevelt. Often, they were openly pro-Nazi and pro-fascist.

After World War II, these same elements fueled the so-called "Red Scare" and the McCarthyite reign of terror against pro-labor elements in the U.S. government and wider society, accusing them of being communist sympathizers or spies. This came just as redoubled efforts at homosexual rights organizations like the Mattachine Society and Daughters of Bilitis were spearheaded by activists like Harry Hay, a former communist, and backers of Henry A. Wallace's Progressive Party presidential campaign of 1948.

In 1953, right wing forces in the newly-formed CIA launched a systematic effort to undermine pro-labor, pro-civil rights currents running strong in the U.S. citizenry at that point. Their covert program was dubbed "MK Ultra," as subsequent Congressional and other investigations revealed in the mid-1970s.

Unable to impose Hitler-style fascism from the top down, "MK Ultra" was designed to undermine the nation's pro-labor current from within by, again, inducing radical individualism and hedonism. From 1952-1972, the project funded and coordinated 149 sub-projects for research of "radiation, electro-shock, various forms of psychology, sociology, anthropology, graphology and paramilitary devises and materials for behavior control, behavior anomaly production and countermeasures."

In 1973, CIA Director Richard Helms ordered all files associated with these operations destroyed, but a cache of 20,000 documents had been misfiled and therefore were eluded destruction. They became the substance of investigations by the Presidential Rockefeller Commission in 1974 and the Congressional Church Committee in 1975 and were made public.

Operating on forty-four U.S. college campuses and with fifteen research foundations, "MK Ultra" involved mass experiments with the psychedelic drug LSD and other drugs, aimed at "behavior control," "behavior anomaly production" and "producing predictable human behavioral and psychological changes."

Ken Kesey was a key figure who emerged in the early 1960s to play a major role in a cultural sea-change of the American consciousness that involved LSD in a self-centering, hedonistic "dumbing down" of society. Kesey was recruited to be part of "MK Ultra" experiments in California, and he became a seminal influence, organizing "Be-Ins" involving mass LSD ingestion by youths at beach parties around the San Francisco Bay Area and his famous cross-country bus trip to meet Harvard's LSD guru Timothy Leary, chronicled in his *Electric Kool Aid Acid Test*.

Thus did America's right wing launch the anarchist, radical hedonist 1960s counterculture that stampeded the gay movement towards AIDS. I saw it first hand. I was an eyewitness.

Chapter 36

The Extraordinary Heart
Of Larry Kramer

Marking an amazing turn of events in the Summer of 2011, veteran gay activist Larry Kramer took the stage to accept a Tony Award for the "Best Revival" of his gritty AIDS-themed 1985 play, *The Normal Heart*.

Kramer stands head-and-shoulders above all the rest as a prophetic champion of the cause of full enfranchisement for LGBT persons, even as he has faced a barely relenting cascade of criticism from among those very persons over his many years of tireless involvement.

The Tony Awards, which brought him not only before a capacity crowd at New York's Beacon Theater but before millions worldwide, was a small reward for his strivings, hardly adequate to the magnitude of his contribution, but something.

Kramer has always been a passionate truth-teller, as the autobiographical content of *The Normal Heart* demonstrates. So unwilling was he to play by rules of civility while pressing for governmental action to address the raging epidemic of AIDS in the early 1980s, Kramer was booted out of the very organization he founded to fight the contagion.

In those earliest days of the outbreak, no one knew what AIDS was. All anyone knew was that gay men began suddenly getting very sick, very fast and in very big numbers. And they were dying like flies.

Kramer, to his everlasting credit, wasted no time taking action. When the first public reports of the syndrome surfaced the summer of 1981, Kramer and a small contingent organized the "Gay Men's

Health Crisis," and began sounding alarms within the community. They put a table at the dock on Fire Island on Labor Day Weekend 1981 to raise money and awareness to "Fight Gay Cancer" (the best anyone could call it then). But as 18,000 gay men walked past them to the beaches that weekend, they absorbed nothing but ridicule and indifference, raising only $124.

I presume most of those 18,000 gay men, coming to Fire Island because of their proclivities for sexual promiscuity, wound up dying from AIDS themselves.

When Kramer wrote *The Normal Heart*, he'd been forced into exile by his own community. Leaving New York, he wrote the play starting in 1983 as a form of personal therapy, to unload his burden through his art.

What he wrote captured the urgency, the frantic hysteria, pain and bewilderment that attended the outbreak of the crisis.

In it, Kramer blamed not only government inaction, but also what had devolved through the 1970s into what had become the urban gay community's normative, dizzying descent toward egregious sexual excess. With a notable prescience, in 1978 Kramer had sounded the warnings of not only the emotionally numbing effects, but also of something yet unnamed, unmanifested that would become some terrible consequence of such behavior.

That was the subject of his novel *Faggots,* written in 1978 even as the HIV virus was raging silently and yet-undetectably through the bloodstreams of thousands who passed their blood multiple times nightly in the back rooms, the truck trailers, parks, bathhouses and sex clubs of New York, San Francisco, Los Angeles, Miami, New Orleans, Houston, Chicago, Boston and elsewhere.

That novel elicited anger and bellicose outcries from leaders of LGBT officialdom, who insisted on silence about such matters from its gay and pro-gay politicians, social and religious leaders. But Kramer insisted on truth.

Yes, as much as anybody, he saw it coming.

But he spent little time blaming gays once the epidemic broke out. He pleaded for them to stop their excessive sexual habits, but more angrily demanded the Koch and Reagan administrations mobilize to address it.

Finishing *The Normal Heart*, Kramer went back onto the streets of New York and elsewhere, founding ACT UP from among the swelling legions of new LGBT activists taking up the cause through peaceful civil disobedience.

A leader on the government side of the AIDS fight, Dr. Anthony Fauci, recently wrote that Kramer's efforts had, indeed, made a crucial difference in eventually bringing the federal government to its senses.

The ruling elite's right-wing efforts to undermine the gay movement in the late 1960s by flooding it with anarchistic, hedonistic calls for "sexual freedom" was critical for pushing gay behavior toward the excesses that invited AIDS.

In *The Normal Heart*, Kramer mentions a rumor widespread in that era of a sinister right-wing conspiracy hatched at Fort Dietrick, Maryland, to develop and spread the HIV virus into the gay scene. He doesn't endorse or deny the rumor, he just mentions it. To my mind, even if such forces didn't conjure up and spread the deadly pestilence, they would have if they could.

Characteristic of his extraordinary heart, in his acceptance speech Sunday, Larry Kramer said, "I could not have written it had not so many of us so needlessly died. Learn from it, and carry on the fight. Let them know that we are a very special people, an exceptional people. And that our day will come."

Chapter 37

Why "Coming Out"
Matters So Much

Mimi Swartz' article in the June 19, 2011's *New York Times Magazine*, "Living the Good Lie: Should Therapists Help God-Fearing Gay People Stay in the Closet," followed by an "ex-gay's" chronicle, seem to miss completely the most fundamental point about what "coming out" means to most gay persons.

Being "in the closet" for the person who is conscious of an erotic attraction to others of his or her own sex is not really about hiding a secret or "giving up any opportunity to have fulfilling relationships as gay men or women," as Swartz contends.

It is about something more personal and important, shall we say, to the soul. The "closet" has most essentially to do with denying integrity, the quality perhaps most important to a healthy, productive human being.

When I came out of the "closet" as a seminary student in the period just preceding the Stonewall Riots in 1969, it was a life-changing decision taken in the midst of a world of turmoil, anti-Vietnam War demonstrations, civil rights marches and ferment in the ghettos that included the assassinations of monumental leaders for constructive change, Dr. Martin Luther King and Bobby Kennedy.

It was a decision to claim my own life, to rip it free from the cruel conventions of an unjust society that demanded and threatened the most severe punishments if I did not live a lie. I had been forced to be two-faced, duplicitous, lying, deceptive and untruthful on a basic level to all those, including those I cared for the most, around me.

The social ferment for justice and equality caused me to realize that, just as Dr. King said about African-Americans, I could not be leaned on if I refused to stoop over. So, I decided to stand up.

It was the most important thing I've ever done, even though my relationship with the gay world has been a spotty one at best, including what I considered extensive periods of virtual exile while the irrepressible surge of radical hedonism in the 1970s set the stage for the AIDS epidemic.

But once I stood up by coming out, it compelled me immediately to devote whatever talents I had to building the gay liberation movement so that my experience could be shared by as many others as possible.

Even more importantly, it provided me with the personal strength, through a new-found integrity of my inner soul, to throw off the accumulated burdens suffered through years of emotional and physical submission to the whims of a tyrannical father.

My father died in 2002 and toward the end of his life we became close as I respected, loved and helped him despite everything. After all, he'd passed onto me certain strengths of character that not only gave me the courage to come out, but also to confront him at the risk of violence when I had to.

It was Christmas Eve 1970, and when I arrived from San Francisco by bus to our family home on the Southern California coast I had long hair and a beard. My father didn't need to know anything more than that. He dictated that I would not be welcome at the family dinner, even though my two brothers and their wives and my grandparents would be there.

It was a long day leading up to the dinner, with my brothers and their wives debating in the living room of our grandparents' home next door whether or not to boycott the meal in my defense, and bemoaning our shared lives of putting up with our father's arbitrary, violent and tyrannical ways for so many years. But in the end, they all decided to cave in and show up, leaving me isolated and excluded.

I decided I could not allow that to be the final word, even though my father's physical strength was legendary and he had a history of inflicting pain on my mom and us boys. I knew if I confronted him, he could pulverize me.

I opened the front door to my parents house to find everyone at the dinner table, all, upon seeing me, frozen with forks and knives in hand and looking at me speechlessly with stunned, wide-open eyes. I assumed a pose as one steeled for a fight, and unleashed a stream of loud, angry invectives against my father.

When I'd spent myself I was surprised that my father made no move toward me. He continued to sit and sputtered, "So, you want to ruin our dinner."

I turned on my heels and strode out, slamming the door. As I walked away, not my father, but my brothers chased after me, threatening me for my violation of their shameful compact of subservience that they knew was wrong.

That night, which I viewed as sealing my "coming out" by claiming my integrity and my life, freed me to become whatever life had in store, never again to cow-tow to unreasonable convention or fear.

Chapter 38

As Any Good Gay
Boy Would Do

A conversation I overheard on a train from New York in late June 2011 involved a very fat fundamentalist minister in shorts, and a middle aged man trying to keep up a meaningless, "manly" conversation with him. When the man debarked, he introduced his effeminate son who'd been sitting behind him having a lively, high-pitched laughter-filled conversation with a female passenger.

The facial expression of the minister suddenly conveyed contempt, mostly, I'd say, for the man for failing as a parent to have "beaten the gay" out of his son. That fat, judgmental minister evoked an archetypal image of angry haters who've made life miserable for gay people from time immemorial, myself included. Such are the real bullies that young gay people suffer.

They drive fearful parents to desperate measures to de-gay their sons and daughters, with disastrous results. Gay youth suffer doubly when "cures" don't take, blamed for not trying hard enough. Love gets dashed by fear and anger, with scars that last lifetimes.

Too often, youth do the suppressing on themselves, seeking acceptance and losing touch with their gay sensibilities until much later in life, if ever.

It is vital, when lacking, for gay people to get in touch with the gayness of their earliest years, to see those special gifts and sensibilities that are so often evident long before any explicitly erotic aspects come into play.

There are those who just can't help but shut the bedroom door and play music to get their dance on. There are those who prefer the accoutrements of the gender opposite their own. There are those overloaded with empathy and compassion, who always do things for others.

I preferred the company of the females among the adults and their friends in my family and I bled, emotionally, for my mother and the cruel, arbitrary conditions she endured at the hands of my father.

My innate skill was as a writer, but not in an introverted mode. Instead, I produced a newspaper, my first at age seven, which reported on news of the family and neighborhood. I went door-to-door in our little California seaside town of 300 to peddle it for a nickel.

My purpose, I realized much later, was to work in legion with my mother to bring harmony to our home. (It was when I started my own newspaper, the *Falls Church News-Press*, forty years later, that this motivation dawned on me, and this has animated my efforts with my paper since).

Yes, I loved being alone with my music in my bedroom! My favorite music was, one could say, unbeknownst to me, that of my first gay romance. It was with the music of the gay composer Peter Ilyich Tchaikovsky. Little did I know he was gay, of course, but I was all over his frilly and rich sounds and themes, and I stood in front of a mirror not dancing in the usual sense, but in the lavish manner of an orchestra conductor. I'd get goose bumps doing the "1812 Overture" or, my favorite, the final movement of his Fifth Symphony.

As a boy, I was known as kind and generous, and I became the best friend of a lonely Jewish boy whose mother survived the Holocaust.

As a teen, I lived in the same time period and much like the gay character in Tobias Wolff's autobiographical *This Boy's Life*, the one who, in the film version, steals a kiss from the Leonardo DiCaprio character on the piano bench. I had no similar outwardly gay mannerisms, but eschewed crowds in favor of intense one-on-

one friendships, and my first was with a straight lad, who I helped a lot.

High school and college days were tortuous, filled with shyness, self-loathing, acne and fear of disclosure. My newspaper talent was my only consolation. I went out for sports and struggled to date girls.

Meanwhile, I lived in the same time period, again, as the high schoolers in Peter Weir's brilliant film *Dead Poet's Society*, set in the late 1950s. The film chronicled a precursor to the youth ferment of the 1960s, and that mood was in the air.

The only time I shared a homoerotic physical moment in all those years came when three of us, ferried by our high school English teacher, rode back from an event in Los Angeles. A girl was in the front passenger seat. A boy was with me in the back. I was very attracted to the boy, but would never act. Dozing off, I suddenly felt something. I turned to see the boy staring at me, with his warm, moist hand on my thigh.

A first, unforgettable erotic touch! But I pulled away, moaning inside even as I instantly imagined dreaded consequences of reciprocity.

I couldn't break this suffocation until after college, when I did what any good gay boy would do: I enrolled in a theological seminary to find a vocation of bringing love and happiness for all.

Chapter 39

Beatniks and Hippies Vs. Progressive Gay Pioneers

The problem is that almost all gay history or criticism written since Stonewall in 1969 has been from the postmodern perspective, where all social reality is defined in terms of pleasure and power facets resulting in many downright errors, if not lies, concerning some basic facts.

Among the handful of notable exceptions are Rictor Norton, who in his book, *The Myth of the Modern Homosexual* (1997), systematically demolishes the postmodern so-called social constructionist dishonesty of Michel Foucault and others.

Another exception is Tennessee Williams. In Williams' case, notwithstanding those who've tried to interpret his work from the postmodern point of view, in his amazingly prolific writings from the 1960s until his death in 1983, he often wrote directly about the homosexual condition, and never let go of his signature worldview defined by the polarities of cruelty and compassion, both notions rejected by postmoderns (for them, cruelty is subsumed by power and compassion by pleasure).

In his late 1970s efforts like *Vieux Carre* and *Something Cloudy, Something Clear*, for example, Williams drew from his own experiences as a young homosexual to speak directly to the particular struggles of the homosexual to retain self-respect, sensitivity, integrity and creative work against the impulse of carnality-for-its-own-sake.

Such was the dominant unwritten morality of the homosexual back then, the Platonic struggle to elevate both the self and the beloved in the context of a love of beauty and creativity, against the gratification of the mere sexual act itself. It was not so much an either/or, as a tension, to a greater or lesser degree, between the two that defined homosexual lives.

Among other things, postmodernism has completely distorted essential components of gay history prior to Stonewall, painting a picture of a monolithic, linear movement that never, in fact existed that way.

For example, in the early 1950s, the Beat poets of the Village in New York, the likes of Jack Kerouak and Allen Ginsberg, had nothing in common with the organizers of the seminal gay rights organizations like the Mattachine Society. The Beatniks were angry, sleazy, dirty, self-indulgent anarchist hedonists living on the fringe, known for their disgusting abuse of women many of whom, in the name of "free love," they forced into prostitution.

The emerging early gay rights movement was an extension of the legacy of FDR and the New Deal, and pro-labor, pro-socialist currents, carried on following FDR's death by his homosexual wife, Eleanor Roosevelt, her promotion of the *Universal Declaration of Human Rights* through the United Nations, the Henry Wallace presidential campaign of 1948, and the likes of Tennessee Williams and Christopher Isherwood. It also had a religious component, as mainstream urban Protestant and Jewish congregations touted the progressive values of this current.

In San Francisco, for example, the "Council on Religion and the Homosexual" forged important gains for gays in the mid-1960s, and served as the pathway for my own coming out as a seminarian.

But make no mistake, there was no love lost between the Beats and the progressives founding the modern gay rights movement in those days, contrary to the official histories of the current post-modern era.

The Beatniks stood for demolishing all moral benchmarks restraining a purely carnal pursuit of sexual pleasures. Anger against society (Ginsberg's *Howl*) was tempered only by unbridled sexual excess.

In the 1950s, right wing elements operating through covert channels established during World War II unleashed a "domestic pacification" operation to blunt the influence of the progressive movement, especially among the young. It involved the mass dissemination of LSD and other drugs (such as heroin in urban ghettos).

In the early 1960s, anti-progressive writer Ken Kesey was formally identified with this effort, and he played a seminal role in promoting mass LSD use in that era, an effort that peaked with the "Summer of Love" in 1967, when millions of young people were recruited into the ranks of the mewling, marginalized moral degenerates of the Beats. These hoards of "hippies" flooded into the cities and seized control of the gay movement, sending it on its tailspin into the boundless sexual excesses of the 1970s that became the context for the emergence of the AIDS epidemic.

One of the more patently absurd claims of postmodern gay history mythology is that gays engaged in their wild excesses during the 1970s because they'd been pent up for so long. Actually, hardly anyone out in urban America had serious limits in the previous decade, and anyone new to the scene was too young to know any long history of repression. So in fact, it was the angry "hippie" repudiation of any social limits, period, that insisted on excessive sex as a revolutionary mantra.

A seismic shift occurred in American culture as a result. The marginalized became the mainstream. The "hippies" brought with them hedonistic, insensitive post-modern thought and a new right wing resurgence in the name of radical individualism, anarchy and the Reagan revolution.

Chapter 40

"Hippie Free Love" Hijacks
The Gay Movement

In his *The Picture of Dorian Gray*, the storied homosexual Oscar Wilde (1854-1900) penned a work for popular audiences that held specific significance for his "Uranian" (a term for homosexuals in his day) brothers and sisters. The original 1889 version had more explicit homo-eroticism than later rewrites but the message was clear, either way.

Wilde made frequent forays into the urban subculture of London, to mingle among young male "panthers," hustlers and prostitutes generally the social heirs of the street urchins Dickens wrote about fifty years earlier in *Oliver Twist*. From that vantage point, in *Dorian Gray*, Wilde signaled extreme caution, warning in the way only a homosexual with first-hand experience of being entangled in such "pleasures" could, against the dismal consequences of the "New Hedonism," embodied in the philosophy of his novel's character Lord Wooton.

Wilde wrote with a strong ring of truth about the dangers of groundless hedonism's descent into jaundiced depersonalization, addiction, deceit, cruelty, disease and death.

Wilde struggled for true romance with his younger lover Bosie against the pitfalls of the urban homosexual underworld. His was a common struggle for homosexuals. Contending with such tensions, homosexuals commonly took their satisfaction from their creative work.

In the 1950s, urban underworld culture was promoted by right-wing elements to stymie a burgeoning morally-grounded progressive movement (that included many gay pioneers). It involved a mass proliferation of LSD, elevation of Beat Poets onto a national platform, and the message of *Dorian Gray*'s hedonistic Dr. Wooten.

For Beat Poet Allen Ginsberg, social dichotomies were not between capital and labor, rich and poor or white and black, but between the "uptight and the turned on," the "square versus the hippie," the "Birchite versus the faggot individualist" (*The Life and Times of Allen Ginsberg*, 1993). No striving for economic or social justice, only the pursuit of "sex, drugs and rock and roll."

Gay icons Tennessee Williams and Christopher Isherwood were not impressed. Williams, speaking through his character Ms. Goforth in *The Milk Train Doesn't Stop Here Anymore* (1961) said about beatniks: "They're writers who don't write, painters that don't paint. A bunch of freeloaders... That's why I'm not so sympathetic to them. Look, I made it, I got it because I made it, but they'll never work for a living as long as there's a name on their sucker list."

Isherwood, in his diaries of the 1960s published last year, wrote of meeting LSD "guru" Timothy Leary in 1967, and described him thus: "He really is a fake. The smile on his face was so slimy that you could hardly bear to look at him."

Attending a Leary "Psychedelic Celebration" the next day, Isherwood wrote, "A lot of it was ass-licking the younger generation, telling them how great they were and how free. Leary sneered at the oldlings and somehow tried to pass himself off as an honorary young man. He appealed to all the young to 'drop out, turn on, tune in,' which means, as near as you could tell, drop all obligations imposed on you by your elders, take pot, acid or whatnot and thus tune into the meaning of life. What was so false and pernicious in Leary's appeal was its complete irresponsibility. He wasn't offering any reliable spiritual help to the young, only inciting them to vaguely rebellious action, and enticing them without really involving himself with them."

Months later, in July 1967 during the so-called "Summer of Love" when "hippies" took over American culture, Isherwood wrote, "10,000 or maybe 100,000 hippies are expected to descend upon California in the near future, and this, say certain doctors, may start a series of epidemics, because the hippies have syphilis, gonorrhea and hepatitis."

That was horribly prescient of the entire next decade, when "hippie free love" hijacked the gay liberation movement and set social behaviors on a path to the AIDS epidemic.

By 1971, gay author Edmund White (*City Boy*, 2009) reported that in the explosion of impersonal sex in New York, San Francisco and other inner cities, contracting a venereal disease, the "clap," monthly was common.

In bathhouses, back rooms, and the trucks at the West Village piers, what public health expert Gabriel Rotello in *Sexual Ecology* (1998) called "core groups" of compulsive disease-compromised homosexuals formed an environment conducive to the introduction of new viruses and germs.

Michael Callen wrote in *Surviving AIDS* (1990) that as a young, effeminate gay man arriving in New York, "Since becoming sexually active in 1973, I racked up more than 3,000 different sex partners... I had also contracted, many more than once... hepatitis A, hepatitis B, hepatitis non-A/non-B (now C), herpes simplex types I and II, venereal warts, *amebiasis*, including *giardia lamblia* and *entamoeba histolytica, shigella flexneri* and salmonella, syphillis, gonorrhea, non-specific urethritis, *chalmydia, cytomegalovirus* and Epstein-Barr virus, mononucleosis, and *cryptosporidiossis*." He died from AIDS in 1993.

Chapter 41

Gay Liberation Formed
Of Two Opposite Currents

Understanding events leading up to and following the Stonewall riots in 1969 is critical for appraising gay culture and gay identity in the U.S. today. I was uniquely positioned to witness what was going on, both before and after, coming to the San Francisco Bay Area in 1966 as a liberal seminarian and journalist with a keen eye to discern the social forces at play.

I am, of course, also gay, and the process of my coming out in that era was also instrumental for my observations.

Much was muddled at the time. It was hard to tell who was who in the midst of events, and much has been clarified only with time. It is, perhaps, a bit simplistic to characterize "hippie free love" as set against "the gay movement," since it all seemed indistinguishable then, but it reflects what was really going on.

There were two distinct social currents that became deliberately entangled. One was the civil rights movement, including the "War on Poverty," outgrowths of the humanitarian, progressive currents that emerged from World War II with a new optimism about the advance of human rights, democracy and progress globally.

The other was the opposite, cynical machinations of what President Eisenhower called the "military and industrial complex," those industrial-financier interests who backed fascism before the war and redoubled their efforts after it.

That latter current was responsible for McCarthyism in the U.S. in the early 1950s and at the same time used its influences in new U.S. domestic intelligence agencies to blunt and reverse progressive impulses in the population.

This covert CIA operation was documented beyond a doubt in U.S. Congressional hearings in the mid-1970s, and included the specific case of the "Merry Pranksters" of Ken Kesey, on the payroll of the CIA when he crisscrossed the U.S. in the 1960s dispensing LSD and anarcho-hedonistic philosophy.

These operations utilized unemployed beat poets, Warhol soup can and mad Basquiat graffiti "art," and more, to diffuse the moral groundings of the progressive movement, advocating radical individualism, amorality, excessive drug use and the mantra to "tune in, turn on and drop out." Right-wingers at the CIA didn't create these currents but did push them, and drugs, onto society's center stage.

Beatniks, hippies and yippies were promoted by some of the most powerful institutions of the time. It was startling to see long-haired hippie group sex and songs praising sodomy and fellatio in the 1968 Broadway hit *Hair*.

Suddenly this new hippie movement was taking over student protests, and violent clashes occurred between pro-socialist and pro-anarchist student groups in Berkeley and elsewhere, spouting rival slogans at anti-war rallies. It was reminiscent of the "Red and Black" number in the *Les Miserables* musical. I drove to seminary daily along roads lined by armed National Guard troops in those days.

The "Blacks"—referring to shirt and flag colors, not race— were the right-wing anarcho-hedonists, perpetrators among other things of nihilistic, radical "sexual freedom" ideology and practice. They exploded with remarkable force and energy onto the national scene during the Kesey-organized "Summer of Love" when enormous hordes of teenagers descended on San Francisco in 1967, accompanied by tons of drugs.

As a seminarian and youth counselor that summer, I encountered this as a license to crude, foul-mouthed and contemptible behavior. There were no principles except the expectation of a nebulous notion of "love" that usually meant an entitlement to get everything, and everyone, for free. Dropping out of jobs and school, signing up for welfare and promoting sexual excess were normative. Suggestions of restraint were denounced as counter-revolutionary. I knew these people very well, and saw how they operated.

Living as street people in big-city urban subcultures was elevated to an ideal. Kesey wrote *One Flew Over the Cuckoo's Nest* to provide a pretext for then-Governor Ronald Reagan of California to shut down state mental health facilities, driving countless thousands of emotionally-vulnerable people, including young gays, into joblessness and homelessness. The same went for veterans returning from Vietnam.

These trends were boosted by CIA influences in Hollywood, with such films as *Skidoo*, a 1968 pro-hippie film featuring a cache of famous stars. Then in 1969, the year of Stonewall, the first-ever mass media portrayal of an actual homosexual act was embedded into a film that won the Oscar for Best Picture.

Midnight Cowboy romanticized down-and-out New York urban street culture, including the depiction of a young man "going down" on a street hustler in a tawdry Times Square movie theater, and throwing up in the men's room after. I recall how shocking that scene was. Everyone in the theater groaned and gasped.

Some way to introduce gay love to mainstream culture! But it was an integral part of how cynical right wing elements sought to steer the gay movement in the direction of radical, urban hedonism, away from high-minded aspirations for creative, wider social reform.

Chapter 42

The *Boys in the Band*
Call to My Liberation

Two contradictory forces collided in the late 1960s—the civil rights movement and the "sexual freedom" movement—and the latter won. Gay liberation soon adopted the trappings of the right-wing inspired "counterculture," while seemingly magically in inner cities, doors opened wide to welcome virtually any kind of hedonistic excess.

In addition to sinister right-wing political and intelligence operations, monied interests who stood to gain fabulously from all the new nightclubs, bars, bathhouses, sex clubs, porn industries, the sex trade and more got their grip on the movement. Philosophers of hedonistic excess filled gay publications with calls to act out social anger with wanton, impersonal sex. Not love, sex.

Anyone who counseled restraint, or even romance, was denounced as counter-revolutionary and "sex negative." It was no longer a matter of enfranchising homosexuals, as by 1971 it became fashionable on college campuses to be drugged and gay. What had been marginal in inner city underworlds—drugs, prostitution, porn and impersonal sex in public bathhouses, tea rooms, parks and sex clubs—became mainstream.

The June 1969 Stonewall riots, not the first involving clashes between police and gay street people (for example, the August 1966 Compton's Cafeteria riot in San Francisco), occurred at the same time as, nearby, long lines were waiting to see Mart Crowley's huge hit play, *The Boys in the Band*.

That play, which began a run of 1,000 performances in January 1968, marked a high point in the civil rights-inspired current of the gay movement.

It was the first of its kind to present the urban homosexual lifestyle to general audiences, and was wildly popular among gays and straights alike. Unlike the tsunami of "sexual freedom" that later took over the movement, it was about two abiding themes: the struggle for genuine self-esteem and the notion of a gay community.

Contrary to those who've trashed *The Boys in the Band* from the standpoint of subsequent, disingenuous post-modern hedonism, the play was not primarily about pre-liberation self-loathing. It was grounded in compassionate truth-telling, in the manner of Tennessee Williams, resonating with authenticity for gay audiences, while holding out for a far better day.

While recited as a taunt by Harold, it was actually important and liberating when the play's character told Michael, "You are a sad and pathetic man. You're a homosexual and you don't want to be. But there is nothing you can do to change it. Not all our prayers to God, not all the analysis you can buy in all the years you've got left to live. You may very well one day be able to know a heterosexual life if you want it desperately enough—if you pursue it with the fervor with which you now annihilate—but you will always be homosexual as well. Always, Michael. Always. Until the day you die."

That "affirmation" was, to me in that era, far more a clarion call to "come out" and to own my identity and integrity than any riot or lure of hedonistic excess.

All that was missing in the lives of the characters of that play, all that was needed for their liberation, was to have them, and the wider world, understand and accept the meaning of that small speech.

And finally, after all the cat fighting and drama, Harold departs by saying simply, "Call you tomorrow." The bonds in this microcosm of our wider homosexual tribe could not have been stronger, despite everything.

For a young gay man, this play made the prospect of my life as an open, and not self-loathing, homosexual not only tolerable, but expectant.

It helped me to resolve, as Christopher Isherwood wrote about himself in *Christopher and His Kind* (1976), "He must never again give way to embarrassment, never deny the rights of his tribe, never apologize for its existence, never think of sacrificing himself masochistically on the altar of that false god of the totalitarians, the Greatest Good for the Greater Number—whose priests are alone empowered to decide what 'good' is."

The play's characters were employed and aspiring, the way most homosexuals were who came to the big city to pursue their often enormous talents. They'd not "turned on, tuned in and dropped out," as the "counterculture" soon after demanded as a central tenet of the movement.

Like the play's characters, I pursued a creative career after graduate seminary as a journalist for a weekly alternative paper, the famous *Berkeley Barb*. I was a leading writer and focused on gay issues.

But by 1971 working for the *Barb* as a gay activist did not met with my radical counterculture gay colleagues' favor. An entourage showed up at the *Barb* and, in publisher Max Scherr's presence, demanded I quit and join them in the ranks of the unemployed, to live off welfare checks ("Aid to the Totally Disabled," to be exact) and food stamps. I didn't.

Chapter 43

Such a Noble and Heroic Breed Are Homosexuals

Almost all the gay-authored literature describing the Stonewall era through the end of the AIDS "automatic death sentence" era, from 1969 to 1996—including compelling writing by the Violet Quill circle of notable gay-themed novelists including Edmund White and Andrew Holleran—presents an overwhelming sense of inevitability.

Lone exceptions among prominent gay figures are playwright/ activist Larry Kramer and the late *San Francisco Chronicle* reporter Randy Shilts (*And the Band Played On*). But even they only alluded to, at best, rather than critically examined the larger social forces that shaped post-Stonewall gay culture, that steered it and reinforced it in the direction of the astonishing radical hedonism in the 1970s, creating the context for AIDS and 600,000 deaths of mostly male homosexuals in the U.S. to date (and, of course, countless more worldwide).

So, my *Gay Science* series over recent months has been pioneering. It is presented not as definitive or the final word, but as a starting point to a fresh examination of not only what happened then, based on, among other things, my journalistic eyewitness leading up to and following Stonewall, but of the "what, why and how" of trends that continue to drive gay culture at its core today.

Dominant gay culture remains defined in that core by circuit parties, recreational drugs, mindless worship of the physical properties of certain endowed young men, boring pornography, sexual excess, the constant abuse of the emotive impulse to love by resort to casual and anonymous sex, outlandish allegedly-sexual extreme behaviors (such as "erotic vomiting," described in glowing terms in a twisted "queer theory" textbook), and the abiding popularity of Grindr, Scruff and other casual sex hook-up sites.

These features are so mainstream in gay culture today it seems hopeless, an invitation to derision, to call them into question. No wonder the yearning for something akin to normalcy among so many gays, seeking it through marriage and other institutions that parrot the even more morally-bankrupt straight society that either still hates or will never really be comfortable with them.

Kramer's character Ned Weeks in his Tony Award-winning *The Normal Heart* cries out as the reality of the AIDS epidemic unfolds, "I belong to a culture that includes Proust, Henry James, Tchaikovsky, Cole Porter, Plato, Socrates, Aristotle, Alexander the Great, Michelangelo, Leonardo da Vinci, Christopher Marlowe, Walt Whitman, Herman Melville, Tennessee Williams, Byron, E.M. Forster, Lorca, Auden, Francis Bacon, James Baldwin, Harry Stack Sullivan, John Maynard Keynes, Dag Hammarskjöld... The only way we'll have real pride is when we demand recognition of a culture that isn't just sexual. It's all there—all through history we've been there; but we have to claim it, and identify who was in it, and articulate what's in our minds and hearts and all our creative contributions to this earth... That's how I want to be defined: as one of the men who fought the war. Being defined by our cocks is literally killing us. Must we all be reduced to becoming our own murderers?"

That has been Larry Kramer's abiding theme.

To my mind, such a noble and heroic breed are homosexuals! We've been an indispensable glue and momentum for the maintenance and advance not only of civilization, but of civility, itself. Nature has put us here for a reason.

Strip us of our rightful role, replace a zeal to create and contribute to a more just and compassionate world, reduce us to "blithe indifference," and the entire world becomes angrier, more paranoid, more selfish and cruel.

Assess the wider social impact of one hundred thousand of the most creative souls in the world, who found their way to New York, the creative capital of the globe, to make their contribution, wiped out by AIDS—most long before they'd come close to achieving their full potential.

How would the world be different today had that not happened? Would the outcome of the razor-thin 2000 presidential election in the U.S. (considered by many the most significant watershed for all the chaos that's followed) been the same? You can't remove that many homosexuals without making the world a less cheery place.

For too many who survived, the cynicism and indifference imbued into gay culture in the 1970s, and the unaddressed "post-traumatic stress" consequences of the AIDS era, turned them away from humanitarian ideals, to parrot their straight oppressors as harsh individualist libertarians, anarchists and jaded arch-conservatives.

Gay people will never "fit" in straight society. Nature provided us to transform it, not conform to it. We're meant to be neither the mindless hedonists of the urban gay culture of the 1970s nor new Ozzie and Harriets. Nobody said this would be easy. It isn't.

But we can speak to each other from the vantage point of, as Abraham Lincoln (one of us) put it, "the better angels of our nature," to love not lust, to urge one another to tackle fears and become important to the mending of an increasingly dysfunctional world.

Chapter 44

The Social Engineering
Of Anarcho-Hedonism

Occasionally it is instructive to take a question from the audience, so to speak, to help clarify certain points.

I present excerpts from thoughtful August 2011 comments of one reader of this series, followed by excerpts from my reply that I emailed to him last weekend:

"Mr. Benton,

"You seem to see most things gay as through a black or white prism. Either conspiracy-laden, or sanctimoniously correct. There are villains and there are saints.

Walt Whitman is good; Allen Ginsburg, bad. Ken Kesey, the devil's own; Christopher Isherwood, a saint...

"You rightfully point out that unbridled hedonism, a primary component to the sexual liberation movement of the 60's and 70's, helped produce STD epidemics and the AIDS pandemic which hit our community especially hard... But then you lose me when you go off on paranoid tangents of inferring that the U.S. government/ CIA were directly instrumental in subverting the gay liberation movement through their proxies: the hippies, Kesey, Leary and company.

"I maintain that the so-called free love movements and anything-goes mentality of that period were entirely self-generated; a reaction to the prudery of the '50's, and merely provided fodder for those who identified themselves as critics or adversaries of our movement."

Here are excerpts from my response:

"Dear Sir,

"When you say 'self-generated,' what 'self' are you referring to? Did it just blossom simultaneously and spontaneously out of everyone's head? That's not how I experienced it at all. It was shoved down our throats (figuratively and literally both, I suppose). Yours is the conventional view, but I saw it differently living it.

"Please do not reduce my observations to simplistic 'black versus white' caricatures. I do not claim the entire U.S. government and its intelligence arms were involved, but specific reactionary elements of them, only. Others were unaware, opposed or condoned them on the grounds of fighting the Cold War domestically.

"I invite you to go back and read the development of my case, the references to the seminal roles of elite institutions like Esalen, the Stanford Research Institute, and the CIA's covert drug-pushing MK-Ultra project run off forty-four college campuses from the early 1950s, including the explicit involvement of Kesey with those.

"In the context of the Cold War, it was a massive cultural 'paradigm shift' these interests were working for, well documented in the mid-1970s findings of the Rockefeller Commission and the Church Committee in Congress (notwithstanding almost all the relevant covert ops-related documents were ordered destroyed by the CIA chief beforehand), and background is also provided in Jeff Sharlet's *The Family*, published two years ago. (Ed. Note—I neglected to add other sources, such as Marilyn Ferguson's *Aquarian Conspiracy*, a 1980 rendition glowingly hailing the cultural shift and its motivating institutions; note the word 'conspiracy' is hers not mine).

"Nobody has applied any of this to what happened to gay culture in the 1970s. I am trying.

"The loaded word, 'paranoid' is only empty name-calling unless it can be demonstrated their are no grounds for the concerns expressed. In that regard, I have more to make my case, I believe, than you have to dismiss it."

When I moved from a small coastal town to the San Francisco Bay Area for graduate school in 1966, little did I imagine what I would encounter: the push for the radical counterculture social paradigm shift was well underway.

I came as a trained journalist, editor of high school and college newspapers who'd worked part-time through school and after full-time as a reporter for my hometown daily. Journalists don't just arrive somewhere and get steeped in living. They can't help but examine the terrain constantly, looking to find connections between and behind events and phenomena, much like intelligence specialists.

My observations were enhanced by two more facets. First, as a graduate seminarian, I studied intensely the varied philosophies and theologies that underpinned and overarched social movements through history.

That enabled me to identify the underlying world view of the pro-Nietzsche anarcho-hedonists who were driving the "sexual freedom" (as distinct from the gay liberation) bandwagon without regard for moral precepts.

The Nietzschian anarcho-hedonists were straight out of the historical strain of the fascist radical right. It was not a big leap from that discovery to, during the 1970s, learning about the CIA's MK-Ultra project behind it.

Second, I am gay. My coming out and becoming a pioneering gay activist provided, with my other advantages, a vantage point from which to see things unfolding more clearly.

The overall right wing-directed quasi-covert operation succeeded in transforming the ethos of American culture from its post-World War II compassionate humanitarianism, the rise of the U.N., Marshall Plan, reconstruction of Japan, civil rights movement and War on Poverty.

Within one decade, from 1965 to 1975, the nation shifted toward selfish self-interest, poised for the Reagan Revolution of 1980. The gay movement was caught up in that shift, driven into urban orgies of mindless hedonism as part of a bigger social plan.

Chapter 45

Radical Sexual Hedonism
Vs. "Rightly-Ordered Love"

"Virtue is rightly-ordered love."
— St. Augustine, City of God.

The concept of "virtue," descriptive through history of the most highly-valued human qualities, is, truth be told, the invention of homosexuals.

But it has almost disappeared from our language, a primary victim of the last forty years' shift in social mores brought on by a "counterculture" that sees "virtue" as a primary target for destruction. "Virtue," after all, centers human behavior on love, courage, consideration and justice, while anarcho-hedonist "counterculture" values are centered entirely on selfish self-interest.

The 19th century philosopher Neitzsche ridiculed "virtue," and he was a seminal influence in the post-World War II rise of the radical anarcho-hedonist movement.

Tragically, anarcho-hedonism smothered the gay liberation movement in its cradle in the late 60s and early 70s, fomenting an urban gay culture of startling sexual excess, among other things, the precondition for the AIDS horror.

But the homosexuals' invention of "virtue" was a lawful product of our natural role in creation as ones not primarily driven by an impulse for physical species procreation, but instead for the procreation of civilization itself.

Concepts of "virtue" appear in the writings of homosexuals Plato and Socrates who defined it as a blend of temperance, prudence, courage and justice. The Apostle Paul defines it as inclusive of "faith, hope and love" in I Corinthians 13, and in his letter to *Galatians*, broadens it to include love, joy, peace, patience, kindness, generosity, faithfulness, gentleness and self-control. Paul's allegedly anti-homosexual commentary in his letter to the Romans was against predatory lust, not virtuous love.

St. Augustine (354-430 A.D.) defines "virtue" as "rightly-ordered love," consisting of all the above-mentioned qualities. Augustine is rightly included in Paul Russell's *The Gay 100* volume (1995) because he acknowledged in his autobiographical *Confessions* passionate same-sex relations as a young man.

But few knew better than Augustine the consequences for civilization of wanton, out of control hedonism, being an eyewitness to the unraveling of the Roman Empire.

Augustine's *City of God* was a critique of the collapsing empire, and how hedonistic rituals, including profuse homosexual acts performed by Galli priest-prostitutes, contributed to it. He observed that Rome's rulers cared not a hoot for morality, but solely for the docility of their subjects.

Like Plato and Paul, Augustine counseled restraint—or better, "virtue"—in cultures where massive hedonistic excess led swiftly to death, both of persons and societies. He was not anti-homosexual, but anti-dehumanizing hedonistic excess. He elevated love and virtue, with particular regard for the well-being of the beloved, over sexual hedonism.

It is a challenge to see St. Augustine for who he really was in his time, and not as distorted by the cloudy prism of 1500 years of subsequent history. A critic of a crumbling civilization, he struggled to build a bastion to salvage humanity. He wrote and preached prolifically. In fact, rather than denounce virtuous same-sex intimacy, he affirmed it. He endorsed the kind of relationships we see exhibited, for example, between medieval priests played by Sean Connery and Christian Slater in the mesmerizing film version of Umberto Eco's novel, *The Name of the Rose* (1986).

Subsequently, of course, brutal repression in the name of religion, including of all same-sex relations, accompanied the advance of civilization.

It was not until the rise of gay liberation in the late 1960s that the opportunity arose for all homosexuals to affirm their true selves openly. Then, it became possible to exercise virtuous same-sex love openly and proudly for the first time. Most homosexuals are, after all, the most beautiful, loving, creative people in the world, especially when we are free to claim our integrity.

The author of the poignant AIDS-era novel *Borrowed Time*, Paul Monette (1945-1995), put it in in a most inspired way in his essay, "On Becoming," in Mark Thompson's *"Gay Soul: Finding the Heart of Gay Spirit and Nature"* (1990).

"It has been my experience," he wrote, "that gay and lesbian people who have fought through their self-hatred and their self-recriminations have a capacity for empathy that is glorious and a capacity to find a laughter in things that is like praising God. There is a kind of flagrant joy about us that goes very deep and is not available to most people."

Echoing what I've affirmed in these chapters all along, he added, "Being gay is about something more profound than my sexual nature."

We homosexuals really did not deserve what the ugly counterculture of anarcho-hedonistic excess imposed on us in the late 1960s, nor did we deserve the consequences. "Virtue" was the targeted enemy of the counterculture, which forcibly imposed incredible vulgarity and selfish disrespect for persons. Women in that male-dominated counterculture were particularly degraded. Drugs were rampant, dulling resistance to this new culture, and all was perpetrated in the name of "revolution," "freedom," and "liberation."

Chapter 46

The 1970's Vortex
Of Sexual Addiction, Part 1

My core argument can be summed up like this: (1) Homosexuals are beautiful, (2) we are important, and (3) we must shift our culture's "center of gravity" away from hedonism.

First, especially when free of self-loathing and oppression, we gays have demonstrated through history unique qualities of heightened sensibility, an alternate perspective and constructive non-conformity that have brought beauty and joy, and have been integral to the humanizing and progress of civilization.

Second, there's no doubt that we gays are an integral component of natural creation whose role has, in general, been to focus on the socializing qualities of education and science, appreciation of the beautiful, humane social governance, and to be the "great poets" described by Walt Whitman. Because we're not inherently focused on species reproduction and the territorial components of that (which lead to wars), we focus on the nurture of widows and orphans, so to speak, and to stand firmly, as unconventional and usually perceived arch-enemies of male-dominated cultures, against the dehumanizing trends of those. Without homosexuals exercising a proper role, societies become harsh, brutal and self-destructive.

Third, hedonism, says the dictionary, is"the pursuit of or devotion to pleasure, especially to the pleasures of the senses." The tragic fact of our gay history that forty years ago, at the time of Stonewall, just when it became possible for the first time in history for us to shed the terrible burden of secret double-existences and self-paralyzing deceit, we were plunged into a maelstrom of destructive anarcho-hedonism. Our current gay culture is inherited from this.

"Anarcho-hedonism" is a novel term I get credit for introducing into serious discourse. It is descriptive of the 1960s-centered so-called "counterculture," the noxious product of sinister conniving by pro-fascist elements in the covert U.S. intelligence structure. I witnessed first hand its evolution and deployment to shift the national cultural ethos away from post-World War II progressive and humanitarian values to, by the early 1970s, a mass movement of depoliticized, self-centered hedonists.

The nation in the early 1970s, including its suddenly-burgeoning urban homosexual scene, was going literally insane. The young went from being principled, idealistic civil rights activists to being deluged with powerful mind-altering drugs, content-less hypnotic music and free sex, the most powerful narcotic of all—it was the "triple threat" of the counterculture: sex, drugs and rock-and-roll.

Whereas it's very cool, of course, to be homosexual and to like what we like, the "counterculture"-led explosion of anonymous, impersonal and relentless gay sex in major urban U.S. centers— egged on by mysteriously suddenly-libertine attitudes by public authorities and gurus of sexual freedom who taunted the fainthearted by accusing any impulse for restraint of being counter-revolutionary—created a serious, massive clinical addiction that eventually led to AIDS.

The addiction was to sex itself, the internal bodily chemistry of the orgasm and its release being most powerful narcotic of all. It was reinforced by peer pressure and, in the haze of instant gratification, the relentless preachers and peddlers of hedonistic excess. Among other things, it was a heyday for rapists, predators and pederasts, emboldened to practice drug-laced seduction and coercion, all in the name of the "sexual revolution." It was too much. By 1973 I'd effectively exited the scene, but observed its relentless deepening and spread until slowed by AIDS beginning in 1981.

The new freedom was, in fact, a new slavery, as with any addiction. Writing about gay culture in that era, Andrew Holleran and Edmund White, even if they didn't acknowledge the problem as addiction, in fact, alluded to its effects repeatedly.

In *Dancers From the Dance* (1978), Holleran's "non-fiction novel" (his term) describing the New York homosexual scene in the pre-AIDS 1970s, he used terms like "prisoner of love," "the hot gloom of lust," "unable to leave," "kept him there against his will," sex as the "extraordinary disease," "doomed queen," "the grim expression of someone living for lust," "the itchy sore of lust," "ceasing, like us, to have any identity at all," "just as lost as we were," "the hope of love getting further and further from any chance of it," "sick with lust," "surrender to the white pill," "the disease, the delirium of the last 10 years," "we were lunatics, I am sorry to say," "addicted," "the madness of it all," "the disease had eaten into his system," "we are doomed."

Hedonistic addiction act like a powerful vortex, a force of destruction hurling victims against their will to utter destruction. Plato knew this. It is the dynamic expressed in Dante's *Inferno*, and in Wilde's *Picture of Dorian Gray*.

This, and not the grinning, PR version of our post-Stonewall history, is what we actually suffered. It led to the unspeakable horror that beautiful gay people could not be deterred from becoming the crazed assassins of 600,000 of their own.

Chapter 47

The 1970's Vortex
Of Sexual Addiction, Part 2

Assessing modern gay culture, consider that two important components from Stonewall forward were the result of external factors.

The first was the explosion of the "sex, drugs and rock and roll" 1960s counterculture in America that shifted—like a gigantic earthquake shifting a tectonic plate of the planet's crust—the national ethos, among other things plunging the emerging gay liberation movement into a toxic sea of unbridled and counterculture-mandated sexual excess. This did not arise from within gay culture, but overwhelmed it from without.

The second was what happened as a result: in major urban centers indulgence in relentless, impersonal and casual sex, often multiple times daily, quickly led not only to a loss of sensibility for genuine romance and love, but to a loss of control. I submit it was due to a ferocious clinical addiction to the potent narcotic of sex itself.

It explains the compulsive behavior of that decade, and its persistence to this day, if on a more limited scale. But addiction, a medical condition, is not inherent to being gay, so to the degree it impacts our culture, it comes from without.

Beyond my own experience and references to addictive casual sex in Andrew Holleran's *Dancer From the Dance*" (1978) in my previous installment, gay writer Edmund White made multiple references to addiction in his autobiographical works. In his *My Lives* (2006), he wrote about being caught "in the grip of a compulsion that didn't have much to do with pleasure."

He wrote, "I was too addicted to its sexual rewards to renounce this system," referencing the 1970s gay scene's "new aesthetic, which I dubbed the Pleasure Machine (that was) frank, hedonistic and devoid of irony," in his *States of Desire: Travels in Gay America* (1980).

(Christopher Isherwood felt that book was "deeply disturbing" as a literary tour because it "used the predicament of the homosexual minority to demonstrate what is very wrong with the social health of the country.")

In his *City Boy: My Life in New York During the 1960s and '70s* (2009), White wrote about an addictive force compelling him in the dark holds of long-haul trucks parked under the piers on the Lower West Side beside the Hudson River, and in the dark abandoned piers themselves.

In the backs of trucks or in the piers, he wrote, "I simply couldn't make myself go home. Even after a satisfying encounter with one man or ten I still wanted to hang around to see what the next ten minutes would bring. What it brought was the morning light." He then confessed, "Not that there was much happiness in a life of pleasure."

Tennessee Williams, the most famous openly-homosexual American of all, also wrote about the addictive nature of frequent, impersonal sex. In his *Small Craft Warnings* (1972), the first openly homosexual character in one of his major plays, Quentin, says, "There's a coarseness, a deadening coarseness, in the experience of most homosexuals. The experiences are quick, and hard, and brutal, and the pattern of them is practically unchanging. Their act of love is like the jabbing of a hypodermic needle to which they're addicted but which is more and more empty of real interest and surprise. This lack of variation and surprise in their 'love life' spreads into other areas of sensibility..."

Thus, Williams, the compassionate truth-teller, the often promiscuous homosexual, was no fan of casual gay sex because of its addictive nature.

The combined external factors of the counterculture and addiction led to AIDS through the formation what public health experts call "core groups," environments in which human immune capacities are compromised, as Gabriel Rotello documented in *Sexual Ecology: AIDS and the Destiny of Gay Men* (1998) and Ronald Bayer in *Private Acts, Social Consequences: AIDS and the Politics of Public Health"* (1989).

The explosion of sexually-transmitted diseases in such "core groups" and their damage to the immune systems of their hosts almost guaranteed that a dormant, inactive virus like HIV would awaken and flourish. And so it did.

Although imposed from without, homosexuals caved in to the pressures of counterculture excess and its addictive, fatal consequence, such that undoing the persisting influence of those factors in homosexual culture today will require enormous effort. It may take generations. So, while my contributions are addressed to readers today, so they are also to homosexuals yet unborn, and it is theirs whose judgments I value most.

White, in a 1991 third edition Afterword to *States of Desire*, conceded that all the 1970s "self-centered pleasure seeking...was a betrayal of an earlier philosophy that had linked homosexual rights with feminism and socialism," a passing, partially adequate reference to what I and my "Effeminist" gay activist colleagues were fighting for at that time.

We lost that fight. We were crushed. The "pleasure-seekers" won. Now it's forty years and 600,000 horrible deaths later.

Chapter 48

The 1970s Vortex
Of Sexual Addiction, Part 3

In *Dancer From the Dance*, Andrew Holleran wrote about the rampant, excessive hedonism that swept the gay world in New York in the 1970s, as Larry Kramer did in his novel *Faggots* and his film documentary *Gay Sex in the '70s*, and Edmund White did in his *States of Desire, My Lives* and other accounts. I witnessed the same phenomena in San Francisco.

In his "non-fiction novel," Holleran described a club called The Twelfth Floor. It was on West 33rd Street, an all-gay, earlier version of Studio 54, where a plethora of drugs and casual hook-ups flowed among elite pretty boys and those who could afford or had sufficient status to be their admirers. No ordinary people allowed, just the beautiful ones—which quickly became elevated as quintessential "gay culture."

There, amid a crunch of beautiful young gays squeezed into the club, a cynical and jaded older homosexual introduces a young novice to the scene, a "thin, pale young fellow in horn-rimmed glasses who looked as if he had just stumbled out of the stacks of the New York Public Library."

The older homosexual addresses the young man's reluctance to plunge into this hedonistic maelstrom by suggesting he abandon his career ambitions ("Please don't feel you have an obligation to be secretary of state," he says), and providing him a drug, persuading him it isn't as bad as the hog tranquilizers (used to induce "the profound ease felt by a Nebraska hog about to be castrated and bled to death") many in the room ingested.

Next, this older "mentor" points out someone "so bitter about his fate (of having a small penis) that when he developed a case of syphilis he went to the baths and infected everyone he could who sported an enormous organ."

He then advises the youth, "You are beginning a journey, far more bizarre than any excursion up the Nile," concluding, "For tonight, my dear, you are a homosexual!"

That scene reflected the reality of the times, but was so horribly wrong on so many levels, especially the infuriating contention that plunging into a sex and drug-laden club scene defines one as a homosexual.

That lad was a homosexual from birth, and with a world full of opportunity to bring his unique gifts to bear, gifts often unique to homosexuals, that can impart a powerful force for love and in the process, find and share it for himself as well.

But there were many, many profoundly immoral older homosexual carnivores like Holleran's character, slyly recruiting neophytes into a world of gross hedonistic excess with the help of drugs and coercion, and using counterculture "philosophies" like "if it feels good, do it," and the subordination of creative aspirations to instant sexual gratification.

For predatory letches, the more youths they can induce into mindless excess, depersonalization and addiction (and, way too soon, a casket), the more they'll become meat for them, if not for sex, as customers to buy their drugs and porn. Also, as with avenging a disadvantage by deliberately spreading syphilis, there's the angry, self-loathing of such aging queens, obsessed with contaminating and ruining the young and pretty.

It didn't have to be that way. By contrast, in 1972, the same era as Holleran's Twelfth Floor scene, I wrote a piece for the *Berkeley Barb,* one of three essays of mine included in the first published collection of post-Stonewall writings, *The Gay Liberation Book* (Ramparts Press, 1973, first edition only). Entitled *David,* I wrote about my experience with a young man from an Iowa farm forced to become a hustler after running away to San Francisco.

He was cold and distant when I befriended him, I wrote. "It wasn't hard for me to understand why," I wrote. "I represented just another older man to him, an older man who didn't really care about him, but just wanted his body. It pained me because it was plain how much he desired honest affection, and how much threat of exploitation there was in every move toward affection with me."

I offered to pay him just to talk with me, and when that happened, he was astonished. A few months later, he knocked on my door. He had overdosed and thought he was dying and I was the only person he knew who, he thought, could help him.

He stayed a few days with me, went home to Iowa (where he'd received electroshock therapy for being gay), couldn't take it, and came back. We spent a lot of time talking after that, and I concluded in my essay that because of his understanding of oppression, and his ability to equate his own with that of women, "David understands gay liberation, I think, better than all those bourgeois queers in gay organizations who talk about their own liberation while continuing to oppress women and younger men like David."

Chapter 49

Sensibility, Alternate Sensuality, Constructive Non-Conformity

Those who will read these installments in their eventual book form will appreciate that with their publication week-to-week, it's often necessary to recapitulate central themes, as each week brings new readers unfamiliar with what had gone before.

Foremost among these themes is the notion that homosexual orientation *per se* is but one part of an individual's total distinctive personality and identity. As total persons, homosexuals are created as among the most beautiful in spirit on the planet, who bring important, unique gifts. Without us around, humanity suffers. We're naturally generated as a portion of the universe's evolution designed to bring unique features necessary for the ultimately harmonious unfolding of life.

Same-sex erotic attraction is but one manifestation of the homosexual's total complement of special gifts. Others I have described as a heightened sense of empathy that can be called "gay sensibility," an alternate sensual perspective, and a constructive non-conformity.

The straight world is not entirely devoid of these qualities. On the contrary, it is our purpose as homosexuals, working with the social emancipation of women, to heighten these qualities for civilization as a whole. But we homosexuals gain from appreciating that they constitute the core of our total personhood, that they are our tribal identity, so to speak.

Our natural adversary is the tyrant, the tyrannies great and small derived from unchallenged straight male dominion. That domination is over women, children and subjugated peoples, and derived territorial and resource perceived requirements that cause wars. That is how nature, in its human social form, is organized—ninety-three percent of it, roughly, that is.

We homosexuals are that percent which stands in the way of male dominion's total lust for conquest and control. We liberate the oppressed, as our great poet laureate Walt Whitman wrote, "The attitude of great poets (that's us!—ed.) is to cheer up slaves and horrify despots" (*Leaves of Grass*). We attend to the widows and orphans, we construct and operate the institutions of mercy and fairness. We emancipate abused women and boys whose fathers train them to fight and die in their wars or become their dulled corporate clones.

Because we are homosexual, we are not obsessed with species reproduction and territorial dominion, but have an alternative sensual perspective directed more to beauty and forms that elevate and humanize the spirit. When a straight brute walks into a room, he orients immediately, in his constant urge to reproduce, to any attractive women there. When a gay person walks into the same room, he or she orients instead toward whether the drapes and the carpet match.

In terms of constructive non-conformity, we are challenged to recognize that we will never, nor should, fit in to male-dominated society, but that it is in our very core to counter its influence in a myriad of ways—from camp and acting out, to public service, scientific discovery, invention, education, design and higher art in myriad forms. These are all ways in which "constructive non-conformity" gets expressed, and the natural impulse of the unbridled straight male is always threatened by this at one or another level.

When emancipated women and gays rule the world, we will impose a lasting, if uneasy, peace that will eventually evolve into a more humane, enlightened and productive species.

It should come as no surprise that we've been responsible for the very notion of "virtue" in global civilization for millennia, as derived from our "founding fathers," Plato and Socrates, persisting and evolving into the notion of the "Christian prince (or princess)" as expounded by Erasmus during the Renaissance (*The Education of the Christian Prince*), as contrasted to the tyrant. From that developed modern concepts of democratic republics (after Plato's *The Republic*) that underpinned the Constitution of the U.S. and the enlightened, universal humanitarian values contained in the United Nation's *Universal Declaration of Human Rights*, championed after World War II by one of us, Eleanor Roosevelt, and advanced by another, U.N. Secretary General Dag Hammarskjöld. All this was, and is, us.

What's the point? It's so that waves upon waves of new homosexuals, whether they want to call themselves that or not, that nature propagates in each new generation, can know that this is who they are, this is the tribe into which they've been born.

They need to know it is this, and not the current, dominant so-called "gay culture" definition which says it's really only their sex drive that matters, that lures them into the mindless club scene of drugs, musical monotony and thoughtless promiscuity.

The club scene dulls the sensibilities, destroys the passion for real creativity, and routinely creates the most dreaded fate of all, to become hopelessly jaded.

Gay people naturally have the most gentle, beautiful spirits in creation. We love to sing, laugh and bring comfort to the afflicted. But alas, we are not immune from the brutality and injustice of male dominated society, and can become inflicted with its traits.

Chapter 50

Our Gay Movement's Colossal Failure

W hen I became a vocal gay liberation leader in San Francisco after completing graduate seminary and coming out with a bang in 1969 (shortly before the Stonewall riots across the continent), I quickly came under fire for contending our liberation called for fundamental socio-political change, rather than just boundless sex.

Using my journalistic skills, I became the most prolific writer on all matters gay in the Bay Area, contributing weekly to the *Berkeley Barb*, often to its rival the *Berkeley Tribe*, to the *Gay Sunshine* newspaper, authoring its first editorial, to my own paper, *The Effeminist*, and a variety of San Francisco gay bar rags, like the *Kalendar*.

I co-founded the Berkeley chapter of the Gay Liberation Front, and I was voted by my peers to be the first gay spokesman formally invited to speak at a major anti-war rally. When the first collection of post-Stonewall gay writings was assembled, *The Gay Liberation Book* (Ramparts Press, 1973), including entries by Allen Ginsberg, Gore Vidal, William Burroughs and other big names, I was the only one among those who had more than one entry. I had three.

This was all before the legendary Harvey Milk migrated from New York, where he'd been a Wall Street Republican, to set up shop in San Francisco. I had many exchanges with Milk, who dismissed all initiatives except electoral and legislative ones.

Milk and others did a great deal to win political gains for homosexuals. I ran on the same ballot with him in San Francisco in 1975. He ran for supervisor, I ran for mayor, losing with a dozen others to George Moscone, who was killed along with Milk by Dan White in November 1978.

By 1972, from my vantage point as a gay leader, it was clear that a countercultural, anarcho-hedonistic tsunami was turning the movement away from any sensibility for wider social change to focus solely on unbridled sex and license to it.

The gay "The Age of Contagion" (my term) ran from 1972 to 1996, AIDS being phase two. It was fueled by unlimited impersonal sex, which became not only normative, but a "politically correct" imperative. It was common for gays in urban centers to be infected with venereal disease almost monthly, compromising immune systems to provide opportunity for the HIV virus, while crippling the emotional capacity for sustainable romance.

I became sharper in my arguments against all this. I wrote against, and even picketed, Allen Ginsberg, the gay beat poet with two decent compositions to his credit, because Ginsburg bragged publicly about masturbating to images of young boys, ran a help-wanted ad in the *Barb* for a personal assistant, providing a physical description of the kind of boy he wanted, and was a founding member of the North American Man-Boy Love Association (NAMBLA).

Ginsberg assailed me in the *Barb*, contending I was "obviously in need of a good f**k." (My fiery redheaded boyfriend at the time insisted on writing a reply that I was not lacking in that regard).

Ginsberg, elevated to countercultural sainthood, and the gay French post-modernist philosopher, Michel Foucault, were highly visible Pied Pipers of "The Age of Contagion."

Lecturing at the University of California at Berkeley in the mid-1970s on the "history of sex," Foucault was notorious for spending his nights at leather S&M bars on Folsom Street in San Francisco.

Enticing young gay students and anyone else toward what he called "limit experiences" that led them to degrees of sexual degradation they normally avoided, Foucault mused, with all the trappings of academia, that the only novel invention in all the sex of the post-Stonewall era was "fisting."

The words, "love" and "romance," of course, never appear in any of Foucault's teachings, only "pleasure" and "limit experiences."

Foucault reportedly laughed cynically upon hearing the news that what became known as AIDS began appearing in the summer of 1981. In 1983, he returned to the Bay Area, manifesting symptoms of AIDS, himself, which did not deter him from almost surely spreading the virus at nightly bath house engagements until his death in mid-1984.

Overwhelmed by all this, I chose exile from the gay movement in mid-1973, and bailed out. Subsequently, despite the urban gay culture's descent into dangerous sexual excess, no one in the gay movement spoke out about it. No one. Not one leader. Not one, except for a single angry playwright, Larry Kramer who wrote *Faggots* in 1978 and was accused, as I'd been, of being "sex negative."

The terrible truth about AIDS is that, while outside factors introduced and perpetuated the 1970s sexual excesses, virtually every lethal infection was passed by one gay person to another. We did it to ourselves, even after knowing the consequences. Our actions caused the "Age of Contagion," starting about 1972, and our movement failed, abjectly failed, to prevent within in our own ranks what became the horrible, premature deaths of 600,000 of our beautiful, very own.

Chapter 51

In the Valley of the Shadow
Of Death and Sorrow

The "AIDS Dark Age" was horrific beyond words. For most of us, it extended from July 5, 1981 to December 30, 1996, starting with the *New York Times'* first public report of a new "gay cancer" and ending when *Time* magazine named Dr. David Ho the "Man of the Year" for finding how to prevent AIDS from being an automatic death sentence.

Its toll among gay men is estimated at 600,000 deaths. Every gay man who'd been within spitting distance of a gay establishment in the previous decade feared, if not learned, the worst, never knowing if a cough or a blemish might signal the onset of a monstrous death.

The HIV virus causing AIDS was especially cruel because of its long incubation period, leaving unsuspecting carriers symptom-free an average of five years, all the while unwittingly spreading it in an era when condoms were never used. It began silently spreading among core groups of hyper-promiscuous urban gay men in the mid-1970s, before first erupting as "frank" AIDS in the summer of 1981.

Once headlines began appearing about a new, mysterious "gay cancer," panic, horror, fear and pain set in. In the first years of explosive outbreaks, its cause, nature, and mode of transmission were not known, and no tests existed to identify who had it. The deaths mounted steadily through the early nineties, and even after 1996. My close friend's brother hung on until 2002 before passing.

The government turned its back and thousands of gays stepped up in the midst of their own fears to become heroic caregivers to friends and strangers. The emotional toll for survivors was so acute, it undoubtedly exists to this day.

Important works written in that era described its impact, foremost being Larry Kramer's play, *The Normal Heart* (1984) that portrayed with grit, terror and compassion the period after AIDS first manifested in that summer of 1981. Its revival on Broadway in 2011, and its Tony Awards accolades are heartening indicators that after fifteen years since the end of that "Dark Age" era, with all the post-traumatic stress it caused, we may now be moving beyond it.

Other accounts written in the era include Andrew Holleran's collection of 23 essays written during the mid-1980s, published together as *Ground Zero* in 1988 and re-published recently as *Chronicle of a Plague Revisited*. Paul Monette wrote *Borrowed Time, an AIDS Memoir* (1988). Randy Shilts wrote the epic tome, as a journalist chronicling the era for the *San Francisco Chronicle*, called *And the Band Played On* (1987). Tony Kushner wrote the magnificent, Pulitzer Prize-winning *Angels in America* (first performed in 1990). Both Shilts' and Kushner's works later became important television films. Many victims wrote poetry in that time, too, a sampling assembled by Philip Clark and David Groff in the recent volume, *Persistent Voices: Poetry By Writers Lost to AIDS* (2009).

The acute pain and sorrow of that time were also captured in songs written about AIDS, including Elton John's *The Last Song* (1992) and Bruce Springsteen's haunting Academy Award-winning *Streets of Philadelphia* (1993) featured in the compassionate, first major U.S. film about AIDS, *Philadelphia*.

Called "The Horror" by Africans on whose continent it now still rages, AIDS, Holleran wrote, "quickly converted people in their twenties into old men who were blind, mad, wasting away, racked with fevers, chills, pneumonia, diarrhea, Kaposi's sarcoma, dementia, and other diseases made possible by the total breakdown in the immune system."

In addition to being terminal, AIDS forced "outing" to parents, relatives and employers, often resulting in anger and shunning, terrible feelings of personal guilt, grueling suffering and loneliness, dying virtually alone (many already alienated from their families for "coming out" before moving to the city), premature total decimation of bodies and faces once so beautiful and valued, incontinence and frightening dementia.

The many uncontrollable tears shed by audiences at Kramer's play in 2011, or by readers of other works of that era, are balm even now for breaking through the hardened emotional defenses erected in that horrid time. Clive Jones' AIDS Quilt project, the AIDS rides in the 1990s, the National AIDS Memorial Grove in San Francisco's Golden Gate Park and more have also provided opportunities.

My mind goes to the so many I knew devastated by that era, and the countless faces I remember from the 1970s I admired but never knew. I think of young models in Mel Roberts photographs, of chorus line twinks I espy on 1970s TV variety show reruns, and by imagining that in hospital wards, young gay men abandoned by their parents as they withered away sung along while the biggest hit of the early '80s, Foreigner's *I Want to Know What Love Is*, played on the radio.

My dedication to the National AIDS Memorial Grove reads, "To all the beautiful gay angels, on earth and in heaven."

Chapter 52

The Valley of the Shadow
Of Death and Madness

Gay men during the "AIDS Dark Age" (1981-1996) were frightened out of their minds, especially in the first years of its outbreak when so little was known about it, or about who or how many among the still symptom-free harbored the deadly virus.

Behaviors under these conditions varied radically—from the caring to the insane.

Voluntary caregivers provided extraordinary support for their stricken fellow homosexuals, friends and strangers alike, so many alienated from family and former friends and otherwise alone, as documented in David Weissman's film, *We Were Here*.

Strident activists took to the streets. Playwright Larry Kramer was first to leap to his political feet when the public reports started coming out about the new, mysterious "gay cancer" in July 1981.

Then there was the madness, as journalist Randy Shilts, destined to die of AIDS in 1994, witnessed first hand and reported in his *And the Band Played On: Politics, People and the AIDS Epidemic 1980-1985"* (1987).

That 630-page book is the most thorough testament to the first years of AIDS, a critically important chronicle of the professional journalist's "who, what, where, when and how" of what happened. Shilts was an openly gay reporter for the *San Francisco Chronicle*.

His book ran afoul of the gay establishment at the time, as it was deemed to cast too negative a light on the gay community. But it was made into a powerful, Emmy Award-winning HBO documentary film in 1993 though still, as good as that film was, it didn't begin to reach the depth and gritty detail of the book.

Most shocking is the book's description of the unfathomable resistance to standard public health measures, designed to prevent the virus from spreading, that came from leaders of the gay establishment, caught in the grip of their radical hedonism, in those early years of the epidemic.

Sadly, many leaders of gay organizations were people with significant vested financial interests in the promiscuous sex of the urban gay subculture. They were owners of bars (many with sexually-active "dark rooms" in the rear), porn bookstores (many with "glory hole"-equipped peep show compartments in the back), sex clubs and bathhouses.

It was suspected very early that these kinds of establishments were major points of transmission of the virus, and there developed a pitched battle between public health officials and those in the gay community, either with financial interests or deeply entrenched from a decade's worth of collective, clinical addiction to frequent and impersonal sex, who fought to keep these places open and unchanged.

Clinical addiction to sex in the face of AIDS became hysterical insanity.

Three years into the epidemic, when some gay leaders began realizing that measures like closing the bathhouses were required to save lives, an editorial entitled "Killing the Movement" appeared in the April 4, 1984 edition of the *Bay Area Reporter* in San Francisco. It equated closing the bathhouses with "killing off" the gay liberation movement, saying the move spelled "the annihilation of gay life." The paper publicized a "traitor's list" of the sixteen gay leaders who called for the bathhouse closings.

As Shilts wrote, "A homosexual McCarthyism descended on the gay community...McCarthy felt he could proscribe all the political views a true American should have; the *Bay Area Reporter* and its like-minded gay leaders now felt they could order all homosexuals to think exactly as they did or be branded unhomosexual traitors."

Under such a logic, Shilts added, "The heroes had become the bathhouse owners, who had assured doctors at the AIDS Clinic that bathhouses were fine because 'we both make our money off' the people who were killing themselves there.'"

Even more disturbing, he said, "was the fact that there was no one in the gay community who would censure this verbal terrorism. Not one gay politico, writer, or thinker would step forward and say, simply, 'This is madness.' Insanity triumphed because sane people were silent."

It's hard to know which was more outrageous: fanatical resistance to preventing the spread of the deadly virus or the equation of gay liberation with unprotected bathhouse sex.

It took a gay activist from the pre-Stonewall era to force the issue on closing the baths. In 1984, Larry Littlejohn, a founder of the Society of Individual Rights (SIR), moved to place a referendum on the ballot to ban sexual activity in the San Francisco's fifteen bathhouses. Threatening to "out" the issue like this forced city and gay leaders to act, neither wanting it on the ballot, and the bathhouses were soon closed. Other U.S. cities quickly followed suit.

The same madness persisted among those gay leaders who a year later resisted testing for the virus, once an effective test was finally devised.

The plague was extended for years longer than it might have, at the cost of hundreds of thousands of lives, by the combination of government inaction and astonishing insanity in the gay establishment.

Chapter 53

In the Valley of the Shadow
Of Death and Contrition

I am asked why I focus so much in these installments on what I call our gay "Age of Contagion" from 1972-96. Isn't it ancient history? Isn't it better to just move on?

Hardly, I reply. First of all, much of the information I've highlighted is new to any who've not searched heavy tomes to find it. Not only is most confined to scholarly discourse, but much has been suppressed within the gay movement because of its unflattering nature.

An important component of what I have been doing with these weekly installments over the past year is that I have made them accessible to a wide general audience, posting them on two websites and reprinting them in a popular weekly gay news magazine in the nation's capital. In that format, younger and older, neophyte student and noble senior survivor, all have had access to the same information and perspective.

Thus, this series, entering briefly into a second year, is not just words, but in its totality constitutes an "event" in itself of some historic relevance.

Making the history of the "Age of Contagion" accessible is vital for the future of gay liberation. I've first made the case that homosexuals are beautiful and essential components of the natural order of creation.

So, when it comes to the "Age of Contagion," the axiom applies that he who does not learn from history is condemned to repeat it.

But more than that, the need to face up to the horror of what really happened is an essential precondition for embracing a new collective gay identity, a "new gay morality" as playwright Tony Kushner calls it.

Facts relevant to the "Age of Contagion" begin with the socially-engineered "counterculture" tsunami of "sex, drugs and rock and roll" that swept the nation in the 1960s and flooded a fledgling post-Stonewall gay movement with an anarcho-hedonistic urgency for rampant, depersonalized sex.

Mass hysteria in the form of a clinical addition to sex resulted, and the proliferation of sexually-transmitted diseases compromised immune systems that became conveyors by 1975 for the silent spread of the HIV virus.

While no gay movement leader (apart from Larry Kramer) issued a single public cautionary statement about this, "frank" AIDS hit in July 1981 and thousands quickly became sick, horribly tormented, demented and dead.

Sadly, sex addiction compelled many in the gay movement to furiously resist effective public health measures to stem the epidemic. No leader of the gay establishment spoke against this either. Thus, hundreds of thousands of additional gay people became infected and died who might not have otherwise.

A hostile wider society and government inaction contributed to the death toll, but the ghastly reality is that we alone spread this epidemic by ourselves to ourselves.

Denial and emotional recoil sealed hardened hearts, perpetuating the paradigm of behavior that drove the epidemic. But beneath that, a level of sorrow and remorse can be tapped by grasping the magnitude of the AIDS horror, which can serve as a wellspring of penitence for a collective moral healing and rebirth.

Our great genius Oscar Wilde (1854-1900), brought down from the heights of fame and celebrity to humiliation and shunning when convicted of "the love that dare not speak its name" (homosexuality), wrote a letter from prison in 1897 entitled *De Profundis*. The first part directed to his beloved Alfred Douglas ("Bosie"), its second part counts among the magnificent short works in literature.

Wilde's remorse was not for being gay, or for the "crime" for which he was convicted, but for the arrogance that ignored the consequences of flagrant behavior, which by ruining him, ruined his benefit to humanity.

"Sorrow," he wrote, "is the supreme emotion of which man is capable," adding "I must say to myself that I ruined myself and that nobody great or small can be ruined except by his own hand."

He wrote, "Nothing in the whole world is meaningless and suffering least of all... Hidden away in my nature, like a treasure in a field, is Humility. It is the last thing left in me, and the best: the ultimate discovery at which I have arrived, the starting point for a fresh development."

He referenced Dante's *La Vita Nuova* ("The New Life"), written in 1295, a short poetic essay whose Beatrice is the assimilation of beauty, reason and love into a singular desire, the pursuit of "virtue."

Wilde referred to "the fierce misery of those who live for pleasure." Then he wrote of "that imaginative sympathy in the entire sphere of human relations, which is the sole secret of creation."

"Pleasure's fierce misery" is set against "imaginative sympathy:" rival animators of personhood.

Male chauvinist civilization's great vice is arrogance, a wanton disregard for the consequences of behavior on general social well-being. In our "Age of Contagion," homosexuals aped that arrogance. Through contrition comes a restart.

Chapter 54

Franklin Kameny and the
Birth of Our Movement

It was by a remarkable and gracious coincidence that the first weekend after the passing on Oct. 11, 2011 of our gay movement's greatest pioneer, Franklin Kameny, the Martin Luther King Jr. Memorial was dedicated on the National Mall.

The ceremony included a viewing of the entirety of Dr. King's seventeen-minute "I Have a Dream" speech delivered on the steps of the Lincoln Memorial to 300,000 in the "Great March on Washington" of August 28, 1963, the year of the 100th anniversary of Lincoln's signing of the Emancipation Proclamation.

Seven of the handful of original gay members of the Mattachine Society of Washington, led by Kameny, attended that historic rally and heard that speech. It was with its echoes ringing in their ears that in 1965, Kameny and a tiny cadre of fellow homosexuals carried out the first-ever organized picket line demanding homosexual equality held at the White House gates.

In his 1963 speech, Dr. King welcomed the racially-diverse makeup of the rally. "Many of our white brothers, as evidenced by their presence here today, have come to realize that their destiny is tied up with our destiny. They have come to realize that their freedom is inextricably bound to our freedom," he intoned.

"We hold these truths to be self-evident: that all men are created equal," Dr. King declared. "I have a dream that my four little children will one day live in a nation where they will not be judged by the color of their skin but by the content of their character."

That speech directly inspired the rise of our modern gay movement, led by Kameny (May 21, 1925-October 11, 2011), Lilli

Vincenz, Barbara Gittings and a handful of others, as chronicled in the film documentary, *Gay Pioneers* (2004), produced by the Philadelphia Equality Forum.

Frank Kameny, I am proud to say, was my friend in recent years. He was arguably the single most seminal influence in the history of our movement, so claimed at a Rainbow History Project forum last week. Kameny was scheduled to speak at that forum before his untimely death at age 86 just two days before.

His was the strident, compelling force that led the effort against the 1950s McCarthyite anti-homosexual witch hunts in the government (David K. Johnson, *The Lavender Scare, The Cold War Persecution of Gays and Lesbians in the Federal Government,* 2004).

He organized picket lines when no one else was doing it and carried on a relentless, lifelong fight for equality. He ran for public office and railed loudly against injustice in an era when no one, except in rarefied circles of literary or artistic elites, dared publicly declare their homosexuality.

His crowning achievement was his relentless, eventually successful campaign to get the American Psychiatric Association to remove homosexuality from its list of mental disorders in 1973. That signal achievement changed the public perception of homosexuality, laying the groundwork for growing public acceptance and affirmation since.

Kameny invented the slogan, "Gay is Good," far more controversial in its time than it seems now. I defended it then against objections of dedicated gay friends who considered it too radical.

When I first met Frank, I was a young gay activist in 1970 in San Francisco. with Dr. King's speech permeating the national ethos, I'd made two life-changing decisions: entering seminary in 1966 and joining Kameny and his San Francisco counterparts prior to Stonewall in early 1969 to "come out" and join the struggle for gay, and human, liberation.

Our fight, I wrote in the editorial for the first *Gay Sunshine* newspaper, "should harken to a greater cause, the cause of human liberation, of which homosexual liberation is just one aspect."

Regrettably, about that same time, the onslaught of the right wing, socially-engineered anarcho-hedonist counterculture hijacked our movement, dashing Dr. King's appeal to the "content of character" in the process. We've had to live, and die, with the consequences of that since.

I reconnected with Frank in recent years, while his contributions became more recognized and appreciated. A milestone came when the many picket signs, leaflets, speeches and photographs he'd kept from his earliest activist days were formally received as a special collection at the Smithsonian Institution. He was honored at the White House by President Obama, and a photo of him and me with Vice President Biden hangs in my office.

Along with another other early activist and mutual friend, Lilli Vincenz, and her long-time partner Nancy Davis, I hosted Frank as my guest at the national dinner of the Human Rights Campaign in 2005, and often invited him to lunches at The Palm restaurant in downtown D.C.

Those many lunches were not only to enjoy his company, but to provide opportunities for my friends, especially younger ones, gay and otherwise, to meet and appreciate this genuine hero of our movement. Recently, of this *Gay Science* project, Kameny smiled and quipped, "I think we wind up in the same place." I concurred.

Chapter 55

Life, Liberation and the Pursuit of Happiness

It is important to treat the issues of our gay identity, new (or, very ancient) gay morality and our future from the standpoint of the American revolutionary promise of "life, liberty and the pursuit of happiness."

On liberty, I take the liberty of substituting "liberation." Also, it is noted that the phrase, "pursuit of happiness," wound up in the "Declaration of Independence" over objections from some who wanted "property" there instead. "The pursuit of happiness," by contrast to property, is at the heart of what the American experience is intended to be. Not happiness, mind you, but the pursuit of it.

The American notion of the democratic republic, and how it has progressed against all odds toward the achievement of its founding goals, grounded as it is in the affirmation that "all are created equal," has among its greatest progenitors in history, us!

One can start with our Plato (author of *The Republic*) and Socrates, with the poetry, valor and nation-building of our David, inspired by his love for Jonathan, with those who advanced Platonic notions in Judeo-Christian and Islamic traditions, influencing government at all levels, from the local to the education of princes.

Such notions were democratized by our Shakespeare's plays, including his love sonnets to young Willie, and the shaping of America's unprecedented democratic nationhood by our Alexander Hamilton, writing the *Federalist Papers* and marshaling the country's economic potential, to our Abraham Lincoln, who preserved the union, freed the slaves and instituted the "American system" economic and social engines of growth, opportunity and prosperity. These accomplishments were hailed by our Walt Whitman and their compassionate side elevated by our Tennessee Williams. Then, they took on a global dimension in the advancement of the *Universal Declaration of Human Rights* by our Eleanor Roosevelt.

Our beloved late Franklin Kameny led the cause to extend all this to the full, open enfranchisement of homosexuals. And there have been countless more.

It is worth examining this history, as I have in this series, as a form of self-discovery of what it really means to be gay, a member of the LGBT tribe. We are that indispensable component of creation and civilization, that nature's purpose has provided to engineer the highest, most noble aspirations and inspirations, and to translate those into modes of just and compassionate governing. In this current, government becomes the will of the people behaving collectively on the basis of universal principles of fairness, justice and provision for the opportunity of all to attain their fullest potentials.

Naturally, we are not the only ones who embody all this, as it is precisely our purpose and our success to spread it far and wide. But there is this special role for us, we who are empowered to love in a Platonic manner, rather than being driven by natural erotic impulses primarily to reproduce the species.

I have looked at the history and impact of our tribe from this point of view, seeing the imprint of our influence on history in these forms, and not from today's popular historical reductionism and shallow empirical investigations into evidences of mere sexual activity.

The movement for our liberation has come through a terrible time—the Age of Contagion (1973-1996) that included the AIDS Dark Age (1981-1996)—when an estimated 600,000 of us perished prematurely in the most horrible of ways. Accounting time for the trauma of all that, the manifestations of post-traumatic stress, to recede, we're in a time now when it's right to look at that heinous era squarely, and to mourn in a contrite manner that cleanses and frees our collective spirit to move ahead. So the revival of Larry Kramer's drama, *The Normal Heart*, did for us with its remarkable Broadway success the summer of 2011.

But two misguided tangents grip our cause in ways we can see more clearly now than in the fog of the Age of Contagion and its aftermath.

The first is society's pressure on us to "assimilate," to be clones of today's dominant, banal consumerist culture, and it's understandable to want that, given our history of repression and pain. The second is the unproductive reaction against that in a modern variant of anarcho-hedonism, the destructive force that drove our movement into the ground in the 1970s, known today as "Queer Theory." For many, a combination creates the assimilation-obsessed political anarchist, or radical libertarian.

This wouldn't be trending at all now but for AIDS, I fear. Not only were 600,000 of the most creative, caring and compassionate of human beings prematurely wiped off the national landscape in two decades, but for survivors, a trauma-driven assimilation wish, on the one hand, and jaded negativism, on the other, is shaping the identity of too many.

One can only imagine how the history of our nation, and world, might be different had not so many of our tribe perished before their fullest potentials were matured.

Chapter 56

Life, Liberation and Happiness, Part 1: *Angels in America*

For gay men during the AIDS Dark Age (1981-1996), during which time an estimated 600,000 of us died horribly and way too soon, there was nothing more valued than life itself, and as Prior, the main character in Tony Kushner's amazing play about that era, *Angels in America,* insists on, "Life...more life!"

The promise of "life, liberty (liberation) and the pursuit of happiness" as "inalienable rights" involves not only enjoying them, but empowerment to provide them to others as well (something we homosexuals are very good at). It's because the promise was not only written, but delivered by the Founding Fathers, who made a revolution to secure it for all. Each of its components—life, liberty and happiness—is properly defined in terms of the other two.

In Kushner's epic Pulitzer, Tony and Emmy Award winning play, the two-part *Angels in America,* subtitled *A Gay Fantasia on National Themes,* (1993), life is the reality most affirmed in the seven-hour (presented in separate parts) drama about struggling to cope in the AIDS Dark Age.

The play is about insisting upon life while confused angels counsel against the idea, and ends with its AIDS-wracked but still standing hero Prior blessing all of us at the healing pond of the angel Bethesda—this one not in Jerusalem, but Central Park—and by so doing bestowing life upon us.

Drawing the exhaustive *Angels in America* to a close—after God is absent, angels are befuddled as heaven is crumbling, a Jewish activist prays for her enemy, a Mormon mother makes a breakthrough and puts love ahead of everything, a saucy male nurse steals from the rich for a friend in need, a depressed housewife breaks free, Prior breaks a fever, and much more—Prior turns from his friends sitting at the Bethesda fountain to speak to the audience, to us homosexuals. He says:

"The fountain's not flowing now, they turn it off in the winter, ice in the pipes. But in the summer it's a sight to see. I want to be around to see it. I plan to be. I hope to be.

"This disease will be the end of many of us, but not nearly all, and the dead will be commemorated and will struggle on with the living, and we are not going away. We don't die secret deaths anymore. The world only spins forward. We will be citizens. The time has come.

"Bye now.

"You are fabulous creatures, each and every one.

"And I bless you: *More Life*.

"The Great Work Begins."

For non-gays asking, "What about us?" this play is not about them, but for homosexuals in our darkest hours. Others can watch and learn.

Especially for any homosexuals, and our friends and loved ones who lived in that era, *Angels in America* is amazing beyond words. It was made into an HBO mini-series in 2003 that won and astounding eleven Emmys (directed by Mike Nichols and with a star-studded cast that included Al Pacino, Meryl Streep, Emma Thompson, Patrick Wilson and Mary-Louise Parker).

An overarching theme is the unspoken alliance between women and gays against white male brutes, with the brutes in the play—the notorious Roy Cohn and his young lawyer ally—both being right-wing closet queens. Their closets are the product of the straight white male dominated culture that they bought into, and by so doing brought misery upon others. (Such gay assimilationists become, practically speaking in life, political reactionaries because assimilation doesn't come naturally to them. They have to work hard at it.)

This points to the role of homosexuals in nature's wider order, to protect and provide for the advance of civilization by allying with independent-minded women to resist the cruelty and brutality of unbridled male supremacist behavior.

The archetypal male supremacist order is death-centered. Territorial by nature, it raises its young to fight its wars and to generate more fodder. Young males are raised to kill and die, or spiritually die to the monotony of its convention, and young females to bury them, actually and metaphorically, and make more.

Core homosexual traits—heightened sensibility, alternate perspective and constructive non-conformity—resist the dynamics of this archetype, combining with awakened women to fight it by... giving life!

Life in this sense—not as birthing to fuel the machinations of death, but a life that flares up and empowers the human spirit—is fundamental to who we are as homosexuals. We collaborate with women to break the death-cycle of male supremacy and create great, just and enlightened civilizations.

Our power to give this life—through humor, irony, education, music, dance, art, poetry and invention—is compromised only when we lose a passion for it.

Thus, it's so critical to fight against resignation and jaded cynicism and insist on this life in "Angels in America."

Chapter 57

Life, Liberation and Happiness, Part 2: Prophetic Anger

Gay activist and playwright Larry Kramer, interviewed in advance of a November 2011 reading in Washington, D.C. of his 1985 AIDS era play, *The Normal Heart*, has changed little over the years.

He remains like an Old Testament prophet, an image he first adopted in the gay movement writing the controversial *Faggots* in 1978. That novel warned presciently that sexual excesses within core urban gay subcultures of the 1970s was headed toward some form of disaster.

Only three years later, AIDS manifested. Kramer leaped to action in that summer of 1981, founding the Gay Men's Health Crisis. When he pushed his colleagues harder than they wanted, they voted him off the board of his own organization. He left town to write about it all, creating *The Normal Heart*.

Kramer exhibited the same fire in an interview with the *Metro Weekly* magazine last week that fueled his play and his leadership of the ACT UP organization he later founded that is universally credited with spurring the government to find a way to keep AIDS victims alive.

Uneasy gay leaders today, still feeling the abrasive heat of Kramer's stridency, have chosen a single word to blunt, if not dismiss, his message: "angry." Kramer is almost universally called "angry," "too angry," as if that's a bad thing.

In particular, they are irritated by Kramer's insistence that nothing has really changed in the gay community since the 1970s. He claims advances in laws and social attitudes favoring the LGBT community are due to factors outside the community, while levels of apathy and complacency remain as endemic within it as before.

First, people must face the unpleasant fact that Kramer, despite his allegedly off-putting manner, has been right, historically, when everyone else was wrong. He was right to place the blame for AIDS flatly onto the behavior patterns of gay men themselves. It made everyone uncomfortable, but was true.

(He's like the French. Reviled by Americans when they refused to join in the invasion of Iraq in 2003—many changed "French fries" to "freedom fries"—they turned out to be right for eschewing the invasion, but they're distrusted still.)

Second, as he said in the interview, Kramer insists that there is no real leadership in the LGBT movement. While there are important organizations providing for needs in our community, everything in terms of advocacy is geared toward incremental gains in equal rights laws and after-the-fact protests against incidents of harassment and prejudice. No one is out front *demanding* full enfranchisement.

Throwing bones to well-behaved advocacy groups leave LGBT persons, those who can afford to be, comfortable and unthreatened. While they mimic straight society in their outward appearances, they enable the same patterns of anarcho-hedonistic behavior that led to the excesses of the 1970s, in the first place, to persist within the community.

That's what Kramer meant about the lack of real change. The internal mental state of the gay community remains the same.

I concur. It has been my effort over the course of these *Gay Science* installments to cause some phalanx of gay people to take seriously what the natural role of gay people within the wider society means for us. The gifts homosexuals bring, taken as a whole through history, include natural propensities toward heightened sensibility, alternate perspectives and constructive non-conformity. They lead us to constantly strive for the transformation of social orders toward justice, compassion and progress.

We cannot be content with our own so-called "equality." Equality with what? Equality in a society that is as unequal as ours requires far more than equal rights laws for homosexuals alone.

Those laws will come. But in a society where the average income of the top one percent is $1.4 million a year, and for the remaining ninety-nine percent is $30,000 per year, there is a structural inequality that will take enormous courage, and the full exercise of our collective creative power, to set right. A new, menacing wave of hateful reaction is rising to not only threaten us, but women, workers and immigrants as well.

Equality? Gay people historically have stood staunchly for the enfranchisement of all persons. We demand and claim our enfranchisement only to empower us to extend that claim universally. African-Americans in our society received full equality under the law forty-seven years ago. Do they feel equal, in fact, today?

Smug, comfortably self-indulgent, apathetic cynicism are symptoms of a suffocated gay soul. The hopelessly jaded homosexual is a sad sight to see, a visible setback to the aspirations of humanity as a whole.

We will never be "equal" in the sense of some hypothetical societal equilibrium. We will never be "equal," except in an inadequate legal sense, because we are not "equal" with the prevailing structures and mores of a brutal, straight-male dominated society. We should be deeply thankful for that.

"Equality" and "liberation" are two fundamentally different things. Liberation is our biggest challenge.

Chapter 58

Life, Liberation and Happiness,
Part 3—Innocence Armed

Thanks to a swift intervention by GLAAD, a PBS commentator quickly apologized for allowing bigoted comments on his show by a leader of the Family Forum that associated the heinous Fall 2011 child rape case at Penn State with the issue of gay adoptions.

Our gay sensibility—a gay self-identity and new morality that are the focus of this series —is the polar opposite to the abuse charged in that case, which is similar to patterns of what has likely been eons of abuse in the Catholic Church.

Our identity is rooted in our heightened empathy, especially for women and children. Clearly, anyone with that attribute cannot tolerate the kind of cruel rape that is perpetrated by authoritative adults against helpless children, whose psyches are often shattered and crippled for life as a result.

Empathy and compassion have to be stripped away, if there in the first place, from the souls of any who become consumed by the ravenous and perverse passions that fuel relentless abuse.

Through history, since the time of Socrates and Plato, the special role in the natural order of creation that homosexuals play involves standing against the excessive abuses of straight male dominion in defense of women and children. We form the buffer that resists the brutality associated with unbridled rape-like behaviors of male supremacist practitioners. We set up institutions grounded in notions of virtue and compassion to not only protect, but to advance the self-empowerment of the downtrodden.

It is the moral and political enemies of our gay sensibility—our heightened empathy, alternate sensual perspective and constructive non-conformity—that have encouraged through history the kind of male chauvinist anarcho-hedonism that condones, sometimes encourages rape.

This was rampant in the right wing so-called "counterculture" that swept through the fledgling post-Stonewall gay movement in the late 1960s and 1970s, the perverse and twisted offspring of the 19th-century German philosopher Friedrich Nietzsche's "superman" and his "will to power."

Nietzsche's cosmology involved man's struggle between Apollonian and Dionysian opposites, between obedience to laws out of a sense of duty and the wanton abandonment of them in the pursuit of pure pleasure. The Nietzschean "superman" conquers social convention on behalf of his true self, his Dionysian impulse, his "will to power."

Such a system justified the worst, most brutal excesses of the 20th century, particularly the rise of fascism in Germany and its systematic genocide of innocents.

It also informed the "counterculture's" efforts to undermine morally-grounded sensibility with a savage pursuit of relentless, lawless hedonism.

Systematic rape and child abuse were endemic to the so-called "sexual revolution" of that era. It was almost as if the whole movement had been precipitated by predators to alienate the young from their families and then to snare them when they headed to the urban centers for their "summers of love" and yearnings for freedom. I fought against it as long as I could.

In late 1971, I wrote about the German-born author Thomas Mann (1875-1955), who was trapped in the Nietzschean dichotomy when he wrote *Death in Venice* in 1912. It was about the attraction of an older, burnt-out composer to the beauty of Tadzio, a young adolescent Polish boy, during a summer on the beach of Venice. The composer, Aschenbach, became obsessed with the youth's beauty and manner, and his coy acknowledgments of the older man's admiration.

But Aschenbach uttered no words to the youth, because he was emotionally trapped between his Apollonean duty and, what he dreamed, a descent into the hellish world of Dionysus. The only resolution was death.

In 1971, when *Death in Venice* was produced as a film by Luchino Visconti, I wrote an essay in the Nov. 11, 1971 *Berkeley Barb* entitled, "Death in Venice: Plague of Silence."

"The contradictions between root human feelings and a bondage to a way of speaking and a way of acting which do not represent those feelings is the contradiction of the male experience," I wrote. "This (is)...the root of gay oppression."

What Aschenbach "is not free to recognize is that his infatuation is actually subliminal recognition of the youth's looking-and-not-speaking as the call for help of a fellow human creature falling into the same male-trap (conventional male dominated society—ed.) that has driven him to this point of existential despair."

"He longs to break through to the youth with a language that doesn't exist, to 'save' him...from being 'turned under' in the male world."

The gay revolution, I wrote, "is now making possible the creation of a new language...a language of liberation, ultimately a language of self-determination, something really new... And with this new language, a genuine recreation of the world in its totality is occurring as the plague of silence is passing away."

I hailed liberation through a new language of self-determination, against a destiny defined by male dominated culture. I saw gay liberation as empowerment, wielded as a weapon against the prevailing anarcho-hedonism.

Chapter 59

Life, Liberation and Happiness, Part 4—Prometheus Unbound

Launching this series in October 2010, I explained that my title, *Gay Science*, came not only because it was apt in its own right, but also because it referred to a work of the same name by the 19th-century German philosopher Friedrich Nietzsche, *The Gay Science*, written in 1882. Nietzsche, I wrote, had his *Gay Science*, of which I am no fan, and I have mine.

The world view presented by Nietzsche proved to be wildly influential for more than a century, advocating a form of anti-conformity which placed the core of human identity on a "will to power" that is manifested in "supermen" who demolish the burdens of forced mediocrity and slavery to convention.

Sadly, his "superman" concept gave rise to notions like the Nazi's claim to an Aryan "super race," and the convenient, completely false identification of the Jewish people as its oppressors. Later in the last century, Nietzschean philosophy fed the rise of the anarcho-hedonist so-called "counterculture," breaking the bonds of convention in the same paradigmatic manner through a modified form. (Appreciating the common roots of Nazism and the counterculture helps unravel the history of the 20th century, and in particular, what happened to the gay movement in the 1970s.)

Nietzsche posited a world where man's existential condition was caught between two opposites, using archetypes taken from Greek and Roman mythology. On the one side is the archetype of Apollo, of the state, its laws and their call to duty. On the other side is Dionysus, the lure of the individual to abandon duty in his pursuit of self-serving pleasure.

In my previous installment, I wrote that in Thomas Mann's 1912 novella, *Death in Venice*, the protagonist Aschenbach's obsession with beauty is caught in this Nietzschean vice between Apollonian and Dionysian polarities, and it does him in.

As I pointed out in my 1971 *Berkeley Barb* essay, "Death in Venice, Plague of Silence," the way out of the vice for both Aschenbach and the object of his obsession, young Tadzio, was "the creation of a new language...a language of liberation."

But what exactly is that "new language" that shatters the suffocating vice of Nietzsche's system? Nietzsche proposed shattering it by a force of individual will, by angry imposition of an ultimate selfishness.

There is a "third way," alluded to in everything I have written in this series about nature's role for homosexuals in the creative order. It embodies all the attributes I have derived from the homosexual experience, outside of sexuality *per se*, such as a gay "sensibility," including a heightened empathy, an alternative sensual perspective, and a constructive non-conformity.

In the context of Greek mythological archetypes, it is identified with the mythological role of Prometheus.

Prometheus! Who would have thought of him in association with homosexual identity?

That's the nature of our gay revolution, to call into being something new, a new idea, and thereby to redefine ourselves and, thus, the world around us.

The myth of Prometheus fits. He was the Titan deity who stole fire from Zeus and gave it to mortals, a great champion of mankind that the fifth-century B.C. playwright Aeschylus, who in his *Prometheus Bound* credits him with also providing mankind the arts of civilization, including science, math, agriculture, writing and medicine. His gift of divine fire symbolizes the spirit of creativity and constructive revolution, of humanity's liberation to reach its full potential.

Zeus punished Prometheus for what he did for man by tying him to a rock and having an eagle eat away at his gut every day, only to be regenerated nightly and the cycle repeated. That, symbolically, corresponds to the emotional and social alienation such champions often experience, including resentment and repression by the defenders of the power structures of the *status quo*. Prometheus' punishment reflects the oppression of gay people, whose unique gifts deployed to the liberation of women and children from brutal male supremacy, to the betterment of all mankind, commonly bring hostility against us.

But, for the happy ending, Prometheus is ultimately freed by Hercules, the demigod who, on behalf of humanity, fully appreciates Prometheus' great gifts.

(In art, Prometheus is best known as the gilded bronze statue in the sunken plaza at the Rockefeller Center in New York, the 1934 work of Paul Manship. On the granite wall behind the breathtaking image, called the fourth most popular sculpture in the U.S., is an inscription from Aeschylus: "Prometheus, teacher of every art, brought fire that had proved to mortals a means to mighty ends.")

So, the alternative to Apollonian conventionality, including tyranny, is not Dionysian hedonism, but Promethean creative innovation and human liberation. That would be us.

The post-Stonewall gay movement's descent into Dionysian anarcho-hedonism did not reflect us. Instead, by recognizing and pursuing our core Promethean-like identity, we are empowered to unlock in others their Promethean potentials. Indeed, doing thus *is* the "pursuit of happiness."

Chapter 60

We Are Prometheans,
Not Dionysians

It has taken over a year of these weekly installments to lay a proper groundwork for the important, veritably-revolutionary notion I introduced last week: the core identity defining our homosexual tribe is, in terms of archetypes taken from Greek mythology, not Dionysian in nature, but Promethean. This has important implications for every gay person.

Dionysus was the god whose archetype represents pleasure-seeking hedonistic excess. Prometheus was the Titan who stole fire from Mt. Olympus and gave it to man, who also provided man with the "arts of civilization," science, mathematics, agriculture, writing and medicine. In fact, in some ancient mythological accounts, he is attributed with the very creation of the human race.

In the post-Stonewall gay movement, Dionysian anarcho-hedonism came to define gays and our culture. As set against the Greek archetype of the god Apollo, who represented authoritative order and structure of the dominant, conformist culture, Dionysus was touted as the anti-culture. Dionysus marked the rebellion against the *status quo* that acted out in the form of "sexual freedom" and the radically-excessive, impersonal, addictive sex that came to dominate urban gay subcultures.

We know how this came to drive the post-Stonewall movement into the ground, resulting in over 600,000 self-inflicted deaths from AIDS. While Dionysus persists to this day as the dominant paradigm defining the gay community, among other things enabled by those who profit from it, this identity did not arise from within our tribe. As I have documented, it was imposed by, and imported from, the right wing "sex, drugs and rock and roll" so-called "counterculture" that arose in the 1960s.

Gays are not naturally Dionysian, but succumb to such tendencies when pressures arise from dominating cultural influences. In the U.S., self-centered, pleasure-seeking Dionysian "rebellion" has increasingly dominated the entire cultural landscape of individual lives since the rise of "consumerism" in the 1950s. It's led to today's serious epidemic of Internet-fueled sex addiction (Chris Lee's article, "The Sex Addiction Epidemic" in the November 2011 *Newsweek*), akin to what urban gays experienced so intensely in the 1970s, with the consequential "emotional curtains" that such addictions draw down within victims, causing "intimacy disorders," crippling abilities to relate in loving ways to others.

The prevailing straight Apollonian-archetype male-chauvinist, patriarchal over-culture, and Dionysian rebellion under-culture are flip sides of the same coin. This was the view of the 19th century German philosopher Friedrich Nietzsche. He posed the double-sided notion of the Apollonian-Dionysian struggle in his book, *The Birth of Tragedy* (1872), claiming that human "existential being" is defined by this tension.

But this doesn't apply to the natural disposition of gays, whose distinguishing characteristics suggest a "third way." Nietzsche and major currents of modern culture fail to acknowledge this, although ironically it has played a massive role in the development of civilization and notions underlying the American experience.

Prometheus is the mythical figure whose archetype has been compared to that of Jesus of Nazareth in the Biblical tradition. He sacrificed himself in order to serve humankind, to provide it with fire (the spark inflaming the human spirit), science, the arts and learning. Hungarian scholar Carl Kerenyi, in his 1946 book, *Prometheus: Archetypal Image of Human Existence* (part of a series published by the Princeton University Press), claims the Prometheus-Jesus correlation breaks down because Prometheus was a god and not also "fully man." But that seems a flimsy deference to religious authority, because the myths of ancient

Greek gods were allegories co-mingled with oral histories in which gods were more properly glorified legends and heroes.

The sensibilities unique to gay people I've explored in this series include a heightened empathy, an alternative sensual perspective and a constructive non-conformity. As our early pioneer Andre Gide wrote in his Socratic dialogues on the purposefulness and natural basis for same-sex erotic attraction called *Corydon* (1920), because we gays question nature from a different viewpoint, nature gives us different answers.

The "different viewpoint and different answers" define us. They have compelled us toward a form of constructive non-conformity that has stood for eons against Apollonian male-dominated culture, which at its core is territorial and brutal in its treatment of women and children as chattel and slaves in the maintenance and expansion of territories.

By putting fire (the spirit of human empowerment), science and art into the hands of humanity, in general, and not restricting it to the province of the dominant Zeus-like males, the Promethean interrupts male-dominated culture on behalf of a more egalitarian, compassionate culture. He and she are revolutionaries interceding on behalf of the oppressed to move humanity forward through enlightenment.

The great heroes of our long history, from the psalmist, tyrant-slayer, lover of Jonathan and king, David of the Old Testament, to the fathers of progressive western thought and morals, Socrates and Plato, and key founders and defenders of the American republic, Hamilton, Lincoln, Whitman and Eleanor Roosevelt, all reflect this powerful archetype.

We are Promethean nation builders, not Dionysian hedonists.

Chapter 61

The Case for the Gay
Promethean Archetype

The novel discovery made over the course of these installments is that the archetype identifying the proper role of gay people in history smashes modern culture's straitjacketed, commonly-accepted dualism of Apollonian (law abiding) versus Dionysian (law breaking) with a "third way."

The "third way" is Promethean, the notion of those with heightened empathy and compassion for humanity, passionately driven by an alternative perspective about the prevailing order of things, and engaged in a constructive non-conformity, defying the existing order on behalf of mankind.

Those characteristics define Prometheus, the Titan god of ancient Greek mythology, who stole fire from Olympus to give it and much more to mankind, and they also define, as I have articulated in these chapters, the core characteristics of historic gay identity and personality.

It is delightfully astonishing that the rediscovery of Promethean gay identity, after thousands of years, comes now, in the wake of the Stonewall reawakening of the full potential of gay persons in the shaping of culture.

This is lawful, after all. The last time gays played the kind of open role in a society as we are claiming now was in ancient Greece. In those days, the Promethean connection to gay sensibility did not need to be explicitly tied to same-sex erotic attraction, because the latter was such an accepted factor in the social norms of the time.

Still, the Promethean was understood to suffer for his and her gifts to mankind. In the myth, Prometheus is punished by Zeus (the archetypal figure symbolizing straight-male dominant society) for his work on behalf of mankind by being tied to a rock where an eagle, the symbol of Zeus' authority, came to eat out his liver every day.

The notion of having one's liver torn out, and regrown, on a daily basis, corresponds to the tolls, emotional and otherwise, so many of us pay for being gay.

So, after 3,000 years, gay people are poised for the first time to regain the mantle of the Promethean archetype, and by so doing, shedding the erroneous and destructive Dionysian (pleasure-seeking "outlaw") archetype heaped upon us by straight male-dominated culture.

Many gays seek to shift their archetypal identity away from Dionysian, especially given the cataclysm of sexual excesses that led to AIDS, by pursuing the Apollonian archetype—that is, seeking to conform and assimilate within the cultural parameters of violent straight-male dominated society.

But that assumes the straitjacket of a social Apollonian-Dionysian dichotomy advanced by Nietzsche, Freud and gay philosophers Michel Foucault and Arthur Evans (*The God of Ecstasy: Sex-Roles and the Madness of Dionysos*, 1988).

Now, however, we can see ourselves as constructively non-conformist, as Prometheans with our own distinct, important identity in the wider social order, neither Apollonian nor Dionysian.

What are some implications?

For one, we must reconsider our history in ways I've proposed in this series. Instead of looking for explicit same-sex activity to cite evidences of us, we instead look for evidences of Promethean impulses and behavior, knowing that opportunities for same-sex activity have been overwhelmingly repressed, or expressed only in licentious forms, for eons. It means reinventing our gay history in this way, starting by eliminating entirely "post-Stonewall reductionism" from scholarship.

For another, we can define our sensible creative proclivities in terms of the Promethean archetype, on the one hand, and define the Promethean archetype on the basis of our sensible creative proclivities, on the other.

For example, the ancient Prometheus' gift to mankind of fire represents not only invention and civilization, but the animating spark that inflames human souls (in some myths, in fact, Prometheus actually created mankind). Every act that fuels and enlarges the fire animating human souls, then, is Promethean.

There is nothing that gay people are inclined to do more than fuel fires of human souls! Offering encouragement, selfless generosity, optimism through tears, gifts of beauty, song, comedy, camp and laughter as well as science, medicine, art and design, these are core characteristics of our tribe, and they're all Promethean.

The fabulous production number that honored the great Broadway vocalist Barbara Cook at the December 2011 Kennedy Center Honors, replete with an abundance of magnificent divas and dancing boys, captured the very epitome of Broadway, and was, I thought to myself, so totally Promethean!

The hallmark of Promethean nature is a dedication to excellence and achievement that everyone on that stage demonstrated. When we embrace our true Promethean identity, we don't just do good deeds, we aspire to them, and are driven to pursue them.

Not that we don't seek reciprocal romance. But nature uses same-sex erotic attraction as a social glue, binding persons of the same sex, often not reciprocally, alas, but to make a better, more humane society, overall. We are naturally inclined to provide a kind of love that is too often not returned in kind. Thus, our livers are eaten out daily.

Such may be our destiny, but remember also that Prometheus was eventually freed by a handsome young god-man Hercules.

Chapter 62

Re-Branding Ourselves as Promethean, Not Dionysian

It is fair to ask, in response to my proposition that the gay Promethean archetype represents "constructive non-conformity," who defines "constructive." Does it come from some authoritarian source defining it for us?

When asked that question last week, I replied as follows:

"I say no one decides. It comes from within the individual, as has been the whole point of my series. The individual discovers an impulse within him or her that can be called empathy which seeks the well-being of others.

"This leads to a desire to learn how that can best be achieved, which leads to an appreciation of how one's own individual gifts can contribute. From the standpoint of erotic attraction to the same sex, this places an added emphasis on the well-being of persons of the same sex, something hierarchical male dominated straight society does not permit or offer to either sex.

"Yes, it is all derived from empathy, nature's tool for our survival and the unfolding of our full enfranchisement and potential. In the old days, we could call it love, but that word is so out of fashion these days."

Prometheus, in the ancient Greek myth, was punished by Zeus (the archetype of straight male dominated culture) for stealing fire, reason and other benefits to give to mankind.

He was punished, as the Greek playwright Aeschylus wrote in his play, *Prometheus Bound* (ca. 415 B.C.) because of his "excessive love for man" and defiant refusal to "quit his man-loving disposition." In so doing, he "did not tremble at the name of Zeus."

He was defined by his "excessive love for man" in defiance of the straight male dominated cultural model. Such is the paradigm for our gay identity.

Love, or empathy, is a natural human predisposition that we gays do not limit to the dominant culture's accepted norms, but experience as a natural defiance of them. But it is not a negative, angry defiance. It is a passionate, often erotic desire to present mankind with the gift of fire in the form of a creative expression that powers and inflames human souls to become Promethean themselves.

Empathy is contained in each "unit of action" of human development, and identity derived from the succession of them. Empathy is a form of direct connectivity with others that exists on a sub-atomic level where the apparent space separating persons is revealed as an unbroken continuum.

Heightened empathy in individuals derives from an enhanced power of their sensors, so to speak, within this continuum. Persons lacking empathy are those with broken, or destroyed, sensors.

It is out of such empathy-driven "units of action" that the desire for "constructive non-conformity" comes.

We are at our roots, far from the destructive, anarchist and anarcho-hedonist forms of non-conformity, whose "units of action" are animated by anger and negativity. But dominant culture has defined us in those terms, as being within that camp, because, in fact, the Dionysian anarchist paradigm is nothing more than the flip side of conformist male-dominated society.

The pure anarchist, the likes of David Graeber, an anthropology professor at the University of London who's a key organizer of the "Occupy Wall Street" movement (author of *Possibilities: Essays on Hierarchy, Rebellion and Desire*, 2007, and much more), proposes an individualist defiance of norms that is, at its core, no different than the asocial actions of the greed-driven Wall Street scions he opposes.

The self-centered "units of action" are identical, which is why the paragons of our culture have no problem with angry anarchists. They are cut of the same cloth.

In fact, it has been a long-standing form of counterinsurgency against genuine civil rights and labor movements for constructive reform to unleash anarchist elements upon them to confuse and misdirect them.

That's what happened to the gay liberation movement in the period after Stonewall. Fueled by the civil rights movement of the 1960s, the gay movement was swiftly co-opted by an anarcho-hedonist, "sex, drugs and rock and roll" counterculture that disassembled the movement and turned it into a mandate for engaging in the kind of massively excessive impersonal sex that led to AIDS.

Gays were swept under the convenient umbrella of Dionysian anarchy, a form of "rebellion" over which the prevailing forces in straight male-dominated culture have had complete containment and control.

That became our "brand," so to speak. I propose it is time to "re-brand" ourselves as Prometheans, not Dionysians. It is both accurate and necessary.

As Promethean givers of life and love, consider the impact on the overall society in the U.S. that 600,000 of us—600,000 Prometheans—were wiped out by AIDS before beginning to fulfill their potentials and contributions.

Many of our society's current problems stem from this gaping absence. We are challenged to reclaim our proper role at every level from the bottom to the top of our society to rekindle the Promethean fire.

Chapter 63

Promethean Love and the "Gay Jesus" Question, Part 1

The unprecedented claim I make in this series—that gay identity is best associated with the ancient Greek myth of Prometheus, a "third way" distinct from the dual options of Apollonian law or Dionysian hedonism in the German philosopher Nietzsche's system—could not have been made in all of history before now, before Stonewall, when the fullest realization of the implications of an open, affirming gay identity has become possible for the first time.

History indicates there were similar circumstances in ancient Greece, when the Prometheus myth developed, and Aeschylus wrote *Prometheus Bound*. That was when gay identity, if not hegemonic in that culture, was nearly so. It has not been that way since, especially not in the context of a rising civilization steeped in profound thought, as opposed to something dying and degenerate, like Rome's latter days.

In the European Renaissance, moral reference points were attached to Judeo-Christian imagery, thus it was the Old Testament David, the psalmist, slayer of Goliath and just ruler, whose love for Jonathan was famous, that became the symbol for a noble (gay) identity.

But appreciation of Prometheus, the Titan who stole fire from Zeus and, along with knowledge and reason, gave it to man, was held back because Prometheus was too Christ-like and thereby posed a threat to the authority of church. Like Christ, Prometheus came down to offer great gifts to man, and for doing so was punished by Zeus and caused to suffer for eternity, tied to a stone as an eagle ate out his liver every day.

Therefore, characterizations of Prometheus have been skewed.

In *Prometheus, Archetypal Image of Human Existence*, (1944) Carl Kerenyi wrote Prometheus and Christ were incompatible concepts because Prometheus remained a Titan while Christ became "fully man."

The German poet Johann W. von Goethe wrote a definitive poem about Prometheus in 1772, defining him as a defiant rebel, railing against the tyranny of Zeus. That image became prevalent, some equating him with the ultimate rebel against God, Satan in John Milton's *Paradise Lost*.

Because he gave man fire and invention, Prometheus was also assailed for unleashing man's arrogance over nature, as in Mary Shelley's novel, *Frankenstein or the Modern Prometheus* (1818).

Ayn Rand's defiant rebel in *Anthem* (1938) describes the Promethean as struggling for individual freedom against hated statist repression.

In 1970, Jesuit scholar William Lynch, in *Christ and Prometheus, New Image of the Secular*, depicts Prometheus as a rebel, too, but claims his real story is an eventual reconciliation with Zeus.

All these characterizations are terribly flawed because they misrepresent what, at his core, motivated Prometheus. The great English poet Percy Bysshe Shelley in his beautiful lyric drama, *Prometheus Unbound* (1820), came closest to getting it. Prometheus, Shelley dared say (in defiance of the church), was motivated not by hate or rebellion, but by love, a deep, profound and universal love for man.

Prometheus, as Aeschylus wrote in 440 B.C., was motivated by and punished for his "excessive love for man."

He stood against the arbitrary authority of Zeus on behalf of man's weal, giving mankind fire, the fire of the human spirit, and the tools for his advance and liberation from want, ignorance and pain.

His "impulse tendency" being love, it is enacted by a resolute determination to provide that spiritual fire. Love and fire are thus one, and they trace their origins to the corners of, and to the origin of, the universe, itself. Love and fire united for the "Big Bang" that got it all started. (That's my *Big Bang Theory*. I love you, Sheldon!)

Among humans, love unfettered by the natural demands for species reproduction is purer, thus gays embody a greater potential empathy, undiluted by the reproductive urge.

Only in this context can the issue of whether Jesus was gay be addressed. I was given the pseudonym "Gay Jesus" in a book about the early post-Stonewall days, when as a seminary graduate, I wrote mostly about gay issues for the *Berkeley Barb*, the nation's pioneer alternative weekly.

Art Seeger called me that in *The Berkeley Barb, Social Control of an Underground Newsroom* (1983) because, as the thug empiricist I knew him to be, he wrongly claimed that I proclaimed Jesus was gay.

Associating Jesus with gay identity was, for me, in the sense I've described in this installment. I published that view in 1970 in *God and My Gay Soul*.

Reductionist treatments of the issue, such as *The Man Jesus Loved: Homoerotic Narratives from* the *New Testament* (2003) by Theodore W. Jennings Jr. miss the most basic point. Same sex love is not discovered by picking through scriptures for evidence of explicitly gay behavior.

It cries out from the totality of the passionate Promethean love that Christ was, in his parables, prayers and Sermon on the Mount, for unqualified love in defiance of authority, and for love suffering on a cross.

Chapter 64

Promethean Love and the "Gay Jesus" Question, Part 2

The purpose of this series has been to determine and define a constructive, natural and purposeful role for gay people in the grand scheme of things, versus our existence as simply random or a corruption. I think it's working.

On the "Gay Jesus" question, there is nothing in the message or life of Jesus that contradicts a constructive non-conformist role for gays in the order of creation.

Jesus' message and life are wholly compatible with the "third way" associated with the ancient Greek archetype of Prometheus, the one that stands between the hostile archetypes of stern law-abiding Apollo and selfish hedonist law-breaking Dionysus.

Prometheus corresponds to nature's purpose for the existence of gay people. He is the giver of fire, the animated spirit of life itself, to mankind.

Distinct from male-dominated species reproduction and associated aggressive territorial dominion, gay Promethean love inflames the spirit through art, creativity, knowledge, humor and beauty in the cause of universal human empowerment.

In like kind, the life of Christ, as (gay) Oscar Wilde expressed it in his *De Profundis* (1897), "is really an idyll," a poem, in which Christ "is the leader of all the lovers." Christ, Wilde wrote, "saw that love was the first secret of the world for which the wise men had been looking, and that it was only through love that one could approach either the heart of the leper or the feet of God."

(The same core notion is embedded in currents of Judaism, through Philo, and Islam, through Ibn Sina).

Just as Prometheus and Christ were cruelly punished by authoritarian, male dominated "powers that be" for kindling mankind's capacity for universal love, so those same powers have twisted, distorted and maligned the images and messages of Prometheus and Christ over the centuries. Some of the worst distortions have been within the church, itself, from Apollonian and Dionysian sides.

On the Apollonian side, idolatry substitutes for Christ where Protestant fundamentalism primarily worships a book and Catholicism its institutions.

The earliest church, influenced by (our) Plato, saw Christ's message and life as an "incarnation" of the causal purpose of creation (God), being "consubstantial" with it. As such, Christ was seen as the "Logos" (in Greek, "Word") of the Gospel of John, the second person of the Trinity.

But fundamentalists, who hold to the bizarre, magic notion that the Bible is inerrant, the literal word-for-word of God, in practice assign the role of the "Logos" not to the message and life of Christ, but to the Bible. They pervert a "Trinitarian" notion of "God, Christ and Holy Spirit," substituting "God, Bible and Holy Spirit," allowing whomever claims to embody the Holy Spirit (any charlatan) to wave the Bible, quote from any passage, and claim he speaks for God, including by condemning gay people to hell.

On the Dionysian side, "consubstantiality" is undermined in a different way, dismissing the message and life of Christ in favor of a reckless and self-serving interpretation often designed to negate guilt associated with excessive hedonism.

For example, the Chicago Theological Seminary's Ted Jennings joined forces with radical Queer Theory hedonists, spawned in the 1970s by the "Pied Piper of AIDS," gay philosopher Michel Foucault, to argue that Jesus had an openly gay lifestyle.

There is nothing new in this argument. It was there in the late 1960s, when I graduated from seminary and helped found the Gay Liberation movement in the San Francisco area.

I don't know, nor do I question Jennings' integrity. But back then the "Jesus was gay" pitch came from many a slimy and deceitful predator. I knew some personally, and they spurred my efforts at a more adequate expression of the relationship between Christ and gays in *God and My Gay Soul* (1970).

The liberal church failed miserably in the late 1960s period of the mainstreaming of the radical counterculture and thereafter.

The moral suasion of the progressive church peaked in the ministry of Dr. Martin Luther King, Jr. But following his assassination in 1968 and the flood of hedonistic "sex, drugs and rock and roll" counterculture influences that ensued, the liberal church fell strangely silent.

Instead of providing a moral compass, it bowed to the counterculture. At the Pacific School of Religion's Earl Lectures in 1970, a rag-tag assemblage of Children of God cultists were marched before the august assembly and given a standing ovation.

Once I became immersed in the gay movement, I learned quickly about the sexual nature of this cult's so-called ministry, a not-so-subtle form of prostitution, and of the rape and physically abusive practices of so much passing for "free love" inside the counterculture, including the urban gay subculture.

Far from inflaming human spirits, gay behavior devolved to the opposite—exploiting, degrading and raping especially the displaced young. That was why I got out of the whole scene as soon as I did.

Chapter 65

Promethean Love and the "Gay Jesus" Question, Part 3

I do not contend that gay people alone express the kind of love that the ancient Greek titan Prometheus exhibited by stealing fire from Mt. Olympus and giving to mankind, fire interpreted as love that inflames the human spirit.

But I feel strongly that within our wider humanity, gay people have always been a prevalent and indispensable component of that inflammation process, so to speak. Throughout human history, gays have manifested a higher and more potent love than the procreative impulse, their love directed toward protecting and advancing the empowerment of those otherwise subservient to brutal straight-male dominion.

Nature has empowered gay love with intense erotic and heroic impulses to achieve this work, to courageously withstand dominant culture, and to carry out its mission even if no fulfillment of modern notions of gay sexual expression occur.

We've been around since the very beginning and, if silently and secretly, in far, far greater numbers than anyone imagines or any historical record, even to the present day, can account for.

In line with the Promethean archetype (as opposed to legalistic Apollonian or hedonistic Dionysian ones, as outlined by Nietzsche and Freud), every evidence in the Biblical record is that the historical Jesus of Nazareth had at the center of his message and life a form of a Promethean "fire giving" of universal love and humble, compassionate creative work to mankind.

His parables, such as of the Good Samaritan and the Pharisee and the Publican, demonstrate this, as does the entire Sermon on the Mount that includes the profound simplicity of the Lord's Prayer.

Such passages reflect the authentic "voice" of the historical Jesus, as my revered professor of New Testament theology while in seminary, Dr. Joachim Jeremias, established so eloquently. Dr. Jeremias is credited with identifying the importance of Jesus' speaking in Aramaic, his native tongue, the word, *Abba*, translated more like a child's familiar "Daddy," rather than "Father," to refer to God.

That word reflects Jesus' call to "become like little children," to tap into native Promethean fire, a natural inclination to love non-judgmentally and feel passion for the beauty of life itself, sensibilities that otherwise tend, in the course of acclimation into rote and legalistic male-dominated society, to become blunted or extinguished.

As our own magnificent Oscar Wilde, not a religious man, wrote in *De Profundis* while in prison, "Far off, like a perfect pearl, one can see the city of God. It is so wonderful that it seems as if a child could reach it in a summer's day. And so a child could." Such is the Kingdom of God that is aglow within one, as Christ proclaimed.

Wilde described Christ as "a lover for whose love the whole world was too small," and wrote of his miracles that "such was the charm of his personality that his mere presence could bring peace to souls in anguish, and that those who touched his garments or his hands forgot their pain."

"People who had seen nothing of life's mystery, saw it clearly, and others who had been deaf to every voice but that of pleasure heard for the first time the voice of love," he wrote, such that "evil passions fled at his approach and men whose dull unimaginative lives had been but a mode of death rose as it were from the grave when he called them; or that when he taught on the hillside the multitude forgot their hunger and thirst and cares for the world, and that to his friends who listened to him as he sat at meal the coarse food seemed delicate, and the water had the taste of good wine."

"He had pity," Wilde wrote, "for the poor, for those who are shut up in prisons, for the lowly, for the wretched," but also "for the rich, for the hard hedonists, for those who waste their freedom in becoming slaves to things. ...Who knew better than he that it is vocation and not volition that determines us?"

Christ understood "the leprosy of the leper, the darkness of the blind, the fierce misery of those who live for pleasure, the strange poverty of the rich," Wilde wrote. "He awakens in us that temper of wonder to which romance always appeals." For him, "every moment should be beautiful. ...His morality is all sympathy, just what morality should be."

By describing Christ this way, Wilde did not win the favor of the church, because to him Christ was a poet, and his life poetry. Wilde criticized organized religion, writing, "Endless repetition, in and out of season, has spoiled for us the freshness, the naiveté, the simple romantic charm of the Gospels. ...All repetition is anti-spiritual."

But the true revelation of this genuinely inspired work of Wilde lay in his identification of his own gay soul with the soul of Christ, the universal soul of the life-giving Promethean.

Chapter 66

Compassionate Gay Genius
Vs. Art as Merely Habit

Oscar Wilde's inspired paean to the life and message of Christ in his prison-authored *De Profundis* (1897)—identifying with Christ's universal love himself (and thereby, as implied, from the standpoint of his identity as a gay man)—sat well with no one.

Wilde's admirers were dismayed by the deeply spiritual nature of the work, attributing it to the degradation of prison life, and church leaders had even less interest in his unconventional, radically humanitarian appreciation of Christ.

But the work was a fuller exposition of themes Wilde presented in earlier works, especially *The Picture of Dorian Gray* (1890), where he drew a sharp distinction between the hedonistic pursuit of pleasure for its own sake and true happiness. In *De Profundis*, he wrote about "the note of doom that like a purple thread runs through the texture of *Dorian Gray*."

Embracing such a perspective on life, including his own gay life, Wilde remained a happy soul until his untimely death, contrary to the popular view that, after prison, he was penniless, depressed and doomed to ignominy in Paris. His close lifelong friend, Robbie Ross, insisted it was quite otherwise, and it was Ross who saw to the publication of *De Profundis* following Wilde's death.

If flamboyant and filled with wry and ironic humor, Wilde's life and work was completely contrary in its sentiment and intent to the outrageous misrepresentation by Neil McKenna in his book, *The Secret Life of Oscar Wilde* (2005). McKenna dared to falsely assert that Wilde wrote *Dorian Gray* to seduce readers into the hedonistic excesses of the London underworld.

But then, postmodernists have a habit of shamelessly recasting historical figures in their own anarcho-hedonist image, eagerly dragging the legacies of great women and men through the mud with uncommon zeal.

So it is with British playwright Alan Bennett (who penned *The History Boys*), who performed a hatchet job on three important gay creative giants, poet W. H. Auden, composer Benjamin Britten and author Thomas Mann, in his recent work, *The Habit of Art* (2009).

To Bennett, there exists no nobility or virtue in gay sensibility. He recognizes only thinly-veiled social constraints on vulgar hedonistic, predatory lust. Whatever it may suggest about his own gay life, such a conviction reveals a jaded inability to appreciate how creative genius can focus the compassionate gay impulse on great, loving achievements, including the uplifting and edification of objects of affection, rather than their defilement.

Bennett's comedy, *The Habit of Art*, details the lives and careers of its main characters Auden and Britten (and the oft-referenced Mann). But it treats their interest in adolescents as simply open or barely repressed craving, rather than a creator's love of their potential.

Thus, to Bennett's mind, the subjects of their interest are, just beneath the surface, objects to be devoured by lust, rather than recipients of a gay love whose creative energy strives to free them from the stranglehold of male-dominated straight society, and to transform them into loving creative individuals, in turn.

In Bennett's play, the circumstances surround a fictional meeting between Auden and Britten in the early 1970s (the two had, in fact, briefly collaborated 30 years earlier). Britten seeks Auden's validation for his desire to use Mann's novella, *Death in Venice* (1912) , as the subject of an opera. *Death in Venice* had been written by Mann as an autobiographical account of being smitten by an adolescent boy while on vacation in Venice.

Britten, indeed, composed such an opera before dying in 1976. But the dialogue in Bennett's play surrounds Britten's misgivings about how his widely-rumored interest in adolescents—despite having a lifelong lover in baritone Peter Pears—might impact the receipt of an opera on the *Death in Venice* theme.

In Bennett's play, Auden is characterized as a jaded old queen who hires rent boys to show up promptly at a given hour for dispassionate servicing. Auden, indeed, had a famous gay appetite that included cavorting with Christopher Isherwood in Berlin in the 1920s, as documented by Isherwood in his memoir, *Christopher and His Kind*, written following Auden's death in 1976. (Auden used his enormous talent to pen the powerfully erotic poem, *The Platonic Blow*, that became public against his will.)

But the greatest slander of *The Habit of Art* is contained in its title, that creative geniuses consider their work matters of mere "habit."

The rent boy in *The Habit of Art* sounds off at the end, demanding of Auden, "When do we figure and get to say our say?...When do we take our bow?...We... the fodder of art? ... I want to know."

Auden sighs, "We can't help you."

In the play, that was pretty much the sum of it. In reality, as a compassionate, loving gay genius, the entire purpose of Auden's life and creative work was, actually, to answer precisely the opposite.

Chapter 67

The *Billy Elliot* Case
For Gay Identity

The hit single, *Born This Way*, by Lady Gaga—the enormously-talented Stefani Germanotta—is a huge, obvious "shout out" to gays, a big component of her following. It was her contribution to the "It Gets Better" offensive against bullying and hate that resulted from a spate of high-profile teen gay suicides in the Fall of 2010.

But her "born this way" anthem can also be extended to Gaga herself, as one who exhibited enormous talent at a young age, beginning piano at age four, writing a ballad by thirteen, and bringing her portable keyboard to sing at gay clubs and other venues in Manhattan's Lower East side as a fourteen-year-old. Despite her flamboyant style and staging, at her core she's phenomenally skilled, with a good heart, to boot.

Born This Way, for her, refers to her musical inclination and empathetic sensibility. That's also the "This Way" that defines what sets gays apart in our early years, as well, the root of our most precious and critical contributions to humanity.

Little depicts this better than the amazing *Billy Elliot* story, both as Lee Hall's Academy Award-nominated screenplay for the 2000 film version, and as the stage version, *Billy Elliot the Musical*, which debuted in 2005 in London, and has played worldwide before audiences totaling 7.5 million to date, and counting. In the musical version, which won ten Tony Awards, including Best Musical, upon arriving on Broadway, Hall's story and lyrics are augmented by Elton John's music.

The story is about a youth growing up in British mine country during the historic British Mine Workers' strike in the 1980s, who at age eleven discovers and seeks to pursue his natural affinity for ballet against pressures from his family, community and the strife-ridden times. In the musical, it opens to *The Stars Look Down* sung by a chorus of mine workers, affirming a cosmic dimension to the story.

The movie version, starring Jamie Bell, begins with young Billy using his bed as a trampoline while listening to T-Rex singing "I danced myself right out of the womb" (*Cosmic Dancer*).

The story resonates strongly with gays who as youths found themselves with dispositions contrary to the norm (myself included). In a straight-male dominated conformist world where boys like sports and girls like dolls, inclinations toward other, non-conformist interests run usually encounter resistance.

The worst is brutal suppression of such tendencies. In Peter Weir's brilliant 1989 film, *Dead Poets Society*, set at a prep school in the late 1950s that I consider a "prequel" to the modern gay liberation movement, the strongest pressure against a lad who wanted to pursue acting came from his father.

Such is often the case, but society fears taking that on, focusing instead on bullies in the school yard. The suicide in *Dead Poets Society* resulted from parental, not peer, pressure.

The beautiful film portrayed fellow students, inspired by the works of gay poet Walt Whitman, rising up against boorish, male dominated authoritarianism to cry out to the teacher fired for inspiring the tragic boy.

"O Captain, My Captain!," quoting Whitman's poetic eulogy to the death of Abraham Lincoln, they repeated as, one by one, they defied orders to desist to stand on their desks and pay homage to the man who'd kindled in them the fire of their creative spirits.

In the case of *Billy Elliot*, encouragement from a teacher steeled his resolve to challenge his family's resistance, and he eventually prevailed, buoyed by his grandma and especially a letter from his deceased, loving mother that encouraged him: "In everything you do, always be yourself."

The story underscored how gay creative sensibility can bring the best out in others, including Billy's family and community (while Billy's friend, Michael, is explicitly a "poof," Billy remained, for the sake of mass audiences, ambiguous).

The eventual support by all for pursuing his potential brought Billy, in the musical, to dance with his own future—a stunning duet when Billy at eleven dances with Billy as an adult to the music of gay composer Peter Tchaikovsky's *Swan Lake*.

When auditioning for ballet school, and asked how he felt when dancing, he invoked imagery of an inner fire: "Like a fire deep inside, something bursting me wide open impossible to hide," he sang. "And suddenly I'm flying, flying like a bird. Like electricity, electricity, sparks inside of me. And I'm free, I'm free."

(This is precisely the Promethean gift and life-giving "inner fire" I've associated with our gay sensibility. Getting, or staying, in touch with it is key to life.)

Set against the backdrop of the British miner's strike, the *Billy Elliot* story also affirms how, rightly, gay sensibility casts its lot with the underdog, the downtrodden, just as modern gay movement founder Harry Hay was first inspired by his role in the San Francisco longshoreman strike of 1934.

Chapter 68

The Emerald Pin in
Velvet Goldmine

Gay screenwriter Todd Haynes in his brilliant film, *Velvet Goldmine* (1998), has his own colorful way of depicting the "otherness" of our tribe in its opening segment. The baby Oscar Wilde, the famous gay "pop idol" of his day, arrives in a space ship and is planted on a doorstep in a basket with an emerald pin attached to his blanket.

The subject of the *Velvet Goldmine* story (granted, this is how I view it) is the emerald pin, its passing on from one bearer to the next. In 1955, fifty-five years after Wilde's death, the pin appears in the dirt to a lad whose bloodied face had just been planted there by bullies in a school yard.

That lad grows up to be Jack Fairy, who Haynes describes in the interview by Owen Moverman which appears as a preface to the published screenplay, "remains the kind of lost originator of the whole glam thing," who is "the 'real' thing."

(The movie is ostensibly about the glam rock craze of the early 1970s, when gay liberation exploded).

Jack Fairy comes home with the emerald pin and, according to the screen direction, "Clasps the emerald pin to his shirt, stops in front of the mirror and looks up. Jack's lip is still bleeding. He touches it. Gently, he rubs the blood over his lips like lipstick."

Then a female voice-over says, "Jack would discover that somewhere there were others quite like him, singled out for a great gift. And one day...the whole stinking world would be theirs."

In the film, Jack Fairy is a marginal figure, appearing only at the beginning and at the end. But with his "instinctive need to camp it up" (according to Haynes) he kicks off the glam rock fad, which is then carried to fame by the film's main character, Brian Slade (played by Jonathan Rhys Meyers), a David Bowie-type figure.

While Brian Slade tries out a same-sex relationship with the character Curt Wild (Ewan McGregor), an Iggy Pop-type, it's not real for him, just as his musical act is not Jack Fairy's "real thing." Slade soon arranges for his own disappearance.

But Slade's music and erotic same-sex on-stage antics nonetheless awaken the gay spirit of another player, the journalist character Arthur Stuart (Christian Bale). Thus, the emerald pin is passed behind, so to speak, the main action in the film from Fairy to Stuart, from the one "real thing" to another.

Beneath or behind the fad lay the passing of the emerald pin, the marker of our authentic gay tribe, we who are "singled out for a great gift."

The film accurately depicts both the meteoric rise and, through Brian Slade's figure, the rapid crash of the post-Stonewall gay liberation scene.

While Fairy and Stuart are genuine emerald pin-bearing gays, the ranks of youths pouring into the glam rock scene were swollen massively by a new social encouragement to play with gay sexuality. It became a countercultural imperative to engage in as much sex with as many partners as possible, which soon turned the gay movement from a beautiful liberating experience for gays into a compulsive drug and sex addicted, disease-crawling urban nightmare.

The nightmare of loveless, obsessive, hedonistic excess worsened through the 1970s as gifted gays who'd come to major urban centers to hitch their wagons to stars trashed their creative aspirations in favor of an unrelenting pursuit of sex.

A gay activist in the immediate post-Stonewall period, I was eyewitness to the swarm of young runaways arriving onto the streets of San Francisco. They'd arrive rosy cheeked, precocious and full of fun, even though many had been kicked out of their homes because they'd "come out" or otherwise offended their parents.

But within weeks, I'd see them undergo what became a painfully-predictable transformation. Their appearance and demeanor turned pale, sunken and ashen. I couldn't figure out why: Was it due to drugs, lack of sleep, poor nutrition, too much sex? Probably all the above, and more.

Over the course of the 1970s and through the 1980s, this process led to the literal destruction, mostly from HIV / AIDS, of hundreds of thousands of promising young lives. Countless emerald pins, promises to humanity of "great gifts," were lost.

It was too much for me. I bailed from my leadership role in the gay movement in 1973. My "coming out" having cut me off from my family completely, my radicalism alienating me from mainstream career options, I clung savagely to my emerald pin, figuratively speaking, through those tortured years. I struggled on the margins of society, hoping to make a positive difference working with strident activists who secretly held me in contempt because I was gay.

I clung to my emerald pin until something changed, and only when a test for HIV was finally provided in 1985, and I was cleared of an immediate death sentence, did I begin to reclaim my life.

Chapter 69

The Effeminist: Gay Men and Defiant Women

I have undertaken this project drawing on a number of aspects, the overarching being the integrity of my identity as a gay man throughout my adult life, including my accomplishments as a pro-civil rights post-graduate theological seminary honor graduate inspired by Dr. Martin Luther King, a journalist (something of an innate inclination ranging from my first newspaper at age 7 to my last 21 years founding, owning and editing a weekly newspaper), historian, and, in terms of the gay movement, four years of pioneering activism from before Stonewall in 1969 to 1973.

During my gay activist phase, "coming out" in the spirit of Dr. King's admonition to stand tall such that no one can hold you down following my graduation from seminary, I became a pioneer in the founding of the *Gay Sunshine* newspaper, authoring its first editorial, an official spokesman for the gay movement at an anti-Vietnam War rally, a regular contributor to the *Berkeley Barb* alternative weekly and gay-themed papers and, with Jim Rankin, the founder of *The Effeminist,* a combination newspaper and faction in the gay movement.

I was keenly aware of how the "sex, drugs and rock-and-roll" counterculture that was mainstreamed into American culture in the late 1960s swept the gay movement shortly after Stonewall with a blizzard of "sexual freedom" mandates, forcibly brushing away any efforts, including my own, at realizing the potential of the movement for transforming the identity and self-esteem of gays and being a positive force for wider social change.

The Effeminist effort involved arguing for gay men to align politically with the goals of the feminist movement to overthrow the influence of the brutal straight male paradigm dominating society in favor of a new paradigm based on genuine gender, racial and cultural equality.

I wrote about our "Effeminism" current in an essay included in a collection published by City Lights Books in 2010 entitled, *Smash the Church, Smash the State! The Early Years of Gay Liberation* (Tommi Avicolli Mecca, editor). My entry was entitled, *Berkeley and the Fight for an Effeminist, Socially Transformative Gay Identity*.

In the same volume, reflecting the transcontinental influence of the current, Steven F. Dansky wrote a piece entitled, *The Effeminist Movement*.

In my essay, I included excerpts from a piece I wrote in October 1970 in *Gay Sunshine* on the "sociocultural revolution embedded in the very notion of gay liberation." I wrote, "Sex between persons of the same sex is the cultural antithesis to the most fundamental proposition of the whole Western capitalist mentality, which is derived from one fundamental act, the 'missionary position' (male atop female) sexual intercourse."

I continued, "The 'missionary position,' penis in vagina for the explicit purpose of the creation of offspring, is the first presupposition of everything Western civilization represents. From it are derived the concepts of purposeful existence, patriarchy, capitalism, nationalism, imperialism, fascism. From it come the thought patterns of active/passive, dominant/submissive, I/you, we/they, top/bottom, greater/lesser, win/lose and on and on and on...An absolute antithesis of this presupposition is an orgasmic sexual act between persons of the same sex."

In the summer of 1971, Rankin and I "developed the notion of the social paradigm shift that we felt gay liberation represented," I wrote in my essay. "We saw the movement aligned with radical feminism as an effort to end the war and oppression by transforming male-dominated society. To this end, we argued against those who saw gay liberation as only sexual freedom, or even as strictly a fight for legal rights. Many of my articles in the *Berkeley Barb* promoted the notion that, fully actualized, gay liberation had the potential to be socially transformative."

But the "sexual freedom" faction crushed us, and the rest is history, until now.

On my "exile" from the gay movement in 1973 until I launched the corporate structure for my newspaper, the *Falls Church News-Press*, in 1987, I will say only this:

My decision to align my life with a strident, tightly-knit, pro-socialist configuration, if nothing else, saved my life. I struggled with demons by studying classics and advocating in remote places for ways to relieve droughts and feed the world.

I remember the moment when someone came into my office in July 1981 waving a newspaper to announce the news of a "gay cancer." An electric bolt shot through me and I immediately feared the worst. It turned out far worse than I could have imagined.

In 1985, I landed in the hospital with unspecific symptoms, and feared I had AIDS, a death sentence. It turned out not to be so. That, the development of a test for HIV antibodies (I tested negative) and, the moral wheels having come off my associations by their exploitation of homophobia for political gain, compelled my emphatic break, with prejudice.

I proceeded to do what any good gay boy would do. I put my talents for the public good by starting a newspaper.

Chapter 70

Gay Sensibility and the American Revolution, Part 1

This series is not as a history, or a memoir, but an argument, a case for a better perception of gay identity, based on evidence that far from a random phenomenon or corruption, the genus of same-sex erotic attraction is a vital, important and indispensable component of creation, overall, and human development, in particular.

In human society, it is a "seven percent solution," an element built in as an intercession, so to speak, into the species' merely procreative impulse grounded in male dominion over women, children and territory.

Those experiencing primarily same-sex erotic attraction are motivated by something other than the procreative-territorial impulse, and harbor not only a passion for those of their own sex, but also for the disenfranchised victims of male-dominated society, including women, children and, as no longer useful to the perpetuation of male control, the elderly and infirm.

The history of human social development is characterized by two currents in conflict.

• The first is grounded in the male-dominated nuclear family and its extension, in which the male rules the roost, dominating women in the exercise of his reproductive power, and his offspring for purposes of extending his "franchise," so to speak. Boys are raised to be warriors to fight his territorial resource-capture wars or to become corporate clones in the administration of the franchise. Girls are raised to reproduce and care for more offspring in their early years. In this paradigm, the elderly and infirm are cast off, generally, as useless.

Males clash with other males in this "family values" paradigm to compete for territory or resources, or form expedient alliances to gain more collective control and fend off challengers. These form into tribes or nations in which the king male, the most brutish and gains ascendancy stays in power to rule over an extended dominion through the perpetuation of his family line, also known as hereditary succession. While queens are allowed periodically to protect the integrity of the overall process, in general women remain docile second-class citizens, children duly subservient, and populations captured through conquest enslaved to perform rote labor.

Subject peoples are kept in line through ignorance, religious superstition and, of course, downright repression.

• The second current is, in a word, egalitarian. It rejects the dynamics of the "family values" model, asserting that women, children and subject peoples retain as much right to enfranchisement as dominant males. It intercedes to fight on behalf of the subject peoples and is an alliance of defiant women, rebellious slaves and subject peoples, inspired by concepts of democratic, just government and determined to dash the crippling influence of religious superstition through general education to advance scientific knowledge and the power of reason in each and every individual.

There is no middle ground between these two currents, even though history is filled with futile efforts at trying for it.

We know where the first current comes from: nature's mandate for self-preservation through reproduction. But where does the second current come from?

It comes from a push-back by all or part of the those repressed in the first current. But it is more than push-back. It is inspired by concepts of universal harmony, beauty and visions for a free, happy and creative life for all, and they come from persons not captured in the motive dynamics of the "family values" current.

That defines, ladies and gentlemen, us. It is where we gays come in.

While nature operates by its powerful, overriding demand for its reproduction, it also provides for the mitigating effects of that through an equally-powerful expression of erotic passion directed to the same sex, though limited to a small fraction of the total population.

From the earliest human records, egalitarian anti-tyrannical teachings have come from our words and pens, from Socrates and Plato to the psalms and benevolence of King David, through pro-republican leaders of the Italian Renaissance to Shakespeare, and the myriad of our gay sisters and brothers whose lives have gone unrecorded who have populated human history.

Our identity in the long sweep of humanity finds our natural same-sex erotic attraction and fight for egalitarian and democratic values coexisting and inseparable. I call this overall disposition our "gay sensibility."

It accounts for why we are hated by the powerful "alpha males" of the "family values" paradigm. At the heart of the matter, we are their arch enemies who have created the political and other institutions to liberate their enslaved women, children and subjects.

The American Revolution represents a truly radical, history-changing triumph of the egalitarian current against the "family values" one.

The ideas that burned in the hearts of a people inspired to fight for their independence from a brutal "family values" monarchy, on behalf of sustainable institutions of a democratic republic, came from visionaries like Thomas Paine, whose pamphlet, *Common Sense*, railed against the very idea of monarchy and hereditary succession on behalf of a universal vision of a stable egalitarian alternative.

Chapter 71

Gay Sensibility and the American Revolution, Part 2

It can't be overstated how amazingly radical the core tenant underlying the American revolution actually was in its time.

The most important assumption associated with the male-dominated nuclear family was pronounced invalid as a premise for the governance of humankind's affairs. An unprecedented rejection the notion of a monarch ruling through hereditary succession was at the very heart of what the revolution stood for.

Thomas Paine (1737-1809), in his incendiary pamphlet, *Common Sense* (1776), inflaming growing anger in the colonies against British rule at exactly the right moment, made this his most emphatic point.

Mankind's affairs, he insisted, must not be governed by a monarch whose hereditary perpetuation inevitably generates offspring of inferior moral and intellectual powers to rule after him. To Paine, it was not some particularly egregious tax or other policy that was cause for grievance, but the notion of monarchy itself.

Paine's view was far more radical than many other U.S. Founding Fathers, who saw redressing oppressive policies as the primary cause for revolt but who were otherwise content to allow the monarchy to continue.

Paine and his allies were more universally visionary, harkening to a day when all people, regardless of color, gender or current social status, would be free and equal, able to choose their governmental representatives based on their merits and to develop and realize their full talents and potentials.

Tenuous as they remain, such notions are taken for granted today, even as we strive to extend them to the one remaining class of persons in this country still denied them—us. But they were hardly commonly held values on the eve of the American revolution.

It can be credibly argued that gay sensibility—an alternate sensual perspective inherent in our portion of humanity naturally erotically inclined toward the same sex—was an indispensable component in the overthrow of the very notion of monarchy. After all, even if virtually invisible, there were proportionately as many of us around then as now.

Straight men adhering to the privileges of their dominion over women and children were naturally loathe to call for the overthrow of the very system that had given them their advantage for eons. To them, monarchy was a lawful extension of their own vaunted male supremacy.

Those not centered on species reproduction and attendant nuclear families and territorial control would more likely consider a fundamentally alternative way of ordering mankind's affairs. Thus, it was Plato (427-347 BC), author of *The Republic* (380 BC) and others of our tribe, who developed the earliest cogent concepts of how a republic, not tyranny, best serves humanity's interest.

Gays, aligned with free-minded women, children, slaves and others abused by tyranny, were best inclined to push for more than petty reforms, but for a revolution against the monarchical system itself.

There is no evidence that Thomas Paine was gay. He left his wife in England early in his life and never remarried through his exploits sparking both the American revolution and French revolutions. He assailed not only monarchy, but the institutional church that controlled people's minds with religious superstition (*The Age of Reason*, 1795). Eventually too radical for almost everyone (Thomas Jefferson remained one of his few friends), only eight people attended his funeral.

But there is evidence that Paine's revolutionary colleague Alexander Hamilton (1755-1804) was gay. The boyish Hamilton was passionately concerned for the plight of the racially and economically underprivileged, and he authored fifty-one of the *Federalist Papers*, the famous eighty-five essays published in newspapers between October 1787 and May 1788 that argued for the ratification of the U.S. Constitution.

Hamilton and his Federalist allies recognized the potential and importance in a wedding of reason rejecting superstition, anti-monarchical democratic values and organization, and the strength of a union of all the colonies.

Many letters, veritable love letters, from Hamilton to fellow radical abolitionist Col. John Laurens (1754-1782) exist. Laurens and Hamilton were both *aides de camp* under General Washington.

The beloved Laurens represented an interesting link between Hamilton and Paine. It was the same Laurens who paired up with Paine on a trip to France in 1781 to raise money for the American cause. (Laurens subsequently died in battle at age twenty-seven in August 1782).

The first modern feminist, England's Mary Wollstonecraft (1759-1797), author of *A Vindication of the Rights of Woman* (1792), was an ally of Paine.

There are other evidences linking intimate same-sex bonding and revolutionary pro-republican sentiment in that era. Alice A. Kuzniar in *Outing Goethe and His Age* (1996) cited plans by German poet Friedrich Schiller (1759-1805) to write a drama about same-sex love where "the love between/of/for men functions as a complete surrogate for the love of women, and indeed surpasses the latter in its effect."

In his opera based on Schiller's play *Don Carlos*, Italian composer Giuseppi Verdi in 1867 harkened to such a sentiment in the passionate duet between young idealistic freedom fighters Rodrigo and Don Carlos.

Chapter 72

Hamilton, Lincoln and the Varieties of Gay Loving

The novel, stunning insight into the connection between same-sex erotic affection and revolutions overthrowing tyranny is a central theme of these chapters.

The most earth-shaking case was the American Revolution, the unlikely result of a small alliance of European and colonial "Radical Enlightenment" proponents who advocated the overthrow of the very notion of the male-dominated family unit that justified monarchy and its right to "hereditary succession."

Thomas Paine articulated exactly this in a pamphlet, *Common Sense*, that helped spark the revolution.

Among Paine's close allies was Col. John Laurens, who accompanied Paine on a fundraising trip to Paris, and was a very significant love object of Alexander Hamilton.

Hamilton wrote the bulk of the *Federalist Papers* advocating ratification of the U.S. Constitution to "preserve the union" and founded, as the first U.S. Treasury Secretary, the Bank of the U.S. to finance the stability and domestic development of the U.S. His famous *Report on Manufactures* became the blueprint for the economic growth and sustainability of the world's first major democracy for over a century.

Simply pronouncing Hamilton "gay" doesn't work, however. It's complicated, given his heterosexual affairs and many children. But for same-sex attracted persons to live complicated lives was common in those times.

For example, contemporary gays may find it hard to believe that same-sex attracted people did not commonly engage in sexual intercourse back then.

But, notwithstanding different times, coping mechanisms and ranges of allowed behaviors through the ages, it is safe to say that feelings of same-sex erotic arousal, ranging in intensity and mood from the "bathwater drinking" passion to more subtle varieties, has always been the same.

Not counting cases of rape, coercion, prostitution, impersonal bathhouse or t-room varieties of sex or orgies—constituting the bulk of historical records of same-sex encounters—intimate, affectionate and reciprocal erotic dimensions to sustained same-sex relationships are basically of three types, and always have been.

• The first is when one of the parties is erotically attracted to the other, and the relationship is intimate and emotionally reciprocal even through the other party does not share the same kind of erotic attraction and may be, in fact, straight. The straight party may or may not be aware of the friend's erotic feelings. This kind of relationship makes up the vast majority of intimate same-sex relationships where erotic attraction is a factor.

• The second is when there is erotic reciprocity, far more common now than ever before, that is consummated by sexual intercourse.

• The third is when there is erotic reciprocity, but without a context, for any number of reasons, that permits sexual fulfillment or public expressions of affection.

All three types are legitimate and widespread, and are not circumscribed by age difference, masculine or feminine characteristics or any other factors. One or both of the parties in each of the cases often seeks to attain high degrees of exclusivity for the relationship.

In addition, there is a fourth form of same-sex reciprocal relationship involving persons, one or both, with same-sex erotic passions, but which are not factors in the relationship. These are non-sexual friendships that are keenly enhanced by one or both of the parties' special capacity for same-sex empathy that introduces levels of care and consideration surpassing the garden variety usually-superficial and condition-related friendships among straights.

This fourth form is also very common, resulting in some of the most sustained same-sex friendships over lifetimes. It includes what can happen when the erotic passions at play in the other three options fade. It can also apply as gay empathy, or "simpatico," finds affection for genuine spirits regardless of gender or sexual orientation, and among "posses," cliques or circles of gay friends.

Heightened empathy usually makes gays—those not jaded or ground down by their own cynicism—very good employers and collaborators in the workplace. It is a quality that has a strong aversion to cruelty and injustice.

How Hamilton best fits or rides along this spectrum of same-sex erotic and affectionate passions, such was how he was gay.

Likewise for Abraham Lincoln, who like Hamilton, married and had children. Lincoln had a same-sex relationship with Joshua Fry Speed, with whom he shared a bed for four years, 1837 to 1841 (long before becoming president).

As Hamilton wrote love letters to Laurens, Lincoln wrote them to Speed, saying "You know my desire to befriend you is everlasting." Lincoln biographer Carl Sandburg declared each had "a streak of lavender and spots as soft as May violets" for the other.

As Hamilton in his *Federalist Papers*, Lincoln took up the cause to "preserve the union" in the Civil War. As Hamilton was fiercely anti-slavery, Lincoln became the "Great Emancipator" by signing the Emancipation Proclamation.

Both men were passionate same-sex lovers, and champions to the death of sustainable justice and democracy. To the death, indeed. Both died prematurely from gun shots wounds inflicted by enemies.

Chapter 73

Why They Started Calling Us "Homosexuals"

The term, "homosexual," was first coined in 1859, in Germany.

Attentive readers have recognized that some time back, I switched from using the term, "homosexual," and went with "gay." That was intentional, using the former term at first to make it clear, in today's parlance, who I was talking about, and then to lay the basis for a sharp critique of it.

Soft-spoken but intense debates raged among radical Enlightenment figures in 1750-1850 in Europe and the young American republic about ameliorating harsh penalties for sodomy—Thomas Jefferson was considered progressive calling for an end to the death penalty at one point, and all laws against it were abolished for a time following the Napoleonic wars in France.

There was no doubt that same-sex affection and bonding played major roles in the revolutions in the U.S. and France, and continued to inflame political passions elsewhere in Europe.

The core of the revolutionary spirit against political and social tyrannies was a rejection of the paradigm of male domination over women, children, slaves and culture and the associated militaristic zeal for expanding and controlling territory and resources.

Commensurate with this revolutionary zeal, and in the context of a new surge in the value of science and knowledge, rejecting authoritarian church-related mythologies, radical Enlightenment currents orbiting around the collective *Histoire Philosophique* (1770) project led by Denis Diderot (1713-1784), A. G. Raynal (1713-1796) and others in Paris (Jonathan I. Israel, *Democratic Enlightenment*,

2011), began embracing ideas of radical feminism and the validity of same-sex erotic attraction.

That was spurred by historian Johann Joachim Winckelmann (1717-1768) and his extensive published catalogs of images of often homo-erotic ancient Greco-Roman art in his *Reflections Concerning the Imitation of the Greeks* (1755) and *History of Ancient Art* (1763).

Winkelmann's enormous influence in the Enlightenment was of keen interest to the great German poet Johann Wolfgang von Goethe (1749-1832), who was likely also gay (Alice A. Kuzniar, ed., *Outing Goethe and His Age* 1996).

Goethe's embrace of erotic same-sex relations was mirrored in the work of the poet Friedrich Schiller (1759-1805), who elevated same-sex passion to the level of Promethean revolution in *Don Carlos* (1787).

Along with the same-sex erotic passions of such founders and preservers of the American republic as Alexander Hamilton and Abraham Lincoln, this evidence points to the fact that egalitarian, pro-feminist, anti-slavery same-sex erotic passion was an indispensable cornerstone of the Enlightenment's overthrow of tyrannies and struggles for constitutional republics.

This is depicted in David Deitcher's lovely *"Dear Friends: American Photographs of Men Together, 1840-1918"* (2001) and the poetry of gay Walt Whitman (1819-1892), writing in his *Leaves of Grass* (written from 1847 to 1891) that "The attitude of great poets is to cheer up slaves and horrify despots."

In the context of all this, in 1851 a paragraph was added to the Prussian Penal Code, the infamous Paragraph 143, prescribing five years of hard labor for persons convicted of same-sex "unnatural fornication."

It was a key inflection point in the push-back by the forces of counter-revolution that began recognizing the correlation between revolution and same-sex passion.

Suddenly the counter-revolutionary mandate became to define what was "normal," that is, male-dominating patterns and institutions reinforcing the subjugation of women, families and properties, and states deriving from that construct.

Such a blueprint of male dominion required alienating, through social labels and laws, those who failed or refused to "buy in" to that paradigm. Thus, by 1869, the socio-political terms of "heterosexual" and "homosexual" were established to counter-revolutionary ends.

"Heterosexual" became the code word defining behavior encompassing all that was wrapped up in the male-dominion paradigm. "Homosexual," and all its variants described by Richard von Krafft-Ebing (1840-1902) in his "Psychopathia Sexualis" (1886), became the code for all deviations from that model paradigm.

These labels arose for different purposes than explained by conventional wisdom, such as in Charles Upchurch's *Before Wilde: Sex Between Men in Britain's Age of Reform* (2009) or Hanne Blank's *Straight, the Surprisingly Short History of Heterosexuality* (2012). Those explanations fail to grasp the new, late 19th century "science of sexology" in this socio-political context.

Resistance to the counter-revolutionary effort at socio-linguistically restricting same sex erotic passions and their revolutionary corollaries came from those advocating alternative, universalizing terms such as "urnings," or the Platonic term, "Uranians" (Oscar Wilde's preferred option), instead.

Karl Heinrich Ulrichs (1825-1895) wrote a series of five booklets using a pseudonym in 1864 entitled *Researches into the Riddle of Love Between Men* (1864), advancing these alternative labels and providing a constructive, rational theory for the existence of the impulse for erotic love between persons of the same sex.

England's Edward Carpenter (1844-1929) extended this view into the 20th century, talking of "homogenic love" to pull gay identity out of a simply sexual context, although positive theories of same-sex love were not advanced after that, until now.

Chapter 74

In Nature, We Are
Different for a Reason

The recent degeneration of American right wing political dialogue into an angry Neanderthal assault on women—highlighted by the early 2012 Virginia legislature's consideration of mandatory intrusive ultrasound procedures with abortions and Rush Limbaugh's utterly contemptible slurs that should get him fired—illustrates that the root of its similarly bigoted anti-gay venom is a violent and raw male supremacist impulse.

Some one-hundred-and-fifty years ago it was this same impulse, having grudgingly given ground to an advance of egalitarian democratic ideals with the abolition of slavery but as yet far from willing to concede any modicum of equality to women, that devised the socio-psychological categories of heterosexual and homosexual.

The 1869 demarcation for the first time sought to cordon off a strict definition of an acceptable, male chauvinist-grounded social construct from all other "deviations" from that norm. It was a counterrevolutionary reaction to the influence of free-thinking women and same-sex eroticism that was fueling ongoing anti-despotic ferment.

Our society remains trapped in a male chauvinist paradigm. Boys are raised to be soldiers, either in real wars or in a colorless corporate world, and girls are raised to serve their men and nest. All are held, through relentless cultural and religious bombardment, in a matrix of debt slavery. With student loan debt, mortgages and the costs of raising a family, an illusion of freedom is really debt slavery defining the parameters of "normative" lives. Freedom is limited to choice of beers.

By disinterest in, or rejection of, this norm, driven in part by natural same-sex erotic attraction, we are "deviants," who can be called many names. I prefer "gay" because it is not bound by the language of "sexology."

In 1962 Gerald Heard, an early member of the Mattachine Society, called us "isophyls," saying he hoped that "isophyls...can see that they are not a freak but a social psychophysical mutation without which our society can't advance." (James T. Sears, *Behind the Mask of the Mattachine*, 2006).

Heard's concept is, in fact, central to my own argument: In nature, we are different for a reason.

In his exhaustive, 750-page *Biological Exuberance: Animal Homosexuality and Natural Diversity* (1999), author Bruce Bagemihl documents the massive evidence of same-sex behavior in wildlife. From it he coins the term, "biological exuberance," contrasting the notion post-Darwinian concepts of natural selection ("survival of the fittest") evolution, random "chaos theory," or "biodiversity studies."

However, he was the first to admit that the term doesn't explain much, if anything, as animal non-reproductive behaviors remain "paradoxically, inexplicable, since they continue to elude conventional definitions of usefulness. Nothing, in the end, has really been explained."

In *Evolution's Rainbow: Diversity, Gender, and Sexuality in Nature and People* (2004, 2009), Joan Roughgarden presents similar material and argues that "the diversity of gender and sexuality make evolutionary sense." She challenges one of Darwin's three claims that in species changes through natural selection, males and females obey universal templates—the males ardent and the females coy."

She suggests a new theory called "social selection" that envisions "animals as exchanging help in return for access to reproductive opportunity," that "animals evolve (socialinclusionary) traits that qualify them for inclusion in groups that control resources for reproduction and safe places to live and raise offspring." These traits are "interpreted as a secondary sex characteristic," and are attributed to what she calls a "genial gene" that counters the commonly-held "selfish gene."

More light on the view expressed here is shed by Jonah Lehrer in *Kin and Kind: A Fight About the Genetics of Altruism* in the March 5, 2012 edition of *The New Yorker* magazine. He notes that Darwin "regarded the problem of altruism—the act of helping someone else, even if it comes at a steep personal cost—as a potentially fatal challenge to his theory of natural selection."

Lehrer asks, "Can true altruism even exist? Is generosity a sustainable trait? Or are living things inherently selfish, our kindness nothing but a mask?"

He cites the work of entomologist E. O. Wilson, who studied woodpeckers among other things, noting the concept of "group selection, an explanation that most evolutionary biologists now dismiss, because the advantages of generosity are much less tangible than the benefits of selfishness."

But Wilson thinks it is the key to understanding altruism. Citing cases of "cooperating" microbes, plants and even female lions, "clumps of cooperators thrive and replicate, while selfish groups wither and die." Wilson wrote in 2007, "Selfishness beats altruism within groups. Altruistic groups beat selfish groups."

He concludes that "what makes us human is that our history is shaped by both (altruistic and selfish) forces. We're stuck in between."

Altruism as a concept, in the context of normative, fundamentally selfish male dominated society, is akin to preponderant traits of non-normative types, and is indispensable for the success of society. That accounts for us.

Chapter 75

Not Reproductive Variant, But "Species Love"

The thought-through implications of the bio-evolutionary and genetic evidence for what can be called "altruism" as a central, indispensable component for the successful survival and evolution of species are truly astounding and revolutionary, especially as they bear upon questions of the normalcy and necessity of same-sex erotic attraction.

The works I cited in the previous chapter—Joan Roughgarden in her *Evolution's Rainbow: Diversity, Gender and Sexuality in Nature and People* (2004, 2009) and Jonah Lehrer's article about the discoveries of entomologist E. O. Wilson in the March 5, 2012 edition of *The New Yorker*—move the conversation far beyond the commonly-held interpretations of Charles Darwin's "natural selection" and "survival of the fittest" notions of evolution.

Wilson's work focused on the "advantages of generosity" versus the "benefits of selfishness" in the success of species observed in nature, and found that the former trumps the latter when it comes to the ability of groups to "thrive and replicate."

The flawed empiricism that accompanied the late 19th and early 20th century bio-evolutionary and sociological studies succumbed to reductionist categorizations of "heterosexual and homosexual" in the new "sexology" components of their work, perceived to be logical subsets of what rabidly male-chauvinist cultural prejudice superimposed as Darwinian "universal templates" for sexual behavior between males and females.

Given those normative "templates," same sex erotic behavior was categorized as a deviation from the "heterosexual" norm, and

266 Nicholas F. Benton

thereby deviant, either a corruption due to flaws or weaknesses, or a random variant with no real evolutionary consequence. No matter what, deviation from the "heterosexual" norm became viewed through the eyes of religion, morality and the state as, to a greater or lesser degree, potentially eroding the strong, male-chauvinist "template" of normalcy—male dominion of a nuclear family in which women and children were abjectly subservient. A muscular feminist movement had already become more than they could handle, much less this on top of it.

For some "homosexuals," so defined, taking on society's negative verdict was translated into a form of individuality and freedom in urban centers where they could cluster and enjoy a modicum of protection and anonymity. There, some took on a collective, special kind of nominal self-esteem. However, it was barely skin-deep, although it accounted for survival and mutual support, and eventually became a launch-pad for the modern gay liberation movement.

Still, this "verdict" itself was deeply flawed, obfuscating the stunning discovery being introduced to you in this series that the genus of same-sex erotic attraction is not a variant of the heterosexual reproductive impulse or "template" at all. Instead, it is a manifestation of "species love."

Evidence from history has shown since ancient Greece a strong connection between same-sex erotic attraction and social progress. It is a connection, as I have documented extensively in this series, inclined to overthrow arbitrary tyranny in favor of an extension of institutions of justice (including for women, orphans and slaves), legally-constituted democracy, negotiation over war, and the promotion of invention, science and universal education against tyrannically imposed superstition and fear.

This connection represents in human evolution and progress the operation of the same kind of "altruism" that Wilson observed in his natural studies.

As with Wilson's studies, that impulse is in constant tension with that of selfishness, and especially with those prevailing in "might makes right" and "survival of the fittest" struggles by the strongest, most always aggressive and deadly males among a species.

This tension exists throughout nature and throughout human history. Its pervasiveness and permanence accounts for why forces of "altruism" have always fought to establish lasting institutions as bastions of strength and perseverance against perennial onslaughts of "might makes right" tyrannical impulses.

That's why Platonists established city-states in Greece, King David solidified a just kingdom, Augustine strengthened the church against the unraveling of a brutal empire and imminent Dark Age, Italian Renaissance leaders replicated the Greek city-state model, Erasmus sought to educate Christian princes, and the enlightened leaders of the Enlightenment saw crafting democratic constitutions as important to overthrowing tyrannies as the revolutions themselves.

That's why Alexander Hamilton and Abraham Lincoln both invoked the notion of "preservation of the union"—Hamilton in the *Federalist Papers* and Lincoln in the prosecution of the Civil War—to secure institutions of justice against tyranny.

Hamilton and Lincoln both saw the horny hand of greed and tyranny lurking behind the calls for division in their times. Hamilton knew that the colonies could not endure unless united, and the War of 1812 proved him right. Lincoln knew the same fate awaited a divided union, that the Confederacy would soon revert to British colonial subjugation, the dependency of a slave-based cotton trade. The Civil War was both to emancipate the slaves and to preserve the young nation in a century when the main European powers were unbridled in their lust for empire.

Chapter 76

Philia, Agape, Eros and Tadzio's Savage Century

The genus of same-sex erotic attraction is not a corruption or variant of a procreative sexual impulse, but is a vital component of nature's effective survival and evolutionary impulse through altruism, empathy and bonding.

This important realization not only redefines same-sex attraction outside the reductionist concepts of "sexology," but extends even to more primordial forces in nature, including as evidenced by the "left-handed neutrino" phenomenon discovered by atomic physicist Maurice Goldhaber (discussed in an earlier entry here as "violating mirror symmetry" of the universe).

Not only does this point to an engine of an underlying "negative-entropic" tendency for the universe to self-develop, it is of the same order of reality as the evidence of an indispensable "altruism" in social development of species discovered by entomologist E. O. Wilson that defies empiricist interpretations of Darwin's theories.

Same-sex erotic attraction plays a critical role in this process—its progenitor being no less than the self-development of the universe itself—in human social contexts, working to progress society from non-productive male chauvinist-dominated tyranny forms to constitutional, egalitarian democratic ones.

The 18th century mathematician and philosopher Gottfried Wilhelm Leibniz (1646-1710) espoused a concept of the "monad," the notion that everything in the universe is recapitulated in its every singularity, that applies here.

Platonists in ancient Greece understood the concept of "species love," defining it in terms of the broad spectrum of "loves" that range from *philia* (brotherly) to *agape* (spiritual) to *eros* (erotic). Although almost no one operating within the matrix defined by a male-dominant species reproduction mode understands this, none of these Platonic-defined "loves" are associated with procreation, either the act of intercourse or the subsequent "motherly love" of child rearing, but instead that they are singled out to define a range for the kind of love that bonds and develops cultures.

Same-sex erotic (*"eros"*) attraction is a natural variant among these, no matter how much it may appear to emulate the procreative impulse. For any individual "called" to this kind of loving, that loving can be expressed in any one of the three ways, and can also express such loving as *"agape"* or *"philia"* without an *"eros"* component at all. But they are all related.

In 1912, one-hundred years ago, the sinking of the Titanic on April 15 was perhaps an omen for a century sparked by the June 1914 launch of the Great War, the first of two World Wars, the rise of totalitarian regimes, mass genocides, the AIDS epidemic, a Great Depression and perhaps a second.

Another omen was German author Thomas Mann's 1912 novella, *Death in Venice*, about a doomed relationship between a burned out, aging composer and a young teenage lad, a relationship in which no words were exchanged.

Smitten by the Polish lad staying in the same vacation hotel in Venice, the composer, Aschenbach, was unable to either hide his interest or speak to the boy. The boy, Tadzio, responded to the interest, but also remained mute. The story ends with the composer's death from cholera on the beach, watching the slightly effeminate object of his attraction wade into the water and pause, left arm extended in a contraposto pose.

Mann's story was based on actual events on a vacation he took to Venice in the summer of 1911, and the boy was discovered decades later to be a real person, Wladyslaw Moes (1900-1986).

American author Gilbert Adair reconstructed Moes' life history and wrote a short biography, *The Real Tadzio: Thomas Mann's Death in Venice and the Boy Who Inspired It* (2001). "Tadzio," living in Poland, was pushed and pulled his whole life between the two great wars and fascist German and communist Soviet occupations, serving in the Polish military and as a prisoner of war.

He grew into and remained "something of a dandy to the end of his life, no mean achievement in Communist Poland," Adair wrote. "Capable of charming the birds off trees," he "prided himself on his grace as a dancer." He married and had children, but otherwise had an uninspired life buffeted by the great social and military convulsions of his age.

There was more than physical beauty that attracted Aschenbach to young Tadzio in the novella. There was something in Tadzio's demeanor, his charm, his way of carrying himself. Also, as Tadzio gazed back at Aschenbach, almost as if he foresaw his future trapped into conformity with a straight male-dominated century of war and fascism, was his silent plea, "Aren't you going to save me?" Aschenbach couldn't.

"Gay Liberation" is supposed to save the Tadzios of our time, to give them the space and the language to fulfill their full potentials to the benefit of all mankind.

Still, two important loves, one of a man for Franklin D. Roosevelt, the other of a woman for Eleanor Roosevelt, played vital roles in the past century's survival of America.

Chapter 77

Two Same-Sex Bonds
That Saved America

It is a critical realization that same-sex erotic attraction is a variant within the role that nature has assigned for its organic survival and evolutionary self-sustenance to the altruistic impulse among persons. A recent scientific discovery is revolutionary, that species survival and evolution are not driven only by self-preservation, reproduction and accidental mutation, but also by an altruistic impulse.

Until this discovery, modern Darwinian evolutionary science has dismissed notions of altruism, selfless behavior or love as, effectively, chimeras or extensions of behaviors defined within narrow confinements of "survival of the fittest" and "natural selection" dogma.

Within that, the only explanation for same-sex erotic attraction has been as a corruption or deviation from the reproductive impulse. All modern "sexology" theory over the last hundred-and-fifty years has adopted this core assumption.

As such, this flawed epistemology of "sexology" theory was associated with a current of thought developed in the 19th century as the rise of modern industrialism and imperialism compelled ruling elites to design sociological means to maintain their advantage against much larger bodies of workers and subject peoples and prevent, for example, something like the American Revolution from ever happening again.

They sought to isolate persons from each other by promoting theories of anarchy and nihilism, reshaping self-perceptions and individual behaviors away from tendencies to bond together and act on the basis of common interests in social development. A seminal influence for this was German philosopher Max Stirner (1806-1856), a founder of nihilism, existentialism, post-modernism, anarchism and post-structuralists like Michel Foucault.

Stirner's *The Ego and His Own: The Case of the Individual Against Authority* (1844) shaped similar theories espoused later by the nihilist philosopher Friedrich Nietzsche (1844-1900) and the Italian fascist dictator Benito Mussolini (1883-1945), demonstrating the cohesion between radical anarchy and fascist dictatorships that represses popular will through totalitarian force.

The psychologist Sigmund Freud (1856-1939), the most influential figure in the "sexology" movement, developed his theories under the umbrella of the same flawed constructs as Stirner and Nietzsche. In his thought, they took the form of a tension between the Id (in terms taken by Nietzsche from Greek mythology, Dionysian) and the Ego (Apollonian), or between raw hedonistic selfish impulse and socially-acceptable identity.

But as I established earlier, in terms of Greek mythology, there is a third current, the Promethean, which corresponds to the critical bonding, altruistic influences associated with same-sex attraction that Stirner, Nietzsche, Freud, Mussolini and Foucault denied exists.

Still, our current in fact does exist, and always has, as a substantial reality. In the last century, two powerful manifestations— at least one of a non-erotic variety—can be credited with no less than saving America, defeating tyrannies on two global war fronts and preventing the impact of two World Wars and a Depression from resulting in tyranny at home.

Franklin D. Roosevelt (1882-1945) and Eleanor Roosevelt (1884-1962), in tandem the most powerful, unitary influence for good during the entire 20th century, each were beneficiaries of highly influential same-sex bonding experiences.

In H. W. Brands' *Traitor to His Class: the Privileged Life and Radical Presidency of Franklin Delano Roosevelt* (2008), writings by Secretary of the Navy Josephus Daniels (1862-1948) state that when

Daniels first met Roosevelt in 1912 "I thought he was as handsome a figure of an attractive young man as I had ever seen...Franklin and I became friends—a case of love at first sight—for when men are attracted to each other there is born a feeling that Mexicans call 'simpatica,' a word that has no counterpart in English."

Daniels adopted Roosevelt as his Assistant Secretary of the Navy and became his first political sponsor. There is no doubt that Daniels' self-declared intense emotional attachment with FDR played an indispensable role in the launch of FDR's career toward the presidency. Daniels stuck with Roosevelt all the way, while also continuing a successful newspaper publishing career in North Carolina and growing a large family.

In Eleanor Roosevelt's case, the critical same-sex relationship was with Lorena Hickok (1893-1968) during FDR's 1932 campaign for president and in the touchy years of his first term, including a period when Wall Street sought a fascist military coup against them (Sally Denton, *The Plots Against the President: FDR, a Nation in Crisis and the Rise of the American Right*, 2012).

The intense bond between Eleanor and Lorena, a known lesbian, propelled Eleanor to overcome her shyness and step forward as a revolutionary First Lady, as documented by Maurine H. Beasley in her *Eleanor Roosevelt: Transformative First Lady* (2010). Their relationship faded by 1935, but in 1954, Eleanor helped a destitute Lorena financially by co-authoring a book with her, *Ladies of Courage* (1954).

Living on after FDR's death in 1945, Eleanor spearheaded adoption at the United Nations in 1948 of its *Universal Declaration of Human Rights*, perhaps the most important political document in history.

Despite abstentions from the Soviet Bloc countries at the time, it passed all the nations of the world unanimously.

Chapter 78

Conceived In the Shadow
Of Tennessee Williams, Part 1

The book by openly-gay Christopher Bram, *Eminent Outlaws: The Gay Writers Who Changed America* (2012), his eleventh one, makes an enormous contribution to an appreciation of gay writers in the post-World War II period.

Eminent Outlaws is full of history, including love stories and anecdotes about a gay literary scene that was seminal in the emergence of gay liberation, beginning before the war, actually, and chronicling the slow, painful emergence and social acceptance of openly gay topics and story lines in their works.

Gore Vidal, Truman Capote, James Baldwin, Tennessee Williams, Allen Ginsberg, Christopher Isherwood, Larry Kramer, Edmund White, Andrew Holleran, Armistead Maupin and Tony Kushner are among those featured.

Admittedly beyond its scope of work, it differs from what I am addressing in this series. I seek to provide a more three-dimensional context for these and other figures in a profoundly uneven gay movement buffeted by wider social forces.

The touchstone for my work is an article by James Grauerholz in the May 16, 1977 *Village Voice* that involved a conversation between Tennessee Williams and William Burroughs.

In the summer of 2010, I was at my condominium pool reading *Conversations With Tennessee Williams* (1986), an anthology edited by Albert J. Devlin, when I stumbled onto it, and a light went off, more like a nuclear explosion, in my head. My own understanding as an early gay pioneer and of the subsequent unfolding of the movement, including the AIDS crisis, suddenly broke forth with angelic music.

I quoted the exchange in Number 7 of this series. In it, Williams is stunned to discover that Burroughs repudiates the notion that there is any such thing as "right" or "wrong" in human behavior.

The depths of Burroughs' nihilism and amorality genuinely startled Williams, and I recalled afresh the powerful influence of Burrough's worldview in the early gay liberation movement.

There were three trends that fed into the gay liberation movement in the post-Stonewall era.

The first was the colorful, courageous and enormously talented work of Williams and Isherwood (my favorites) and early founders of the gay movement, including my friends, the late Frank Kameny and Lilli Vincenz and others aligned more broadly with the causes of civil rights and justice.

The second was entirely different, a 1960's countercultural "paradigm shift" fueled by radical anarcho-hedonist theory and practice, expounding "sex, drugs and rock-and-roll." This "revolution" repudiated the progressive values-based work of earlier periods in favor of postmodern and post-structural nihilism and radical hedonism. Ginsberg, Burroughs and others fell into this current, which had an influential and ultimate cynic as a leader, Michel Foucault.

The third current was made up of those of us who saw "gay liberation" as a world-historical opportunity to assert a new offensive against the male-dominated cultural paradigm, including its preoccupation with the subjugation of women, children, workers and other exploited peoples in its lust for expanding territories through tyranny and war.

We aligned with radical feminists and for want of a better term, called ourselves "effeminists." We drew on the tradition of the earlier gay movement, seeing ourselves as its new cutting edge.

But the anarcho-hedonists swept like a tsunami over the gay movement. Free and frequent impersonal sex was not only sanctioned in urban centers, it became a veritable imperative.

Anyone preferring romance and respect for persons was assailed as "sex negative."

In this context, I observe these things about *Eminent Outlaws:*

First, Winston Leyland did not "found" *Gay Sunshine,* the nation's first gay liberation-based alternative newspaper, in 1970. It was founded by a collective in which Leyland was a member, as was I. I wrote the editorial for that newspaper's first edition, quoted in part in Don Teal's *The Gay Militants* (1971). If the collective had any leader, it was Konstantin Berlandt (1946-1994). After the first few editions, Leyland effectively hijacked *Gay Sunshine* from the collective against its will, something not hard to do in those disheveled days.

Second, Bram's contention that "gay liberation did not create gay promiscuity" does not take into account the anarcho-hedonist paradigm shift, which changed the very nature of promiscuity.

Third, writing about the first news of AIDS, Bram states "In terms of what was known about the illness at the time, (Larry) Kramer was overreacting. Yet he turned out to be right." That odd contradiction is the popular dig at Kramer. How can someone be "overreacting" when he is "right?"

Fourth, Bram says of Tennessee Williams' death that he had "died as a writer" years earlier. This conventional wisdom is now being challenged by Williams scholars who are finding tremendous creativity in Williams' later works, including one he was working on at his death, *In Masks Outrageous and Austere.*

It was not Williams who changed, or declined, but the wider culture, no longer interested in his compassionate truth-telling. It became far too jaded to appreciate him.

Chapter 79

Conceived in the Shadow
Of Tennessee Williams, Part 2

The powerful influence on American culture by prominent post-World War II gay authors, as documented in Christopher Bram's new book, *Eminent Outlaws: The Gay Writers Who Changed America* (2012), raises the question of just how they contributed to the explosion of the modern gay liberation movement, when countless people burst out of their closets more forcefully and openly than any of those authors had, at least up to that point in the late 1960s.

After all, for most of them—the likes of Tennessee Williams, Christopher Isherwood, Truman Capote, Gore Vidal, James Baldwin and others—references to gay issues were very muted, at best, in their popular works.

How, then, did they impact someone like myself, born near the end of World War II, growing up in the 1950s in a remote community, never knowingly encountering another gay person, entering graduate seminary in Berkeley, Calif., in the late 1960s and suddenly bursting out of my closet to co-found the Berkeley Gay Liberation Front?

Surely, I was influenced by Tennessee Williams' famous plays. But I learned only later how much closer to their influence I actually was, and how one movie by two members of their inner circle actually changed my life.

My title, "Conceived in the Shadow of Tennessee Williams," is more than metaphor. In Williams' extensive diaries, his fascinating 828-page *Notebooks* published in 2006, he wrote lavishly about his gay experiences. Cavorting among young soldiers during nightly blackouts (precautionary measures throughout the West Coast against the prospect of a Japanese attack) on the palisades above Santa Monica brought him very close, geographically, to me.

On Sept. 12, 1943, he wrote, "The unprecedented sex activity continues. The night that I don't desecrate the little god all over again is exceptional." There were expressions of remorse: sex, he wrote, "is about like a dog pissing on a tree," adding on Sept. 26, "I have accepted sex as a way of life and found it empty, empty knuckles on a hollow drum." But on Nov. 15 he reported "a record for me of five times perfectly reciprocal pleasure."

While he was doing all this on the palisades, often bringing men to his modest dwelling, I was busy being conceived in the Santa Monica below. Thus the title for this chapter. Could a rag from one of Tennessee's trysts have floated down off the palisades and magically impregnated my mom such that Williams is my real father? Haha!

This happened at almost the same time that Williams and Isherwood met for the first time, the beginning of a very long friendship.

Isherwood's diaries also revealed a surprisingly immediate brush with my world. He and his young partner Don Bachardy (now, at age 78, my friend) rented a house from my Aunt Ginny in Santa Monica, and he wrote about her.

Writing on May 28, 1955, he called her "Ms. Hoerner," she being my dad's older sister and a frequent visitor to our home in Santa Barbara, a two-hour drive away, where I'd just turned 11.

"Yesterday morning, I talked to Mrs. Hoerner," Isherwood wrote. "She tells me she is looking for a Buddha. She wants to put it in a shrine and light incense sticks in front of it. The Buddha she has now is unsatisfactory, but she burns the incense, just the same; and if she's out, her son Griff does it—although he squirms if ever she talks about religion."

"We got to know her well," Don Bachardy told me. "I can still remember the sound of her voice." He noted that Isherwood "took an interest in her son," my first cousin Griff.

In his diary, Isherwood wrote, "Griff is nearly seventeen, and the other day she found he'd started flying lessons without her permission. Eleven dollars a lesson—he makes the money by washing cars."

Griff carried his passion for flying throughout his life, giving flight lessons for a living before dying in an accident doing that in 2010.

Aunt Ginny commented years later about the wild parties Isherwood and Bachardy threw. The diaries chronicled the many luminaries who attended.

(Ginny was extraordinary, clairvoyant, and my principal correspondent after I became a gay activist in San Francisco in 1970 and was banished, consequently, from my family by my father, her brother.)

In the early 1960s, I was the same age and traversing the same turf as Isherwood's character, Kenny, in his novel, *A Single Man* (1964), played by Nicholas Hoult in the movie version (2009). A college student in Santa Barbara, I played baseball on the same Los Angeles campus and at the same time identified in that story.

Those days, I'd vowed to take my gay secret to the grave. But then I saw a life-changing film, written by William Inge and directed by Elia Kazan, both tight in the Isherwood-Williams circles, *Splendor in the Grass* (1961).

Chapter 80

Tennessee Williams' Shadow,
Part 3: *Splendor in the Grass*

The American playwright William Inge (1913-1973) was so tight with Tennessee Williams that scholars speculate they might have been lovers at some point. He was in the intimate gay literary circles of Williams, Christopher Isherwood, Gore Vidal and others, and among the most successful, winning a Pulitzer Prize for his 1953 play, *Picnic*, and an Academy Award for his 1961 film, *Splendor in the Grass*.

But in his *Eminent Outlaws: Gay Writers Who Changed America* (2012), author Christopher Bram mostly overlooks Inge and generally he has not enjoyed the same stature as his gay literary colleagues of that era, possibly because he insisted on remaining more closeted than they were.

The important interconnections between Inge, Williams and the others (*Williams and His Contemporaries: William Inge*, the transcript of a panel moderated by Annette Saddik at the 2006 Tennessee Williams Scholars' Conference) helps define the impact all these great literary figures had collectively on post-World War II American culture.

It was a life-changing, transformative impact with a bang in the case of what Inge's film, *Splendor in the Grass*, did to me when I saw it in my late teens. It was a powerful punch to my psychic gut like none I've experienced before or since. It contributed to big decisions I made and the world view I carried with me my entire adult life, informing of my contributions to the gay liberation movement among other things.

Tennessee Williams brought a similar theme to his earliest and most important explicit contribution to the early gay liberation dialogue (in his play, *Small Craft Warnings*, 1972), confirming that Inge's work was an offspring of discourses within those tight gay literary circles of the 1950s.

I saw *Splendor in the Grass*—written by Inge, directed by Elia Kazan and starring Natalie Wood and Warren Beatty (in his first film)—when I was roughly the same age, maybe a couple years older, as the main characters, as I was looking the rest of my life in the face with some big decisions to make.

The characters of Wood (Wilma Dean) and Beatty (Bud) were passionate high school sweethearts in a small town in Inge's home state of Kansas about the same age as Inge was in 1928-29 when the story took place, subsuming the great stock market crash of October 1929.

The long and short of the story is contained in its title, a line from a lengthy poem by English poet William Wordsworth (1770-1850) entitled *Ode: Imitations of Immortality from Recollections of Early Childhood* (1807):

"What through the radiance which was once so bright/Be now forever taken from my sight,/Though nothing can bring back the hour/Of splendor in the grass, of glory in the flower/We will grieve not, rather find/Strength in what remains behind;/In the primal sympathy/Which having been must ever be..."

In the movie, the power and passion of Wilma Dean's and Bud's young love is beaten down by convention and parental expectations, ripping them apart, driving Wilma Dean to a mental institution and Bud, pressured by his father, to Yale.

The market crash wiping out his father's fortune, Bud returns to Kansas married to a pizza parlor waitress he met in college to work a small farm. Wilma Dean leaves the mental institution after two and a half years and, coming home, decides to look in on Bud. She hides her surprise at discovering Bud's wife and young child.

"Are you happy, Bud?," Wilma Dean asks in monotone. "I guess so. I don't ask myself that question very much," Bud replies.

"I don't think too much about happiness, either," Wilma Dean then says, and Bud responds, "You have to take what comes." That was it.

I was deeply troubled by that film, and can remember coming home to take a very long look at myself in the living room mirror. I had no words to verbalize my feeling, but I have come to realize that my resolve from that night was to not allow the deadening of the human spirit I had just witnessed to happen to me.

Little did I know it was the gay literary circle of Williams, Isherwood, Inge and others that had just drilled down into my gay soul.

If a life of monotony and passionless mediocrity was to be the fate of most people as they grew out of their childhood idealism, it would be even more deadly to a closeted gay boy, pressured to conform in those ways to cover up and deny himself to himself and everybody else.

As my life had begun to trend toward that kind of mediocrity, it soon began to take a dramatically different course. Settled as I was in my home town, with a solid career ahead and assurances by my powerful boss that I would not be drafted for Vietnam, instead I decided to leave for a graduate theological seminary in Berkeley, Calif.

Chapter 81

Tennessee Williams and Christopher Isherwood, Part 1

William Inge's screenplay combined with Elia Kazan's direction and a young Natalie Wood's acting to produce a classic cultural intervention into the numbing routine of life in America in the 1950s and early 1960s, the film *Splendor in the Grass* (1961). It set millions of teenagers, including myself, pondering the correlation between growing into conformity with the adult values of a dull yet savage society and the quashing of the idealistic passions of youth.

All three major players in this project, the gay but closeted Inge, Kazan and Wood, were tight in the circles of the eminent gay writers of that era, generally orbiting around the life-long friendship of Tennessee Williams and Christopher Isherwood. Kazan directed Williams' classic *A Streetcar Named Desire* and other triumphs, and Wood was among the many fine performers such as Elizabeth Taylor who often preferred the company of such gay geniuses.

In fact, Wood's closest personal aide, the gay Mart Crowley, went on to write the first major Broadway (1968) and film (1970) play devoted entirely to the urban gay lifestyle of that period, *Boys in the Band*. It's a little-known fact that Crowley appeared in drag in a brief cameo role in the final scene of *Splendor in the Grass* as one of the girls driving the truck carrying the Wood character away from the farm of her once-passionate lover.

The friendship between Williams (1911-1983) and Isherwood (1904-1986) is a fascinating study in its own right, if only because both gay men as prolific writers devoted great energy to keeping diaries, published only many years after their deaths. Both diaries recorded, from their differing standpoints, the time that the two first met in Santa Monica, California, in 1943.

Williams' diary was published as *Notebooks: Tennessee Williams* in 2006. In there, on May 23, 1943, Williams wrote, "I met Christopher Isherwood. Liked him, he was so much as I had thought he would be. But he has ignored me since the one meeting, in spite of a letter I sent him. It was foolishly done, the letter."

Isherwood's diary has been published as two volumes so far, going to the end of the 1960s. In the first volume, *Diaries, Volume One, 1939-1960*, published in 1996, he wrote of meeting Williams for the first time. Dated May 13, 1943, the entry read, "Yesterday I had lunch with Tennessee Williams, the writer. He's a strange boy, small, plump and muscular, with a slight cast in one eye; full of amused malice. He has a job with Metro. He wanted to buy an autoglide to ride to work on. I tried to dissuade him, but he insisted. We went to a dealer's, and he selected a very junky old machine which is obviously going to give trouble."

Much later, in 1972 Williams first published his *Memoirs*, his major, general public-directed "coming out" life testament. It appeared in the midst of the early, most explosive period of the modern gay liberation movement, and in it he wrote again of meeting Isherwood in 1943:

"We became great friends. We used to go out on the pier at Santa Monica for fish dinners. This was during World War II when almost everything was blacked out. There was an almost sentimental attachment between us but it didn't come to romance: instead, it turned into a great friendship, one of the continuing friendships of my life, and one of the most important ones."

(Nearby at the same time, as I reported earlier, I was being conceived by my parents.)

In his *Memoirs*, Williams wrote from his heart, more concerned for that than any memory lapses or deviations from his own earlier diaries. But he identified four features of his personality as a youth that I can directly relate to from my own life, and perhaps holds for many other gays, as well.

First, he suffered a "phobia about the process of thought." He wrote, "Abruptly, it occurred to me that the process of thought was a terrifyingly complex mystery of human life." He called it, "The terrifying nature of cerebration," which was lifted from him as if by a miracle as a teen and never returned.

Secondly, he wrote, "My adolescent problems took their most violent form in a shyness of a pathological degree....I developed the habit of blushing whenever anyone looked me in the eyes....I don't think I had effeminate mannerisms but somewhere deep in my nerves there was an imprisoned young girl."

Thirdly, he had an "early childhood disposition to his art."

Fourthly, he held a belief in God, though not of religion or ceremony. He wrote. "I have never doubted the existence of God nor have I ever neglected to kneel in prayer when a situation in which I found myself (and there have been many) seemed critical enough in my opinion to merit the Lord's attention and, I trust, intervention."

Chapter 82

Tennessee Williams and Christopher Isherwood, Part 2

In a century defined by the most savage of brutal wars and genocides, among those things that legendary gay writers Tennessee Williams and Christopher Isherwood held in common were their pacifist political sensibilities and remarkable attention to their creative work, despite innumerable distractions, to express them.

Williams wrote in his *Memoirs* that he voted only once for president, for the perennial socialist/pacifist candidate Norman Thomas in 1932. But through his works he contributed to the rise of the civil rights, anti-war and gay liberation movements of the 1960s, as well as the elections of John F. Kennedy and Lyndon Johnson, and he was fully aware of his role in these effects.

(If 600,000 gays had not died of AIDS after that, how might American electoral history be different?).

The British-born Isherwood (1904-1986) was an eyewitness to Hitler's thuggish rise to power in Berlin that forced him to leave. But he chronicled it all in *Goodbye to Berlin* (1939), which morphed into the play and film, *I Am a Camera* (1951, 1955) and eventually into the musical and film, *Cabaret* (1966, 1971).

In 1976, he did a rewrite of *Goodbye to Berlin* entitled, *Christopher and His Kind*. It was his "coming out" work, revealing the central role of his pursuit of gay encounters while in Germany, invisible in the earlier work. A dramatized version of *Christopher and His Kind* was released on DVD in 2010.

Isherwood suffered as his first true love, Heinz Neddermeyer, fled, was arrested and forced to join Hitler's army. Isherwood came to New York in 1939, and when he applied for U.S. citizenship in 1945, he filled out his application saying he would "defend his country" in non-combatant roles only.

He became a devout follower of the pacifist Vedanta faith, and his diaries show that from the time he met the eighteen-year-old who was to become his life partner, Don Bachardy, in 1953 until his death in 1986, Isherwood's spirituality played a big role in his ability to hold his relationship together through stormy times and despite the great difference in their ages, while helping Bachardy develop his own considerable artistic talent. Bachardy, now 78 and a friend, was the subject of countless entries in Isherwood's diaries, dedicated to him.

Williams' pacifism was expressed against the brutality of society overall, focusing on the microcosmic male chauvinist violence of which great wars are a predicate.

He characterized prevailing culture as "a society whose elite was so grossly affluent, I mean a society that numbered its billions of dollars as he counted our nickels...a nation ruled by that numerically tiny gang which has fitted itself on the top of the totem pole and is scared of getting dizzy if it glances down...our Babylonian plutocracy."

The impact of the structural brutality of culture on the weak and sensitive forms the core of most of Williams' works, including as driven by the horror of experiencing his own sister subjected to the widespread practice in those days, a lobotomy.

Williams worked tirelessly, formulating new experiments to assail the evils and injustices of such brutalities until the day he died accidentally in a New York hotel room in February 1983.

The play that he completed while writing his *Memoirs* in 1972, entitled *Small Craft Warnings*, was dedicated to "a good many other young writers and/or artists" like him, all "disregarding the small craft warnings" while sailing into the teeth of a brutal and indifferent society.

He cited the case of "such a tremendous yet fragile artist as Hart Crane," one "small craft" that crashed. The only possession

Williams carried with him when he plucked chickens in Southern California and went to Mexico in the Depression-ridden late 1930s was a book of poems by the closeted gay American poet Crane (1899-1932).

The subject of a new movie *The Broken Tower*, Crane, brilliant and an optimist in his poetry, committed suicide after being rebuffed and beaten by a sailor during a cruise in the Gulf of Mexico.

Williams was greatly influenced by Crane in his own poetry, and, as he declared in remarks he'd prepared for delivery the morning after he tragically died, insofar as he thought of all his work as, most fundamentally, poetry.

As Plato wrote, "Poetry is nearer to vital truth than history."

Don Bachardy recounted to me about Williams' great triumph, the Pulitzer Prize-winning *"Cat on a Hot Tin Roof* (1955). It opened in Philadelphia prior to moving to Broadway.

Williams invited Isherwood and Bachardy to the opening. On the eve of the first performance, he invited them to his hotel suite, and did a one-man reading of the entire play, changing his voice for each of the different characters.

Bachardy said that he's seen the play performed a half dozen times since, including the 1958 film version, but he's never seen it done as well as Williams did it that night.

Chapter 83

Tennessee Williams and Christopher Isherwood, Part 3

It is one of the incomparable blessings of the modern gay liberation movement, leading up to and following the Stonewall riots moment in 1969, that it both enabled and compelled two of the greatest literary geniuses of our or any age, the close friends Tennessee Williams and Christopher Isherwood, to reveal to the whole world the fundamental role of their homosexuality in the inspiration and content of their work.

Both had become great heroes by virtue of their efforts—Isherwood with his compelling chronicles of the rise of Hitler and fascism in Germany in the early 1930s and Williams with his incomparably sensitive and bravely frank windows into the brutality of our culture—without explicit references to their same-sex erotic attractions.

Going into the 1970s, no one not privy to their intimate circles knew. But with Williams' *Memoirs* (1972) and Isherwood's *Christopher and His Kind* (1975), this changed. By infusing their work with the rich details of their gay lives through these and other works, these two literary giants made a compelling case, strongly implied, that they didn't achieve their provocative triumphs in spite of being gay, but due to it.

While some romanticize being gay prior to Stonewall, apart from very privileged and rarefied circumstances, it was not a pretty existence at all. Two of the only films made on the subject, the German-made *Different From the Others* (1920), remade in 1927 as *Laws of Love,* and the British-made *Victim* (1960), both centered on the themes of homophobic violence, legal repression (Germany's infamous Paragraph 175), blackmail, self-loathing and suicide.

Even as late as 1968, the Broadway play and film, *Boys in the Band*, while having its tender moments, underscored the self-hatred internalized by so many gays up to that point, even those able to live out their lives in large urban centers where they could be at least partially open and enjoy the company of others like themselves.

Tennessee Williams was limited in his plays to discrete references to off-stage gay tragedies, such as in *A Streetcar Named Desire* (1947) where his character Blanche tells of having married "a boy who wrote poetry" and "thought him almost too fine to be human," but then found out, "this beautiful and talented young man was a degenerate." She confronted him cruelly, and he committed suicide.

Then, twenty-five years later in his *Small Craft Warnings* (1972), Williams again portrayed an off-stage sensitive and talented youth who suffered the same fate, although in this play, there were also explicit homosexual references and characters. It is likely that Williams had in mind in these references the sensitive young gay American poet whose work he so admired who had committed suicide in 1932, Hart Crane.

Williams' *Small Craft Warnings* was a companion piece to his *Memoirs*. In the latter he makes references to it being written while *Small Craft Warnings* was initially performed in New York. Written amidst the gay liberation explosion going on, the play struck a cautionary tone embedded in its title that I will have more to say about later.

Prior to 1975, while Isherwood alluded to gay figures in his *Goodbye to Berlin* and other works, it was never in connection with either himself, as the presumptive narrator, or his main characters.

In *Christopher and His Kind*, he went back to diaries and letters in the late 1920s and 1930s to show how he had cloaked his gay relationships in his works from that period. Isherwood was, among other things, able to enlighten us with the amazing continuity that ran from E.M. Forster (1879-1970), author of *Maurice* (written in 1913 but not published until after Stonewall in 1971) and his friend, a pioneering theorist of the unique role of gay sensibility in culture, Edward Carpenter (1844-1929), through him, his associations and to the present, his still-active long-time companion, Don Bachardy.

In it, Isherwood wrote of his efforts to compose a novel about Berlin in 1932 he called *The Lost*, the title operating on three levels: the first, he wrote, being "those who have lost their own way, that mass of Germans who were now being herded blindly into the future by their Nazi shepherds." Second were "the doomed," those "already marked down as Hitler's victims," and, third were "those whom respectable society regards as moral outcasts."

He cited an entry from his diary then: "The link which binds all the chief characters together is that in some way or other, each one of them is conscious of the mental, economic, and ideological bankruptcy of the world in which they live. And all this must echo and re-echo the refrain: It can't go on like this. I'm the lost, we're the Lost."

It was eventually published as *The Last of Mr. Norris* (1935).

Presented was a perspective that a gay genius could by far embody best.

Chapter 84

Christopher Isherwood
And His Kind

Much is contained in Christopher Isherwood's classic memoir, *Christopher and His Kind* (1976), which speaks directly to the matters of gay identity and purpose that have been the subject of this series.

His formidable works written in the tumultuous era from the late 1920s to the onset of World War II contain enormously beneficial insights into the dehumanizing horrors of tyrannical extremism in that era taking the form of national regimes, fascists in Germany, Italy and Spain, Stalinists in the U.S.S.R.

Isherwood's contributions were to the good of humankind as a whole, written in a literary form that was not preachy, not succumbing to parroting the popular political rhetoric of the time, although there is no doubt that his sentiments were, if not entirely pro-Communist, at least fervently anti-fascist.

Many, many years later, after World War II, after the civil rights and anti-war ferment of the 1960s in the U.S. (born in England, Isherwood moved to the U.S. in 1939 and never left), after the rise of the modern gay liberation movement surrounding the Stonewall riots of 1969, Isherwood revealed in *Christopher and His Kind* the indispensable ways in which his homosexuality was at the heart of his efforts at benefiting the wider human community.

Indeed, his affirmation early in life to "live according to my nature, and to find a place where I can be what I am" was fundamental to everything he did. Each of us helps humanity best, he wrote, "by using his own weapons." For him his best weapon was obviously writing, but it was also the perspective he brought by virtue of being openly and self-assuredly gay.

His alternate perspective explained why he became a pacifist on the eve of World War II, he wrote, even as all the horrors of tyranny and genocide swirled around. It was because, he thought, he had so deeply loved Heinz, a man who'd been forced to join Hitler's army, that he could not bring himself to destroy a unit that might have his lover in it. Then, by extrapolation, "Because every man in that Army could be somebody's Heinz...I have no right to play favorites."

Here, an expression of gay sensibility, of same-sex erotic attraction, arises in society as nature's indispensable antidote to the insanity of war. Indeed, nature provides for and sets apart gay sensibility for just such purposes.

"How could I have dared suggest," Isherwood wrote, "that any of these people—or any people anywhere—*ought* to fight, *ought* to die in defense of *any* principles, however excellent? I must honor those who fight of their own free will...and I must try to imitate their courage by following my path as a pacifist, wherever it takes me."

Here, the same-sex lover seeks to intervene on behalf of the life and happiness of all of his sex.

Nature provides no one else to do this, at least not without the force of such a nudge. Fathers groom their sons for war. Mothers obey their husbands. State leaders give the marching orders. Bands play. Everyone cheers, and the young, rosy cheeked youths of countless nations march off seeking glory, and finding unspeakable pain, fear, the devastation of their souls and inglorious death.

But the gay person is positioned by nature to defy that order from the very core of his nature. He loves those soldiers too much. He hears the echoes in his soul of the Biblical confession, "By the grace of God, I am what I am," and the affirmation, "Love that to which you are inclined. But really love it, with everything that entails. Don't exploit it, don't rape it, don't devour and abandon it, but love it."

This is why the paradigmatic straight male and his institutions—the "Others," in Isherwood's words—will always hate and seek to inflict harm on us, we, in Isherwood's words, of "Our Tribe," we homosexuals.

We are born to stand apart from the herd, a vantage point from which to see that the herd, with its ingrained patterns of brutality and selfish self-interest, is heading to the slaughterhouse. They bully and bruise us because we're not in step with their march, and because we cause their march to be called into question.

This was William Inge's point in his film *Splendor in the Grass* (1962) which spun me as a young student out of the march and headed me, over the course of a few years, toward the gay liberation movement. Inge was, of course, an affiliate of "Our Tribe."

But as with Isherwood, Tennessee Williams and so many others of our pantheon of heroes of all sexes, our purpose lies not solely in our own liberation, but in the kind of work to the benefit of widows, orphans and lives seeking happiness and productivity, not war, injustice and spiritual death, which will always and forever place us in harm's way.

Chapter 85

Simultaneity of the Gay
And Anti-War Movements

There's no coincidence that the modern gay liberation movement, that which associates its founding with the riots at the Stonewall Inn in New York's Greenwich Village in late June 1969, arose in the context of the civil rights movement for racial equality and the growing anti-Vietnam War movement.

Postmodernist historians diminish the importance of this confluence by suggesting that, at best, the gay liberation explosion took the other social movements as a model, or occasion, for its own. However, they were intrinsically interconnected, and it is in that interconnection that a crucial component of what it means to be gay is found.

There was a remarkable correspondence of events the weekend of the Stonewall Riots that underscores this point.

Common wisdom is that the riots, which broke out as the Stonewall Inn was closing at 3 a.m. in the warm summer early morning hours of Saturday, June 28, 1969, were in part sparked by the mourning of thousands of gays on occasion of the funeral of gay icon Judy Garland the afternoon before.

Garland, born in Minnesota as Frances Ethel Gumm, was only forty-seven when she died in London of an accidental drug overdose on June 22, 1969. The young teen star of *The Wizard of Oz* (1939), she struggled in her adult life, marrying four times, and took comfort from gay male friends, often hanging out in gay clubs, as she bravely undertook comebacks in her career.

Her body was flown to New York on Thursday, June 26; more than 20,000 paid their respects at a funeral home that day, an overwhelming number of them gay. On Friday, a closed funeral was held, while thousands held vigil outside. That night, in the wee hours of Saturday, street people lingering outside the Stonewall Inn (not the patrons inside) clashed with police in what sparked a running battle over a number of days.

But something else happened at the same time which, it can be credibly argued, was even more acutely associated with that memorable weekend.

It was the publication of the June 27, 1969 edition of *Life* magazine, which did a first for its time of dedicating its cover and twelve pages inside to a high-school yearbook portraits-style format of 242 photographs of mostly eighteen-to-twenty-year-old rosy-cheeked boys who had been killed in just one week, May 28 to June 3, in Vietnam. The feature included one such face on the cover and the blaring headline, "The Faces of the American Dead: One Week's Toll."

Life's plans for the issue received considerable notoriety prior to its publication, and urging from the U.S. military not to do it. Historians of the anti-Vietnam War movement called it "a significant factor in reducing pro-war sentiment."

As a young gay man on the West Coast who had come out two months earlier by way of my first significant gay encounter, I was unaware of the Stonewall Riots but was mesmerized by that issue of *Life*. I had just graduated, with honors, with a Masters from the Pacific School of Religion in Berkeley, and in my three years there had seen a lot of demonstrations, riots, National Guard troops and tear gas as the anti-war movement grew.

I was anti-war, myself, though it was the civil rights movement, and the assassinations of Martin Luther King, Jr. and Bobby Kennedy in the spring of 1968, that really catalyzed my personal transformation from a small-town boy who completed college on a baseball scholarship into an impassioned political being.

My coming out was facilitated not by post-Stonewall ferment, but by a conference I attended the previous fall of the Council on

Religion and the Homosexual, an outgrowth of the struggles of the earlier gay rights efforts of the Mattachine Society.

My actual coming out on April 24, 1969, and my first intimate encounter then, helped, I believe, to open my physical and emotional sensibilities to respond viscerally to the unspeakable horror of what the June 27 *Life* magazine depicted. Unlike today's volunteer armies, most drafted to die in Vietnam were just teenagers.

My younger brother was in Vietnam on a boat that launched swift boats in the Mekong Delta. I'd already learned that two of my friends had died there, including one who had one of the most amazing personalities, with the good looks to accompany it, I'd ever known. Hispanic, he was just a kid, and had no way to avoid the draft.

My affirmation of my homosexuality became inseparably connected to the empathy I felt for the thousands of boys dying senselessly in Vietnam. This is the point that Christopher Isherwood suggested in what I wrote last week; that we, as homosexuals, play a special role in society by virtue of our propensity for loving our own sex, to resist the savage carnage of war and its brutal disregard for the real human beings suffering it.

Not merely a collateral, it is an indispensable part of our gay identity, of who we are.

Chapter 86

The Postmodernist
Counter Revolution, Part 1

"There is no such thing as a good war, or a bad peace"
—Benjamin Franklin.

The stunning confluence of events that occurred on the weekend of June 27, 1969—*Life's* magazine's extraordinary edition lining up twelve pages of high school yearbook-style photographs of one week's worth of deaths of young American soldiers in Vietnam hitting newsstands the same weekend as the Stonewall Riots in New York's Greenwich Village—is an amazingly poignant, fitting historical testimonial to the symbiotic nature of the civil rights, feminist, anti-war and gay liberation movements.

That the modern gay liberation movement, which later adopted the Stonewall Riots as its point of departure, occurred to the day as one of the strongest national statements against the Vietnam War began confronting the national consciousness, provides a telling and decisive clue: Our gay liberation movement was not born in isolation.

It was part and parcel of a social upheaval which had universal justice and equality as its object. What made the Vietnam War so bad was its sheer lack of credible national purpose. On the contrary, it brought home the warning by President Eisenhower a few years earlier about the danger of a "military industrial complex" running the nation to its own ends.

A general in World War II, Eisenhower knew the abject horror of war, and vowed never to permit America to go to war during his two terms as president. When inaugurated in 1952, America had kicked off another war in Korea, and Eisenhower ended it as soon after being sworn in as he could.

But the escalation toward war in Vietnam in the 1960s had the benefit of no such countervailing resolve. Given the mainstream American resistance to the civil rights and War on Poverty struggles of the 1960s, the assassinations of Martin Luther King, Jr. and Robert Kennedy in 1968 led to a angry surge of opposition to tens of thousands of our nation's young being drafted to die in the jungles of a pointless war.

I was in that surge. It included an imperative to cast off all the trappings of social oppression that the captains of the "military and industrial complex" used to hold us down. Coming out, and the launch of the modern gay movement, was part and parcel of a far wider social convulsion that was happening.

Thus I, after co-founding the Berkeley Gay Liberation Front, wrote the *Gay Sunshine* newspaper's first editorial entitled, "Who Needs It?," saying the movement should "represent all those who understand themselves as oppressed—politically oppressed by an oppressor that not only is down on homosexuality, but equally down on all things that are not white, straight, middle class, pro-establishment...It should harken to a greater cause—the cause of human liberation, of which homosexual liberation is just one aspect." (*Gay Sunshine*, Aug.-Sept. 1970).

I was then chosen to be the first-ever "official" gay liberation spokesman invited to address a major anti-war rally in San Francisco's Golden Gate Park.

All this was entirely in keeping with the kind of fervor and wider social justice purposefulness that ignited the Stonewall movement. We gays, after all, hated the war because we were especially inclined to feel empathetic, same-sex attraction to many of those young men being slaughtered. Dads cheered them on. Moms couldn't defy their husbands. So it was up to us to really spearhead the anti-war movement, and we did.

But none of this happened uncontested, and the counter-punch came with a vengeance, though in a form that caught most unaware. While the strident, militaristic right wing required our focus, an insidious and toxic counter-insurgent influence infiltrated the anti-war ferment from within: the "sex, drugs and rock-and-roll counterculture." I documented earlier the covert, pro-fascist intelligence elements behind this.

It was a noxious mix of radical hedonism and postmodernist social dissembling. I was a first-hand witness. The social disintegration aspect involved socio-political ideologies that rejected the bonds of social justice-inspired solidarity linking the anti-war, civil rights, feminist and gay movements. In the postmodernism of the despicable Michel Foucault and his ilk, it is each against all: no one is trusted and all authority, even scientific authority, is to be questioned, disregarded and resisted.

Therefore, the social justice bonds I wrote about in my *Gay Sunshine* editorial came under fire: to them, the gay movement was about gays, and that was it. Talk about "divide and conquer," it was the oldest counter-insurgency trick in the book! It worked. Moreover, with radical anarcho-hedonism replacing social consciousness with the personal pursuit of pleasure, postmodernist imperatives demanded a rejection of all restraint.

The gay movement devolved quickly into the urban anarcho-hedonist excesses of the 1970s, bearing trappings of sexual addiction and habitual fads, creating the incubator from which AIDS arose.

Social activism thus "taken out," the nation crept back toward war. With Reagan came indifference to gays in crisis, non-democratic precedents to fighting wars, and greed-laden spread of domestic debt slavery.

Chapter 87

The Postmodernist
Counter Revolution, Part 2

What hat happened to America in the quarter-century between 1963, when the national ethos was defined by Martin Luther King, Jr.'s "I Have a Dream" speech, and 1987, when it became defined by the "Greed is Good" speech by Gordon Gekko in the movie, *Wall Street*?

Stemming today's perilous careen toward the "might makes right" radical "social Darwinist" tenants of the Rep. Paul Ryan budget, now embraced by an entire political party, requires a hard look at how the shift in that 1963-1987 period happened.

June 1969 was pivotal. I've written about the confluence of events then that involved, on the one hand, a major ratcheting up of the anti-Vietnam War movement and, on the other, the "big bang" birth of the modern gay liberation movement around the Stonewall riots.

Those two simultaneous factors were the product of one of the most moral and courageous periods in history. Building on earlier achievements of the civil rights movement for racial equality, the U.S. population rose up to, for the first time in the nation's history, actually stop a war.

Led by morally-inspired youth who risked all—jobs, careers, family ties, friends and personal safety—Americans shook the very foundations of traditional power in the U.S. They threatened to bring down that "military and industrial complex" governed by white men, all who felt enfranchised to systematically degrade the role of women, racial minorities and workers, to hate homosexuality, and to order tens of thousands of teenagers to ugly deaths in the jungles of Vietnam.

Such was what we called "The Man," and "The Man" was being seriously shaken by a turbulent sea of righteous anger flooding the streets of his cities, surging like a terrible harbinger of Judgment Day against his cruel injustice.

So came our gay liberation movement. Inspired by the courage around us, legions of our own tribe, risking even more by "coming out" than the rest, stood up and, bursting with our own courage, claimed our right, the right of us all, to full integrity and our rightful, unique role in the progress of humankind.

Overall, it was the most amazing period since the Revolution in American history, spawning and empowered by, both, our gay liberation movement. It was the full force of the "I Have a Dream" speech played out on the streets of America.

But it didn't last. As the war began subsiding, there was a rot spreading within the popular uprising whose effect was to turn people away from a fiery demand for justice for all and instead have them curl inward in pursuit of self-centered excessive hedonism.

The influence had been there all along. But as the fervor of the movement waned, it began to assert itself and take over, the flip side of the pursuit of justice and happiness for all. It involved a shift to a preoccupation with selfish desires over the well-being of the overall community. Spurring this tendency had a long history.

Since the rise of industrialism in the 18th century, captains of industry and privilege sought to devise ways to undermine the capacity to resist among those they sought to exploit. They saw collective resistance as the biggest roadblock to their unfettered success, and specifically, they determined to prevent anything like the American Revolution from ever happening again.

Philosophies of the individual were developed and propagated, from Max Stirner's "The Ego and Its Own," to the theories of Friedrich Nietzsche and Sigmund Freud, and others, about empowering selfish self-obsession against social conscience. The science of "sexology" was devised as one variant.

The approach was formed out of a corruption of Charles Darwin's theory of natural selection, the notion that self-centered humans are by nature driven by two impulses, one toward socially responsible behavior and the other in selfish rebellion against it. The tension was defined in terms of sexual urges.

In typology drawn from Greek mythology, these contending urges were seen as Apollonian (socially responsible) versus Dionysian (pleasure seeking).

Key to this theory was its denial and suppression of a third natural human impulse toward advancing the general good of humankind and associated with the Greek myth of Prometheus.

I assert that the vital role of same sex erotic attraction in society is derived not from a Dionysian corruption of the mating impulse, as "sexology" contends, but from the Promethean impulse to love humanity.

Fast forwarding to the 1960s, the deliberate cultivation and mainstreaming of a Dionysian "sex, drugs and rock and roll" counterculture was unleashed on the social ferment of that era to defuse it. That counterculture lured people to abandon social justice on behalf of individual radical hedonism, to "turn on, tune in and drop out."

The mantra to "drop out," to abandon the pursuit of one's creative potential in an effort to shape a better world—namely, to extinguish the Promethean impulse—was its most insidious component. A massive offensive, it worked.

Chapter 88

We Are Best Defined
By Our Creative Work, Part 1

The events surrounding and subsequent to the modern gay movement-founding Stonewall Riots of June 1969 are relevant to our cause today. It's not just ancient history.

First was the spectacular context that gave rise to the modern movement, a by-product of the greatest surge of popular passion for civil rights, justice and an end to a senseless war in the history of the U.S.

Second was the rapid devolution of that idealism and activism into an excessively self-centered urban anarcho-hedonism in the early 1970s creating the preconditions for the AIDS crisis and, most tragically, involving an abandonment by hundreds of thousands of gays of their creative work.

The creative energy that powered the first-ever successful effort by the people to actually stop a war was, by the socially-engineered "tune in, turn on, drop out" so-called "counterculture," deflated into a selfish, habitual obsession with sensual delights that involved dropping the pursuit of creative work.

In the San Francisco gay ghetto, the social pressure was to quit work and go on welfare, as "Castro clones" spent days on street corners in conformist lumberjack dress and nights at the baths. This was how it went down for Ken Horne, who I wrote about earlier in this series, the first known person to die from AIDS. He'd come to San Francisco seeking a career in ballet, but got caught in the "scene," soon abandoning his dream to take a menial job so he could maximize his time cruising for sex.

I felt the pressure acutely, as my gay liberation colleagues pressured me to quit my job as a reporter for the *Berkeley Barb* and go on "Aid to the Totally Dependent." I didn't.

Ironically, post-Stonewall gay liberation transformed gays from valuing themselves primarily for their creative ability to impact the wider culture, even if it had to be done from the closet, into mind-numbed sex addicts.

Previously marginalized institutions of increasingly graphic pornography, seamy bars, disco clubs, bathhouses, S and M torture chambers, and countless opportunities for anonymous, impersonal sex came to define the gay culture and lifestyle.

Later, gradually recovering from the AIDS horror and the loss of 600,000 beautiful human lives between and 1981-1996, our gay culture suffered an acute post-traumatic stress syndrome of denial and conformist and non-conformist extremism. (Typically, writing his "coming out" book, *The Confession*, in 2006, former New Jersey governor James McGreevey talked about life in the closet as a "divided self," but made no mention of AIDS even as it was obviously swirling all around him during his many dangerous forays into anonymous sex.)

But last year's highly-acclaimed revival of *The Normal Heart*, Larry Kramer's gripping 1984 play about the horrible early days of AIDS, has signaled a shift. A smash on Broadway in 2011, winning Tony Awards and now opening in Washington, D.C., it is the first really hard look at AIDS that our wider community has been willing to face up to since the whole thing broke out.

A new opportunity exists to revisit the assumptions of our current gay culture, especially the components carried forward from the pre-AIDS culture of the 1970s.

While no one is advocating a repudiation of all erotic features of our culture, the move toward institutionalizing stable and loyal gay relationships through marriage is a positive impulse toward something more substantial and humanizing.

On the other hand, "Queer Theory" advocates an escalation of non-conformity, pursuing ever more exotic and bizarre pursuits of perceived pleasure and anti-authoritarianism, trying to establish these as authentic for the future of our culture.

But the debate about gay culture as "assimilationist versus anti-assimilationist" is wrong on both sides.

In the courageous struggle for full equality, gay marriage is now the cutting edge. But the issue is one of full equality, not whether or not marriage is the right thing for everybody.

Who wants to merely assimilate into our present militaristic and testosterone-saturated culture? Marriage doesn't imply assimilation as long as we stay true to our gay nature, which to the core is resistant to the cruel and dehumanizing currents of the dominant culture.

The defining characteristics of gay identity—gay sensibility, an alternate sensual perspective and constructive non-conformity— form the basis of the transformative role our tribe is assigned to play in the evolution of our wider culture. Our job is to engage and transform society, as we always have.

Wars will never save humanity. Humanity will prosper and advance in peace only by the work that we gays and our allies do.

Our own salvation is in our creativity and our work, too. Tennessee Williams knew this. As hard as he partied at night, he was always in his studio to write for hours every morning. His work was his life, it was the core of his gay identity.

Gay culture in the future shall be built around creativity and the unique contributions we bring to forging a better world.

Chapter 89

We Are Best Defined By
Our Creative Work, Part 2

Few can disagree that modern American popular culture has drifted toward increased demands for and obsession with youth, physique and instant gratification. This trend owes to the tectonic shift underlying the rise of the Madison Avenue-based marketing industry that has moved American self-perception from producer to consumer.

Our culture now tells us we, as a democratic nation, are composed not so much of citizens who share in the responsibility for the best interests of our population as a whole, but of consumers. We're no longer knowledge-hungry, discerning, inventive people who build and fix things, but we're inhaling, insatiable repositories of earthly delights.

This shift was facilitated by the introduction of credit cards on a wide scale in the 1960s. People were told they could have whatever they wanted, like big-eyed kids in a candy store. This shifted the population from goal-directed resource marshaling to debt-strangling accumulation of toys and "conveniences."

Now, from student loans to mortgages and credit card debt, millions have become bound by "debt slavery." Fresh out of college and to the grave, lives (like nations) are dictated by the imperative to pay debts to the banks, pressured to cast aside dreams and ambitions of creative work in favor of whatever menial job is available.

Under "debt slavery," mediocrity is the order of the day, and explains why the U.S. is falling behind other nations in science, education and invention.

Our gay tribe is caught in this bind, but often with far worse consequences because many among us lack the same kind of social networks to see us through tough times.

While the lure of hedonistic pleasures permeates all of society, the social bonds of family and friends are more likely to mitigate such impacts on the destiny of a wayward soul. But in gay culture, there is a contrary tendency of fair-weather "friends" to encourage a descent down that path without regard for the consequences.

In the wider culture, as youth and looks fade, families—including spouses, children and in-laws—provide enduring comfort and meaning in the transition from hedonistic pleasure-seeking.

But in gay culture, such alternative options often aren't there. Too many gay people become depressed by the prospect of age and a loss of looks even before such conditions are present.

Rather than cultivating one's capacity to engineer a meaningful life, the passive consumer of earthly delights bemoans his or her fate as a crumbling, fading violet, pumping even more iron in the gym to fend off the inevitable, seeking even more impersonal trysts to prove at least a temporary worth in the world of hedonism for its own sake, and sinking into despair over an inability to maintain a supposedly desirable figure.

All the while, those so obsessed hate what they are unable to prevent from becoming, themselves, by lashing out at those already there, denigrating all those they perceive less attractive than themselves.

It isn't just young gays who commit suicide for being tormented by bullies. It's older gays, too, of all ages, tormented by the sense of emptiness and uselessness in a candy store where only the prettiest cookies have value.

"Who says 'It Gets Better?,'" one astute gay friend observed rhetorically. For gays, unless there are lots of financial security and social bonds, it too often doesn't, or not for long anyway.

Valuing sex and sexual partners as acts and objects of consumption, as encouraged in our whole culture, makes matters worse for gays. There is an emotional short-circuit associated with repeated, habitual impersonal sex that leaves lasting scars. It can become very difficult, nearly impossible, to simply drop impersonal sex and pick up a meaningful relationship (that isn't "open").

It is a special tragedy for so many gay people to fall into such depersonalized patterns, because if anything, we are created as people-centered creatures, inclined more than most to lift up those who are in need by the strength of loving empathy and empower them.

The worst fate for a gay person—the one that takes him or her the farthest from the root of a gay soul—is to become jaded, to become indifferent and cruel.

It is a product of our wider culture, for sure, but there is little in our gay culture to insulate us from it, or to cure us from it.

The 1960s so-called "counterculture" and the mores of postmodernism, as preached by Michel Foucault and others, promoted a form of radical consumerism, including the consumption of people as mere sex objects, in the name of the sexual revolution and rejection of authority.

As such, sexual acts of the postmodern rebel were touted more as acts of defiance against power than anything like love or romance. Regrettably, gay culture fell victim to this madness forty years ago and has yet to cast it off.

If anything, gays should be leading the nation's way back to being a productive, creative, caring people.

Chapter 90

Karl Rove's Pitch for
The Gay Movement?

Echoing the case I made last week about the consequences of the national cultural shift since the 1970s away from productive and generous notions of the individual to selfish self-interested ones, a powerful new film documentary *#reGeneration*, narrated and co-produced by actor Ryan Gosling, has been released, available in limited theater release but on On-Demand and i-Tunes.

#reGeneration tells about the systematic institutional and media-engineered creation of the "Me" generation that has, as a result, effectively "tuned out" wider social realities in favor of self-centered consumerism. This has led to unprecedented encroachments on democratic institutions (such as the U.S. Supreme Court's "Citizens United" decision allowing unlimited and anonymous corporate and individual campaign contributions), a steep decline in the nation's competitiveness intellectually, and an "empathy gap," the level of apathy and cynicism about prospects for real change that threaten the nation's most core values.

Dr. Martin Luther King, Jr. said, "The arc of the moral universe is long but it bends toward justice," but he added, "It does not bend on its own. It bends because each of us in our own ways put our hand on that arc and bend it in the direction of justice."

Remove those hands, abandon what Abraham Lincoln called the "better angels of our nature," in favor of unbridled personal and corporate greed and cultural side effects, such as society's implicit sanctioning of rude and hateful behavior, yelling and honking in traffic, insulting persons without remorse, include, as I pointed out last time, the depersonalization of humans as ravished objects of consumption, as "meat," or not.

In this context, increasingly hollow, bought-and-paid-for democratic institutions are allowing the greatest disparity in the distribution of wealth in the nation's history, as all the while the entire world sinks into a prolonged economic malaise, a potential new great global depression savaged by rampant poverty, war and disease.

The daunting task of reversing these trends confronts everybody, and the gay community in particular because of our considerable talent at orchestrating such reversals shown through history.

Faced with this burden, a puzzling title hit bookstore shelves, proclaiming, *Victory: The Triumphant Gay Revolution* (2012).

Victory? Written by attorney Linda Hirshman, her first work on LGBT matters, the book's title suggests that, well, we've won. What's to worry about now? Are we to forget that we are in the grips of one of the roughest presidential campaigns in U.S. history, the first with the prospects of billions of anonymous campaign contributions thanks to "Citizens United?"

Are we to forget that President Obama has instituted more strides toward full equality and respect for the LGBT community, more by light years, than any other president in history? Are we to forget that if he's beaten this November, his Republican opponent Mitt Romney has promised he will reverse and repeal all of the advances that Obama has instituted? Victory *already*? Really?

One wonders if this notion could deter the kind of extraordinary political mobilization the gay community is being called to this summer and fall, with all that we've gained and hope to gain on the line.

The book by this avowedly heterosexual author panders to the gay community and has a decidedly pro-Republican slant. Notwithstanding considerable shortcomings in its history (the complete absence of reference to Randy Shilts' devastating journalistic work about AIDS, *And the Band Played On,* being one example), it diminishes Obama's role (saying at one point he "insults and ignores the gay community") and elevates those of Republicans like the attorney for the gay Log Cabin Republicans by saying, "He finds his advocacy perfectly consistent with his conservative principle that every man should be treated strictly on his own merit."

The book culminates its cited "march to victory" with the work of super-rich moguls, showing how Republican-led pro-gay organizations threw their weight around in recent elections. "Victory" in this sense implies handing off the movement to the one percent of one percent of the super-rich, who don't care what people do in their bedrooms (for now) as long as they hand over their cash to defeating Obama.

It hints to the secretive "Political OUTgiving Conference" held in May 15-16, 2010 in Chicago that Lou Chibbaro reported in the May 27, 2010 *Washington Blade* entitled, *Rare Peek Behind Closed Doors of Secret Gay Donor Confab*. Key organizers of the conference were Patrick Guerriero, former president of the Log Cabin Republicans, and Bill Smith, former aide to Karl Rove.

Former Bush Chief of Staff Rove headed in 2012 the largest post-"Citizens United" so-called "Super-PAC," American Crossroads, and invented the new strategy of gathering monied interests in secret conferences to raise the unlimited amounts they're now allowed to give.

In fact, the May 2010 gay mogul meeting was closely akin to the one held in Utah for GOP Presidential candidate Romney in 2012. Apparently, this constitutes "victory" in Linda Hirshman's eyes.

Chapter 91

This Series' Core Thesis:
The Promethean Identity

The core thesis of this series is the novel notion that same-sex erotic attraction is a variant and derivative of the natural bond between humans more akin to empathy than the physically reproductive impulse.

It is designed to set a framework for further scientific pursuit of this idea based on its importance in the following ways:

1. It liberates the homosexual impulse from being understood as a form of deviation or corruption of the heterosexual reproductive impulse. If that is how it is seen, even if it is seen as a consequence of natural processes, then it must be that the impulse is somehow inferior to an ideal norm, which is species reproduction. The political response in this construct is to see it either as a dangerous or benign for society—either it must be repressed, or can be tolerated as non-harmful.

2. It links and interconnects the homosexual impulse with other attributes associated with empathy, including its impulse to serve others through natural healing-like gifts, such as for the creative arts, and an affinity for the underdog, such as women, children and the elderly and dispossessed in the face of societal leadership that brutalizes them.

The dominant society has defined false parameters, internalized by homosexuals, for the very definition and expectations of same-sex erotic attraction, linking it unduly to simply sexual contexts, including extreme and bizarre forms, and, overall, consigning the phenomenon to evidences of weakness and inferiority.

But this is based on a false epistemology derived from the very brutal nature of straight male dominated militaristic culture itself.

Straight male dominion and its savage might-makes-right axioms justifying the subjugation of women, children and subordinate labor, including slaves and conquered people, to the tyrant's lust for accumulating and preserving the natural and human resources needed to enhance that dominion, suffered its first major setback in modern times in the radical Enlightenment ferment of the 1700s that resulted in the American revolution.

The core political notion underlying the American revolution was that human beings are valued according to their merits as contributors to the social good, and not simply because they are straight males or straight male heirs of royalty and privilege.

The straight-male premise of monarchy, thus, was violently opposed to this American revolution, and devoted the next century to undoing its impact while also contriving ways to ensure it would never happen again.

On the latter point, it encouraged continental philosophies that argued for the primacy of the isolated individual ego in all arenas of human behavior, undermining and discrediting in the process, notions of human empathy and solidarity as primary.

To the extent they created a philosophical movement to this end, it produced (and promoted) individuals like Nietzsche and Freud, who took the isolated ego and bifurcated it into two parts, the socialized ego and the animalistic, anti-social id. In Nietzsche's *Gay Science*, the title of a book about poetry, the ego is identified with the Greek god Apollo, and the id with Dionysus, the rebellious lover of pleasure for its own sake.

Same-sex erotic impulse was brought under this false construct as a manifestation of Dionysus, and that core notion has persisted to this day.

However, if I am right, as the preponderance of evidence I have accumulated in these papers suggests, then the same-sex erotic impulse is more accurately associated with the Greek god of

Prometheus, the god who acted in defiance of Zeus but on behalf of humanity.

The Promethean archetype was at the heart of the revolutionary ferment of the latter 18th century, both in Europe and the American colonies. It represented exactly what the straight-male dominated old monarchies hated and sought to extinguish.

The rise of the modern gay liberation movement associated with the event surrounding the Stonewall riots in 1969 provided the opportunity for a massive outpouring of the Promethean spirit across the land. The Titan Prometheus was willing to suffer for his disobedience because he had given life, itself, to humanity and he, too, is ultimately liberated.

However, the enemies of the life-giving Promethean spirit that had created American democracy and helped to spread it around the world, pounced on the ferment of the late 1960s with a new, escalated round of self-centered hedonistic extremism that diverted the gay movement, and society as a whole, toward the "me" generation of mindless consumerism.

Among us gays, depersonalized sex for its own sake replaced our native impulse toward creative, humanly-uplifting empathy, and soon we became addicted to sex (and disease) and depleted of our humanity to become jaded, cynical and cruel echoes of the greater culture.

Hated by the wider male-dominated culture, too many of us internalized that hatred, denying the weakness attributed to homosexuality and thus ourselves behind closet doors from which gay-hating rhetoric spewed.

Some of us pander to the gay-haters, a sad reality of our time, and some become haters, as well. A far cry from anything Promethean or bold, they worship the source of their own oppression.

Chapter 92

Tennessee Williams Issues
Small Craft Warnings

No one knew better about the worst fate that can beset a homosexual— to become hopelessly jaded, indifferent and cruel— than gay playwright Tennessee Williams. The subject became, simultaneously, his greatest caution to the new post-Stonewall gay liberation movement, and his proposed remedy his greatest gift.

Williams, whose life and work has been so important to this series, made two critical contributions to the post-Stonewall movement. One was his *Memoirs*, his official "coming out" written mostly in 1972, and the other was a stunning soliloquy delivered by the first openly character to appear in one of his major plays, *Small Craft Warnings*, that opened on stage in New York as his *Memoirs* were being written.

What Williams came up with was undoubtedly not what sunny Gay Lib proponents wanted to either hear or have said at that time. But it was, like everything he did, ruthlessly authentic and truthful after Williams' compassionate manner. Many in Gay Lib at the time said he was reflecting the self-loathing of pre-liberation era gays, but subsequent history compels us to take Williams much more seriously than that.

The message is in the title of his play. To Williams, reflecting on his own experience, gays start out tender and sensitive "small crafts," quickly finding themselves too often in over their heads in choppy waters of a hostile world. In one of his last plays, the autobiographical *Vieux Carre* (1978), Williams recounted his first homosexual encounters while in his mid-20s when he moved to a boarding house in New Orleans' French Quarter. Quickly he learned, and with much pain, that lusting for homosexual sex and naive yearning for love had little, if anything, in common.

Williams was fortunate to be in a position to carry on an active if impersonal sex life while still retaining his empathetic sensibilities through creative work. His "love objects" in his plays became the likes of his sad, lobotomized sister, for example.

Williams sharply juxtaposed his creative passion to impersonal sex in his *Memoirs*, and through the soliloquy by the gay character Quentin in *Small Craft Warnings* he attested to the unhappy severance of sex from love but ending with an astonishing remedy. Quentin, an older gay man, arrives at a sleazy seaside bar with a fresh-faced youth he'd picked up shortly before. (The two characters are each Williams himself, one as he'd grown to become, and other being himself as a youth).

Quentin speaks,

"There's a coarseness, a deadening coarseness, in the experience of most homosexuals. The experiences are quick, and hard, and brutal, and the pattern of them is practically unchanging. Their act of love is like the jabbing of a hypodermic needle to which they're addicted but which is more and more empty of real interest and surprise. This lack of variation and surprise in their 'love life' spreads into other areas of sensibility..."

(How's that as a description for today's addictive Grindr, Scruffy and other modes for impersonal hook-ups?)

But then Quentin, recalling his own youth, reflects on when things were different for him,

"Yes, once, quite a long while ago, I was often startled by the sense of being alive, of being *myself, living!* Present on earth, in the flesh, yes, for some completely mysterious reason a single, separate, intensely conscious being, *myself: living!*...Whenever I would feel this...*feeling*, this...shock of...what?...self-realization?...I would be stunned, I would be thunderstruck by it. And by the existence of everything that exists, I'd be lightning-struck with astonishment... it would do more than astound me, it would give me a feeling of panic, the sudden sense of...I suppose it was like an epileptic seizure, except that I didn't fall to the ground in convulsions..."

Then Quentin looks at the adolescent boy with him, and sees in him his own lost innocence and passion for life,

"This boy I picked up tonight, the kid from the tall corn country, still has the capacity for being surprised by what he sees, hears and feels in this kingdom of earth. All the way up the canyon to my place, he kept saying, *I can't believe it, I'm here, I've come to the Pacific, the world's greatest ocean!*...as if nobody, Magellan or Balboa over even the Indians had ever seen it before him; yes, like he'd discovered this ocean, the largest on earth, and so now, because he found it himself, it existed, now, for the first time, never before... And this excitement of his reminded me of having lost the ability to say: 'My God!' instead of just: 'Oh, well.'"

Williams called this one of his best soliloquies ever. In this speech, he offered his fellow, freshly-liberated homosexuals an antidote to cynicism and despair. It was as if he was saying, in my words, "There is only one sin in life—cynical, selfish and cruel indifference—and there is only one virtue, a passionate love of life, of yours and everyone else's."

Chapter 93

Saint Foucault? Are You Kidding? Part 4

I began this series in October 2010 with three chapters entitled the same as this, and as I prepare to conclude, I'll reiterate why I began that way.

First, the overall series title, *Gay Science,* has a double meaning.

In the first case, it refers to my case against 19th century German philosopher Friedrich Nietzsche, as in his book *Gay Science* that proclaimed among other things the "death of God." My *Gay Science,* is contrasted to the flawed Nietzschean anarchistic "will to power" concept that contributed to the rise of Naziism and in late 1960s to the radical anarcho-hedonist shift in American culture.

That shift was away from humanist values associated with Eleanor Roosevelt's post-World War II *International Declaration of Human Rights* to our current consumerist, selfish self-interest defined culture.

In the second, my *Gay Science* refers to the role of same-sex erotic attraction as a core component in nature, a derivative of the essential dissymmetry of the universe itself, and among organized life forms, in the indispensable role for heightened empathetic and altruistic impulses and behaviors in successful societies.

As such, it is contrary to neo-Darwinian "survival of the fittest" and "social Darwinist" theories. I contend that same-sex erotic attraction, although manifested as strongly sexual, actually derives from empathetic and altruistic components of natural behavior, and not as a deviation of the reproductive impulse.

These two meanings of *Gay Science* combined, I've written about the collision of a newly socially-affirmed natural role for same-sex erotic attraction with its context, namely, the last forty years' cultural paradigm shift.

In so doing, I've challenged, among other things, the prevalent view that the modern post-Stonewall gay liberation movement is a cutting edge of that cultural shift toward selfish hedonism. To the contrary, it was swept into adopting the crazed urban-centered sexual addictive behaviors of the 1970s that led to the AIDS epidemic.

While urban homosexuals have yet to consciously shed such effects and residual patterns remain, positive signs exist, including the push for gay marriage and a better respect for the cultivation of talents manifesting our natural "constructive non-conformity" that benefit society overall.

This series has sought to contribute to a new dialogue on these lines, toward what gay playwright Tony Kushner, in an introduction to a recently-published script of Larry Kramer's *The Normal Heart*, called the need for a "a new gay morality" better reflecting our true nature and purpose.

It is forward-directed, recognizing that many committed to the current gay culture may find it foreign or off-putting. Old terms like "sex-negative" or "self-loathing," born in a bygone era to defame anyone who did not affirm anarcho-hedonistic sexual excess, do not apply here.

As a San Francisco-area pioneer of the modern gay movement, I lived through it all. Overwhelmed by the hedonistic excess of the 1970s, I stepped aside to a self-imposed exile. I survived all that ensued somehow and have since felt compelled to understand what happened and share my insights honestly. Thus, this series.

Little did I realize then—as my 1970s effort was failing to lead the movement toward more universal and compassionate civil rights purposes, free from the maelstrom of depersonalizing radical hedonism—that my colleagues and I had a singular adversary dedicated to fueling that maelstrom's power nearby.

Gay postmodern philosopher Michel Foucault, whose acquired stature was the creation of some foul and malicious social engineering effort I have no doubt, was lecturing in the mid-1970s at U.C. Berkeley on the merit of, no the demand for, angrily casting off authority, including scientific authority, or limits of any kind, in pursuit of sexual excess for its own sake.

Frequenting S-and-M themed gay bathhouses nightly, Foucault fueled among the brightest young minds the false justification for the increasingly impersonal and extreme sexual hedonism that overtook urban gay culture, a process that filtered down to the dregs of the San Francisco's gay sex culture including in the form of his own person, in fact. In 1983, Foucault knew he had AIDS, but came back to San Francisco to revisit the leather bathhouse scene nightly, indifferent to spreading the HIV virus, until he died in 1984.

In his book, *Democratic Enlightenment* (2011), Princeton University's Jonathan Israel assails Foucault, in particular, for proposing to undermine the very humanist basis for the American Revolution and any universal moral and democratic political foundations arising out of the Enlightenment, because Foucault held that "the primacy of reason was ultimately just a mask for the exercise of power."

Foucault and postmodernism, generally, are fiercely against universal human rights, Israel argues, because any notion of universality is a form of oppression. This same influence informed the angry rejection of any authority, not only to ethics or accountability, but also to science or public health. As such, it fueled the preconditions and spread of the AIDS epidemic.

Some contended that Foucault was a "saint" of the gay movement. He was more like a sinister purveyor of unspeakable misery and death who almost destroyed us, and still could.

Chapter 94

Larry Kramer's Play Still
Not Taken to Heart

In conjunction with the 19th International AIDS Conference in July 2012 in Washington, D.C., Larry Kramer's prophetic 1984 play, *The Normal Heart*, was performed at Arena Stage, following its initial Tony Award-winning revival on Broadway in New York a year earlier that included the as-of-then-still-closeted Emmy Award-winning actor, Jim Parsons, in the role of Tommy Boatwright. I wrote extensively about the play at that time.

The play, like Kramer, was widely reviled in the gay community when he first wrote it, although it helped spur his formation of ACT UP, the civil disobedience movement that was the first to make major breakthroughs in the public awareness of and concern for AIDS.

Reading reviews and blogs, and in conversations with many who've seen and praised the 2012 production of *The Normal Heart*, it is troubling to find how little of Kramer's play is being taken to heart as a very contemporary critique of gay culture even now.

It is appreciated as a tragic and sad chapter in the history of the gay movement, way back then, thirty years ago. But now, as then, the notion that gay men should stop having sex in the face of a deadly epidemic, as proposed by the character of Dr. Emma Brookner in the play, gets the biggest laugh of the night. Preposterous then, preposterous now.

All the blame goes onto public officials, Reagan and the Mayor of New York. But Kramer was hardly limiting the blame to them.

Kramer was treated like an outcast by the gay movement's leadership when in 1978, in an amazingly prescient book, *Faggots*, he exposed the extent of urban gay America's descent into a morass of boundless impersonal sexual encounters. His point was how impossible it had become for a young gay man coming to New York looking for love and romance to realize his dream, having to abandon his hopes in favor of a culture of relentless, drug-laden pursuit of pleasure for its own sake.

Despite the venereal diseases ravaging gay scenes in the 1970s, no one saw AIDS coming, and the long incubation period meant that plenty of young men were doomed by exposure to the virus long before AIDS first manifested itself in the summer of 1981. The appearance of the HIV virus in urban gay communities could have been as early as 1974.

I was swept up in the urban gay scene in the early 1970s, after enthusiastically coming out and taking a leading role in the gay liberation movement of the San Francisco Bay Area. But it didn't take too long, or too much of all that promiscuous sex, for me to realize this was taking my life nowhere. I recall more than one opportunity for a serious romantic relationship that was shattered by the sheer volume of easy and casual sexual encounters in bathhouses, in parks, and dark rooms in the rear of bars. In New York there were the infamous long-haul trucks docked at the West Village piers that were stuffed full every night with men who were lucky if a struck match could enable them to catch a fleeting glimpse of some of the others they were performing sex with.

In S&M clubs, those preferred by the likes of Michel Foucault, the practice of "fisting" quickly evolved, spiking Crisco's market share, as well as gerbil adventures and public displays of things like "erotic vomiting."

For all such behaviors, the scions of the gay movement—those profiting from the operation of clubs, baths, sex houses, poppers, intoxication and the proliferation of porn—argued that love and commitment may be out of the equation with all this, but it is replaced by boundless pleasure and "trust."

For me, backing away from this scene was not easy. It involved a personal struggle having nothing to do with being prudish, but with wanting my life to matter for something. Because of the highly-addictive nature of the scene, there was no other way but effective exile. But while I loudly announced my departure from the political movement, I bounced along the urban scene's periphery, struggling with temptations, for years.

So, I was brutally abused by the force of those, like Foucault, who fueled the degeneration of the gay scene in this manner. As a young gay man, I was first abused by a culture that caused me to hate my orientation and to hide it at all cost. Coming out, I was abused by my family. My dad threatened to kill me, and I became *persona non grata* in my home town. I turned to my gay community, but far from finding the love I'd longed for, I found its polar opposite, violently determined to dash my hopes.

In *The Normal Heart*, Larry Kramer's pitch is for love over impersonal sex, for gay lives with meaning and purpose over lives ruled by genitalia. Sad to say that for many, his message is still not getting through.

Chapter 95

AIDS and the Lurking
Next Epidemic

The conclusion of the 19th International AIDS Conference in Washington, D.C. in July 2012 left a lot of uncertainty and unanswered questions about the status of the epidemic and the chances for ending it. It, as with many things in life, is now a function of economic class.

Effective treatment must be dirt cheap to work, and the daunting task achieved of eliminating stigmas still associated with the virus. Among the haunting presentations of such challenges was Art Jones' documentary, *13 Percent*, shown in association with the conference in D.C. to drive home that fifty percent of all new HIV infections in the U.S. are in the African-American population, which is only thirteen percent of the total population. Of all new infections among African-Americans, over half now afflict women.

Harsh stigmas persist and even when the uninsured seek treatment, doctors too often don't know that what they're seeing may be early symptoms of AIDS. Failing to diagnose in a timely fashion can render treatments ineffective.

Larry Kramer's effectively-performed *The Normal Heart*, played at D.C.'s Arena Stage as the conference convened. Written amid the exploding AIDS epidemic in 1984, among the many themes it struck was a highly-charged claim that I heard often in those days. A character in his play cites "top secret Defense Department experiments at Fort Dietrick, Maryland, that have produced a virus that can destroy the immune system. It's code name is Firm Hand. They started testing in 1978 on a group of gays."

Kramer was agnostic at best about this theory, but felt it needed to be mentioned in his play. Other theories about the source of the virus prevailed, and while no one is eager to adopt an unprovable conspiracy theory of that type, there are other ways in which covert, sinister policy objectives of powerful interests *did* shape the environment in which AIDS arose.

They involved the otherwise inexplicable shift in the national ethos following World War II. They were engineered through what I've called the "mainstreaming" of the radical hedonistic values of the urban counterculture, peaking in the late 1960s to blunt the growing social ferment of that era. It featured drugs and violence, targeted against the civil rights movement by flooding the nation's inner cities with riots and heroin, and targeted against the anti-Vietnam War movement by saturating the nation's politically-activated youth with anarchist slogans and LSD.

The "sex, drugs and rock and roll" movement was a product of an active domestic intelligence operation known as MK-Ultra. The well-documented CIA operation was uncovered during the hearings of the Church Committee in the U.S. Senate in the late 1970s. It thrust the theories and practices of radical hedonism against the heightened moral consciousness of that period. It was effective in the general population, and for the fledgling post-Stonewall gay liberation movement, it was devastating.

The impersonal, casual sexual imperative element of the offensive is what created the sociological and public health environment in major cities for what eventually manifested AIDS. Clinical sexual addiction fueled the process, compromising immune systems through repeated, chronic venereal infections and weakening physical constitutions of persons insisting on the same levels of intoxication and sex even as their bodies underwent physiological changes associated with aging. By age twenty-seven many were physically incapable of the levels of activity as before, but ignored the signals.

In San Francisco, where I was a gay activist, I saw it over and over. Young rosy-cheeked runaways and others coming to the big gay city in order to claim a happy gay life were swept with lightning speed into the deflowering grind, exploited, raped, drugged, malnourished and often within just a couple of weeks, appeared sullen, aged and pale even on bright sunny San Francisco days. Addictions and insatiable predatory behaviors prevailed in this context, sanctioned and cheered on by the wider hedonistic environment. Sadly, when news of the strange "gay cancer" first broke in July 1981, I was stunned, but not really surprised.

The opportunity had been created for the HIV virus to awaken from dormancy and spread, taking the lives of as many as 600,000 (the current estimate) mostly young gay lives in the U.S. alone. The hysterical denial of gay activists in the lead up to, break out of, and rapid spread of the deadly epidemic contributed enormously to the eventual magnitude of its reach.

So now, if the epidemic is going to end, so must the context that spawned it. Otherwise, who is to say what new, even deadlier virus is lurking in our ongoing urban hedonistic culture?

There is only one guarantee for ending AIDS, and that is to change our culture, not to wait for the next busted condom to begin the next chapter of horror.

But the high priests of the gay establishment today are as indifferent as they were in the lead up to AIDS to the ways in which our culture depersonalizes, cripples and endangers the precious gay souls that are supposed to be in our care.

Chapter 96

The Proper Care and Feeding
Of Precious Gay Souls

The task of this series has been to juxtapose our essence as gay souls to what passes for our current post-Stonewall gay culture.

In so doing, I have sought to define our essence through a wide array of scientific, historical, biographical and literary means, and to show that the current gay cultural influences from the radical hedonism of the 1970s is at odds with it.

The cumulative influences of the modern hedonistic gay culture may be difficult to shake, especially given that much of it is a subset of modern, self-centered consumerist American culture generally. But grasping its sharp deviation from a better appreciation of our gay souls is a start.

In the final chapters of this effort, due to culminate at No. 100, my focus will be on the title of this one: our "proper care and feeding." In other words, how things ought to be for us, causing a creative tension between what is and what ought to be.

I first coined the term, "gay soul," in a monograph, entitled *God and My Gay Soul*, circulated in 1970 through the San Francisco Bay Area following my graduation for a master's degree with honors from theological seminary, my coming out, and my pioneering activism in the post-Stonewall Gay Liberation Front (all of which happened about the same time, if not exactly in that order).

I have not seen a copy in forty years, and while I have long forgotten what exactly I wrote about, I am certain it had to do with an affirmation of gay identity as an intentional and core component of creation.

While in seminary, the very progressive Pacific School of Religion affiliated with the equally progressive United Church of Christ denomination, perhaps the single most influential work we studied was Viktor Frankl's *Man's Search for Meaning* (1946).

Compiled during Dr. Frankl's imprisonment in a Nazi concentration camp and published with many updated editions after the war, it is a short work that embodies the essence of Frankl's theory and work as a therapist, even among the most despairing facing extermination in the concentration camps. As Rabbi Harold S. Kushner wrote in the introduction to the 1992 edition, one of Frankl's key ideas was that "life is not primarily a quest for pleasure, as Freud believed, or a quest for power, as Alfred Adler taught, but a quest for meaning."

Frankl saw man, as a "meaning-seeking creature," having three possible sources for meaning: "in work (doing something significant), in love (caring for another person) and in courage during difficult times." He believed that "forces beyond your control can take away everything you possess, except one thing, your freedom to choose how you will respond to the situation."

My life took a lot of twists and turns following seminary from coming out, being rejected by my family as a result, confronting and eventually recoiling from the radical hedonism that had taken over the gay culture, finding no apparent options but to align tangentially with a marginalized pro-socialist political entity that held me at arm's length because of my sexual orientation, living fearfully under the cloud of AIDS from the time it broke in the open in 1981 to when an antibody test was finally available in 1985, and then slowly reclaiming my life to, as I like to say, "do what any good gay boy would do," to use the gifts I'd first discovered in childhood to found in 1991 and since serve a community with a darned-good newspaper.

Looking back, I can say with confidence that my world view and approach to life did not deviate during that entire span until now from their core foundations in the teachings of Viktor Frankl.

Hence, I rejected the radical countercultural, nihilistic hedonism that took over gay culture in the 1970s, as I did rigid, cult-like authoritarian currents I found on the social margins, or in the growing selfish materialism of the overall American culture following the "Reagan revolution."

I've held to Frankl's three sources of meaning: in work, in love and in courage. If you want to know what's primarily animated this series, you've just found out.

Last year, Jonathan Sacks, the chief rabbi of Great Britain, authored a book, *The Great Partnership: God, Science and the Search for Meaning* (2011), which draws very heavily on Frankl's work but takes it further in an array of directions.

While much could be said about this incredibly rich book, for purposes here, I note that Sacks adds to Frankl's notion that man is a "meaning-seeking" being with the supplementary notion that "man is a culture-producing animal."

In both ways, mankind is distinct from all other forms of life, which means that we do not simply conform to any prevailing culture—such as what we have now— but that we are capable of, indeed we are challenged to, create a better culture.

Chapter 97

Gay Marriage May Save
The Institution of Marriage

Viktor Frankl, in his monumental work, *Man's Search for Meaning* (1946), drafted in a concentration camp to become a seminal contribution to two decades of post-World War II progressive moral suasion, identified man's inherent pursuit of meaning in life in three areas—in work, in love and in courage.

Discovering what these mean for gay people constitutes our path forward for an altogether new and pioneering basis for gay identity, values and culture.

They represent the vantage point from which, like a prophetic founder of a newly anointed tribe walking away from the burning ruins of a self-imploded village and not looking back, we can catch a glimpse of a bright horizon, freed from the shackles of degraded radical anarcho-hedonism, obsessive habits and addictions and the predatory rape and objectification of persons valued as nothing more than stimulants for insatiable lust.

Indeed, such a pilgrimage seems at present still more like stepping through a minefield in the midst of such collapsing conditions, and there also appears a seamless continuity of this distress through all contemporary culture, distinguishable only by matters of degree.

So we gay people are having to do this for ourselves, using the likes of Frankl for guideposts, pioneering as well, perhaps, a rehabilitation of our entire culture. Such, in fact, has been our role through history.

In the grand scheme of things, we are here for a very important reason. Our same-sex erotic attraction is a creative binding force of nature as strong and purposeful as any in all creation, rooted in the empathic buffering glue that preserves, protects and advances civilizing influences, effectively steering evolution in the right direction.

Our awakening from the sheer degradation and chaos mainstreamed into American culture by the social engineers of the "sex, drugs and rock and roll" counterculture of the late 1960s is a prelude and precondition for a revival of beneficent global culture generally.

A fresh impulse for attaining and affirming enduring, personal hard-fought-for, face-to-face intimate human relationships, involving but not limited to the notion of gay marriage, reflects this awakening. Becoming significantly more self-conscious, this process can become socially transformative.

By providing meaning through loving human connections, in Frankl's formula, marriage and intimate relationships inclusive of family and friends, grandmothers and lovers alike, function as stable platforms for enhancing the kind of empathy and kindness that reaches beyond comfort zones to uplift humanity generally. But they don't come easily. Our culture's demand for instant gratification notwithstanding, they all take work.

But they are the cure for victims of sexual objectification, breaking through barriers imposed by lust-aroused mental, including electronic, fantasy images to see and engage real people and not just their "looks."

In San Francisco in the early 1970s, I walked passed an attractive young man leaning against a storefront. Behind the storefront was one of the countless "peep show" joints where impersonal sex took place in the back. He gave me a typical "come hither" stare, but as I kept walking, I smiled and said, "Hi!" His face was instantly transformed by a huge grin that made his eyes sparkle. "Hi!," he beamed back.

In that memorable case, a barrier of sexual objectification was broken to reach the real person inside, which as it turned out for him, was still right near the surface.

In too many other cases in gay ghettos those days, however, such real persons had receded to hard shells deep within. Everybody viewed everybody as a sexual object, and that was preached as the way it was supposed to be. Friendships were superficial, and in cases where "coming out" alienated family and old friendships, as in my case, leaving little in the way of genuine connections.

Religion was no help. There were only two kinds: that which condemned homosexuality and that which affirmed it by uncritically endorsing the radical anarcho-hedonism dominating its culture. So, despite my seminary training, I found no place for me there.

But now, forty years later, the push for gay marriage has embedded within it a potentially transformative, constructive affirmation of the meaning of persons generally that could save the very institution of marriage itself in our wider culture.

It is not just about equal rights. Far more important is the relentless insistence on a social recognition of a sustainable relationship grounded in trust, faithfulness and commitment that goes to the very core of what it means to be human, and applying that to all relationships, marriage and beyond.

Reactionaries hate gay marriage for more than its same-sex aspect, but because it represents the notion that marriage should be a socially-affirmed bond and commitment of equals, and not composed of a dominant male and subordinate female and children.

The reactionary's notion of the "nuclear family" is, indeed, sorely threatened by gay marriage. But theirs is destroying the institution because it undermines truly human intimacy for the sake of male dominion to the detriment of everybody.

Chapter 98

Beautiful Gay Souls I Know:
Don Bachardy and Johnny Weir

Asking, "What does it mean to be gay?," in this series, I identified three ways in which same-sex erotic attraction is linked to a preponderance of personal qualities of great benefit to humanity. Using self-reflection as a measure, I've identified these qualities in countless gays I've encountered, even if they don't apply to everyone.

First, "gay sensibility" is a heightened empathy and compassion often manifested in early childhood by sympathizing with underdogs and discovering talents that bring happiness to others. Second, "alternate sensual perspective" is an inclination to be drawn to something other, not just erotically but also aesthetically, than the majority. Third, "constructive non-conformity," is the inclination to invent, create or represent a different course than passive conformity in life, in a loving, constructive way.

Amplifying and valuing these qualities away from lust for hard bodies can call into being all that gays have had, through the centuries, to bring to the betterment of society and themselves. Uplifting these qualities in our culture, out from the radical anarcho-hedonism of the 1970s that still dominates it, can empower our cultural reinvention based on genuine human relations rooted in the meaning that people derive from their work, their loves and their courage.

Everything beautiful that humanity brings to the world comes from beautiful souls. All have a capacity for beauty, but too many ignore that for selfish instant gratification. The entire culture suffers from this, and it will take many beautiful self-actualized gay souls to heal it.

I am blessed to have many wonderfully creative, accomplished and beautiful gay friends. Two, well-known openly-gay, extraordinary national treasures, Don Bachardy and Johnny Weir are different in many ways. There's a fifty-year difference in age and a continent of difference in location. Their talents are different, but therein lies their first great commonality: both have striven relentlessly in their lives to cultivate and present their talents as gifts to humanity, Barchardy as a portrait artist in Southern California, Weir as a figure skater in New York.

Barchardy, born in 1934, was the long-time companion of the British-born writer Christopher Isherwood (1904-1986), who was declared by his great friend, the late Gore Vidal, as "the best prose writer in English." Barchardy, under Isherwood's loving patronage, trained to become a prominent artist in his own right, doing portraits of all manner of celebrities and important people, including the official rendering of Gov. Jerry Brown that hangs in the California State Capitol.

Weir, born in 1984, is a three-time U.S. figure skating champion and two time U.S. Olympic contender currently training for a third Olympic run.

Both have tons written both about and by them. In Bachardy's case, Isherwood devoted more ink to him in his posthumously-published diaries (a third volume due out before long) than anyone else by far. Bachardy has published his own material, too, including *Stars in My Eyes* (2000), a catalog of his portraits with personal remembrances of 33 famous people.

Weir published a memoir of the first twenty-six years of his life entitled *Welcome to My World* (2010) that is intelligent, candid and worthwhile. Weir's successes, failures, controversies and irrepressible flamboyance have landed him boatloads of ink and celluloid in newspapers, tabloids and reality TV shows.

I had up-close, intense one-on-one encounters with both when I first met them in person.

I met Weir in March 2004 after he'd won his first national championship. Watching him on TV in January, I wrote in my diary (as I recently rediscovered) that his winning long program was so poetic, emotive, graceful and soaring that it was "what my soul looks like."

I used my newspaper credentials to arrange an interview at his Newark, Delaware home rink on March 11, and we sat across from each other, face-to-face in a practice room for over an hour, a session that included a rather creative photo shoot at the end.

When you engage someone that intently, you can see far into them. I encountered Johnny Weir's resolve to speak the truth with intelligence and articulation, to achieve, and above all, to be himself. So, he'd responded to his Russian coach's urging "to remember the art and beauty, and forget the pettiness of scores." He saw his insistence on doing things his own, if unusual, way to be standing in solidarity with every kid that's ever been treated as an outcast for being different from the norm.

I knew about Don Bachardy before I met him at his home overlooking the Santa Monica canyon to interview him and have him paint a portrait of me. The portrait painting had the same intense, one-on-one engagement as my interview with Weir. It took almost three hours.

As a gazed back at him while he looked into details of my face, my eyes and my soul, I caught a glimpse of what Isherwood saw in him that made it worth working so hard for their relationship to last.

Chapter 99

Not Assimilationist, But Transformative

"Though outwardly we are wasting away, yet inwardly we are being renewed day by day."

This quote from Paul's *Second Letter to the Corinthians* (4:16) in the Bible describes the exact opposite of Oscar Wilde's *"The Picture of Dorian Gray"* (1890), where the inward person wasted away while the outward one remained young and beautiful. The brilliant, gay Wilde's reversal of order was clearly intentional, a harsh critique of the philosophy of hedonism raging in his day.

But the *Dorian Gray* ordering also describes modern urban gay culture to a tee. This culture's fixation is on the "tyranny of hard bodies," and its norm is to waste hours a day at a gym, working tirelessly to forestall aging and "love handles," while any impulse to cultivate the mind and spirit are blurred by nightly intoxication and shallow obsession with acts of impersonal sex performed on the outward flesh of others.

Contrast this to the extensive record of Christopher Isherwood's love for his lifelong partner Don Bachardy. As Isherwood "discovered" his homosexuality, so had he discovered his pacifist sentiment as World War II broke out. In an effort to make sense out of it all, he submitted to the teachings of Hinduism, or Vedanta, which called for the individual to experience "union with what is eternal within oneself" (Isherwood, *My Guru and His Disciple*, 1980).

Through this one learns, Isherwood wrote, that "to feel concern for others is the only realistic attitude, because it is a recognition of the real situation, our oneness with each other."

He approached his new guru about his homosexuality, guarded against a negative response that would have disqualified the pursuit. "Can I lead a spiritual life as long as I'm having a sexual relationship with a young man?," he asked. The guru, Swami, replied, "You must try to see him as the young Lord Krishna."

To the Hindus, Isherwood wrote, Krishna was an avatar, an incarnation of the holy (Isherwood called that "this thing") born on earth from time to time, described as having been extraordinarily beautiful in his youth. "I understood the Swami to mean that I should try to see Vernon's (Isherwood's lover at the time— ed.) beauty—the very aspect of him which attracted me to him sexually—as the beauty of Krishna, which attracts devotees to him spiritually. I should try to see and love what was Krishna-like in Vernon."

From this point of view, one finds in Isherwood's extensive diaries chronicling his relationship with Bachardy, which began about a decade later and lasted until Isherwood's death in 1986, the influence of these teachings on his ability to sustain a genuine, veritably spiritual, love relationship with his much younger partner.

Bachardy told me that Isherwood never tried to convince him to join the faith, but that he was very happy when Bachardy announced on his own that he had become a practicing believer as Isherwood neared death.

This dedication to the inward renewal and development of the other is, to reiterate my point, in sharp contrast to the hedonism that dominates modern gay culture.

Gay academic David Halperin's book, *How to Be Gay* (2012), based on his course at the University of Michigan by the same name, is a shameless, wholesale tribute to this urban gay male culture. It suggests that anyone failing to comply with the accepted icons of this culture is somehow less than really gay.

Halperin's earlier 1995 book, *Saint Foucault,* was the take off point for my *Gay Science* series, with my first three installments entitled, "St. Foucault, Are You Kidding?" So it is apropos as I prepare to conclude this series next week that I address Halperin's latest fiction.

I hold "sexologist" philosopher Michel Foucault (1926-1984) in vile contempt. His influence in San Francisco in the 1970s as a lecturer at U.C. Berkeley not only contributed to the outbreak of AIDS, but made it impossible for me to realize my gay identity within the radical anarcho-hedonist gay culture he helped shape.

Ironically, I could realize my gay soul only by resisting that gay culture. I backed away from its descent into madness (such as its stubborn refusal to deter the spread of AIDS), and was fortunate to find sanctuary in a sequence of intimate, reciprocal loving relationships, my most important one persisting from 1983 to the present.

Halperin's book mentions nothing of the downsides of urban gay male culture, with no talk of alcoholism, career-stagnation, drug abuse, sexually-transmitted diseases or suicide. He goes so far as to contend that AIDS and the 600,000 gay male lives it took in the U.S. alone "a terrible historical accident, and it had nothing to do with us."

But who infected all those beautiful gay souls, even after, like Foucault, they knew they were killing their sex partners? To begin to honestly address our gay culture, we have to begin with fact, not convenient fiction.

Chapter 100

My Finale: *What Now, Lazarus?*

On Gay Pride Sunday, June 13, 2010, marking the 40th anniversary of the first Gay Pride parade, I had the honor of delivering remarks to those assembled a few blocks from the Pride festival at the First Congregational Church in downtown Washington, D.C.

I titled my talk, *What Now Lazarus?*, drawing from the question a seminary professor put to me long ago. The Biblical figure Lazarus was raised from the dead, but there is no account of what he did after that. "Did he go back to growing dates, or did he make something more of his life?," my adroit professor asked.

I applied that question to the gay movement today. We have been raised from the dead, metaphorically, in three ways: from the oppression of our closets, from the terrible AIDS epidemic, and, soon, from second-class status in the eyes of the law (while huge fights still need to be fought against a lot of persisting bigotry and hate, this is inevitable). After all this, then what?

Do we assimilate into the male-dominated, profoundly unequal and militaristic prevailing society, becoming as stupid TV sitcoms or right-wing scions seeking to co-opt us would have it, absorbed into and indistinguishable from all that? Do we angrily repudiate assimilation with radical, postmodern "queer theories" and behaviors that define us in terms of perpetual rage?

Or do we follow the alternative approach that has been the subject of this series, which concludes now after being published weekly since October 2010 in the web edition of my *Falls Church*

News-Press and reprinted on the pages of the superb *Metro Weekly* gay news magazine in Washington, D.C.

This alternative is consistent with what history shows are core expressions of our naturally inherent and vitally important gay souls.

Preponderant qualities of heightened empathy and compassion for the underdog, of an alternate sensual perspective (our same-sex erotic attraction being a natural derivative of humanity's powerful impulse for empathy and not a variant of the drive for species reproduction) applied to all aspects of life, and a constructive non-conformity account for the amazing contributions our "tribe" has brought to the benefit of all humanity for thousands of years.

Contrary to the shallow conceits of current, hedonistic urban gay culture, we gay souls have been a major, constructive factor in civilization since before the beginning. Sensitive to the plight of women, children, the elderly and downtrodden in savage patriarchal male chauvinist, war-mongering cultures, we worked to build the institutions over eons that have advanced compassion over cruelty, science over superstition, beauty over corruption and equality over tyranny.

We, with our natural feminist allies (and our natural inclination to identify and align with strong women struggling in all stations in life), sparked the American Revolution as an epochal blow against the male-chauvinist right of monarchies to hereditary succession, and built a constructive alternative in the U.S. Constitution's framework for fair and just governance that had embedded within it what has slowly progressed to equal rights under the law for everybody.

The enormously positive new development of the post-Stonewall era has been our increasing capacity to "come out," gaining for us a degree of personal integrity before the world that was always denied before. It promises to result in an explosion of our creativity and beneficial role to society as a whole, although that was stalled by the radical, anarcho-hedonism imposed on our urban culture in the 1970s that devolved into the AIDS horror and stubbornly persists to this day in urban centers.

But now, the fight for marriage represents for us a fresh constructive front in the struggle for full human equality, not just because we'll have the right to it, but more importantly, because gay marriage advances the notion of loving bonds of equals, striking another blow against the male supremacist paradigm. Some who favor it on gay rights grounds alone may overlook this.

Like Lazarus in the Bible, gay souls have been raised from the tomb of the closet, of AIDS, and second-hand citizen status to a purpose, to the meaning in life we derive through dedication to our creative work, our love and our courage on behalf of humanity as a whole.

Our gay liberation will be complete only when all humanity enjoys the benefits of the same kind of life, liberty and the pursuit of happiness we set as our purpose long, long ago.

I close quoting again the final words in Tony Kushner's magnificent play, *Angels in America*, spoken by its principle character Prior, living with AIDS. He steps away from his friends at the Bethesda fountain in New York's Central Park, turns to all of us, his gay sisters and brothers, and says,

"We are not going away. We won't die secret deaths anymore. The world only spins forward. We will be citizens. The time has come.

"Bye now.

"You are fabulous creatures, each and every one.

"And I bless you: *More Life*.

"The Great Work Begins."

END

About the Author

Nicholas F. (Nick) Benton emerged as an honor student from a graduate theological seminary in Berkeley, Calif., in the Spring of 1969 to barge out of the closet in the months prior to the East Coast Stonewall Riots. He co-founded the Berkeley chapter of the Gay Liberation Front, wrote the first editorial in the *Gay Sunshine* newspaper, become the first officially recognized GLF leader to speak at an anti-Vietnam War rally, wrote countless articles on gay liberation-themed matters for the region's flagship counterculture newspaper, *The Berkeley Barb*, and co-published *The Effeminist*, an original gay newspaper that argued for orienting the gay movement in tandem with radical feminism toward an overthrow of the white male chauvinist-dominated society. Overwhelmed by what he called the anarcho-hedonist capture of the movement, he withdrew from active involvement in 1974. In 1987 he founded an independent news service in Washington, D.C., and in 1991, he founded a weekly general interest newspaper in the Northern Virginia suburbs of Washington, D.C. area called the *Falls Church News-Press*, which is in its 23rd year of consecutive weekly publication. He has written a weekly national affairs opinion column in this newspaper since 1997, and in 2010 launched his 100 weekly installments of "Nick Benton's Gay Science," reprinted in the D.C. area's gay magazine, *Metro Weekly*. Benton and his newspaper have been widely honored in his local D.C. suburban community and in 2012 Benton was named by the statewide LGBT advocacy organization, Equality Virginia, as an "OUTstanding Virginian."

CPSIA information can be obtained at www.ICGtesting.com
Printed in the USA
LVOW08s0522200216

475903LV00004B/35/P